THE FRUIT OF HER HANDS

IEE

IBERIAN ENCOUNTER AND EXCHANGE 475–1755 | Vol. 7

The Iberian Peninsula has historically been an area of the world that fostered encounters and exchanges among peoples from different societies. For centuries, Iberia acted as a nexus for the circulation of ideas, people, objects, and technology around the premodern western Mediterranean, Atlantic, and eventually the Pacific. Iberian Encounter and Exchange, 475–1755 combines a broad thematic scope with the territorial limits of the Iberian Peninsula and its global contacts. In doing so, works in this series will juxtapose previously disparate areas of study and challenge scholars to rethink the role of encounter and exchange in the formation of the modern world.

OTHER TITLES IN THIS SERIES

Thomas W. Barton, *Contested Treasure: Jews and Authority in the Crown of Aragon*

Mercedes García-Arenal and Gerard Wiegers, eds., *Polemical Encounters: Christians, Jews, and Muslims in Iberia and Beyond*

Nicholas R. Jones, *Staging* Habla de negros*: Radical Performances of the African Diaspora in Early Modern Spain*

Freddy Cristóbal Domínguez, *Radicals in Exile: English Catholic Books During the Reign of Philip II*

Lu Ann Homza, *Village Infernos and Witches' Advocates: Witch-Hunting in Navarre, 1608–1614*

Adam Franklin-Lyons, *Shortage and Famine in the Late Medieval Crown of Aragon*

THE FRUIT OF HER HANDS

JEWISH AND CHRISTIAN WOMEN'S WORK IN MEDIEVAL CATALAN CITIES

SARAH IFFT DECKER

THE PENNSYLVANIA STATE UNIVERSITY PRESS
UNIVERSITY PARK, PENNSYLVANIA

Library of Congress Cataloging-in-Publication Data

Names: Ifft Decker, Sarah, author.
Title: The fruit of her hands : Jewish and Christian women's work in medieval Catalan cities / Sarah Ifft Decker.
Other titles: Iberian encounter and exchange, 475–1755 ; vol. 7.
Description: University Park, Pennsylvania : The Pennsylvania State University Press, [2022] | Series: Iberian encounter and exchange, 475–1755 ; vol. 7 | Includes bibliographical references and index.
Summary: "Explores how gender, socioeconomic status, and religious identity shaped the lives and work of Jewish and Christian women in medieval Catalan cities"— Provided by publisher.
Identifiers: LCCN 2022007204 | ISBN 9780271093307 (hardback)
Subjects: LCSH: Jewish women—Employment—Spain—Catalonia—History—To 1500. | Christian women—Employment—Spain—Catalonia—History—To 1500. | Notaries—Spain—Catalonia—History—To 1500. | Domestic relations—Spain—Catalonia—History—To 1500. | Catalonia (Spain)—Economic conditions.
Classification: LCC HD6178.C38 I44 2022 | DDC 331.409467—dc23/eng/20220411
LC record available at https://lccn.loc.gov/2022007204

Printed in the United States of America
Published by The Pennsylvania State University Press,
University Park, PA 16802–1003

The Pennsylvania State University Press is a member of the Association of University Presses.

It is the policy of The Pennsylvania State University Press to use acid-free paper. Publications on uncoated stock satisfy the minimum requirements of American National Standard for Information Sciences—Permanence of Paper for Printed Library Material, ANSI Z39.48–1992.

To my parents, Beth Greenfeld and Richard Ifft, who instilled in me a lifelong love of books and travel

Contents

Illustrations

Figures

Tables

Map

Acknowledgments

This book has been many years in the making and has undergone numerous transformations since I first began to immerse myself in the lives of the women who lived and worked in medieval Barcelona, Girona, and Vic. I owe particular thanks to Paul Freedman, whose advice, support, and expertise has been invaluable from the beginning of this project. His mentorship and friendship have helped shape me as both a scholar and a person. I also owe thanks to Ivan Marcus, Daniel Lord Smail, Francesca Trivellato, Rebecca Winer, and Anders Winroth for their feedback and continued encouragement. I remain grateful to Stephen Bensch for beginning my training as a medievalist and for inspiring me to turn to the food, wine, and archives of the Mediterranean.

I am fortunate to have enjoyed the intellectual support, camaraderie, and mentorship of excellent colleagues and friends both closer to home and while conducting research in Catalonia, including Abigail Agresta, Michelle Armstrong-Partida, Elisheva Baumgarten, John Burden, Rowan Dorin, Christopher Forney, Alexandra Guerson, Elizabeth Hebbard, Katherine Hindley, Maya Soifer Irish, Marie Kelleher, Rena Lauer, Irene Llop i Jordana, Kevin Lord, Sara McDougall, Mireille Pardon, Jonathan Ray, Agnieszka Rec, Anna Rich Abad, Miranda Sachs, Paola Tartakoff, Lluís To Figueras, Marita von Weissenberg, and Dana Wessell Lightfoot. At a moment when positions in the humanities have declined at an alarming rate, I am lucky to have found supportive intellectual homes at Indiana University and at Rhodes College. Thank you to Judah Cohen, Shannon Gayk, Laura Carlson Hasler, Sarah Imhoff, Carolyn Lipson-Walker, Jason Mokhtarian, and Mark Roseman at Indiana University for their friendship and encouragement, and to Raissa von Doetinchem de Rande, Judy Haas, Charles Hughes, Jeff Jackson, Jonathan Judaken, Tait Keller, Mike LaRosa, Charles McKinney, Samson Ndanyi, and Etty Terem for warmly welcoming me to Rhodes even in the midst of a global pandemic.

This project would not have been possible without the generous financial and intellectual support provided by the Social Sciences Research Council International Dissertation Research Fellowship, the Dr. Elka Klein Memorial Travel Grant, the Olivia Remie Constable Award, the Yale MacMillan Center, the Yale Department of History, the Yale Judaic Studies Program, the Yale Program for the Study of Anti-Semitism, and the Borns Jewish Studies Program at Indiana University. Mn. Josep Baucells i Reig and Immaculada Ferrer at the Arxiu Capitular de Barcelona, Joan Ferrer i Godoy at the Arxiu Històric de Girona, and Rafel Ginebra i Molins and Mn. Miquel Gros at the Arxiu i Biblioteca Episcopal de Vic deserve special thanks for their gracious assistance, along with the staff of the Arxiu Històric de Protocols de Barcelona and the Arxiu Històric de la Ciutat de Barcelona.

I also thank Ellie Goodman at Penn State University Press as well as Erin Rowe and Mike Ryan, editors for the Iberian Encounter and Exchange series, for helping bring this book to fruition. I feel fortunate to have benefited from the gracious assistance and careful attention to detail of the press's editorial staff, especially Maddie Caso and Laura Reed-Morrisson. The two anonymous reviewers improved this book immeasurably; all remaining errors are my own. An earlier version of portions of chapter 6 appears in the article "Minding Manors: Gender, Acculturation, and Jewish Women's Landholding in Medieval Catalonia," *Hispania Judaica* 14 (2019): 15–38; a previous version of part of chapter 7 appears in the article "Credit and Connections: Jewish Women Between Communities in Vic, 1250–1350," in *Women and Community in Medieval and Early Modern Iberia*, ed. Michelle Armstrong-Partida, Alexandra Guerson, and Dana Wessell Lightfoot (Lincoln: University of Nebraska Press, 2020), 17–40. I thank the Hebrew University Institute of Jewish Studies and the University of Nebraska Press for permission to reprint versions of both articles here.

I am eternally grateful to my friends for reminding me that there is life outside the archives: Elizabeth Baumel, Oliver Brady, Kristin Caldwell, Robyn Cohen, Ileana Garcia, Dawn Gildenmeister, Nicole Kolenic, Ben Raphel, Mara Shindell, and Benjamin White. Lourdes Sabé has been both a teacher and a friend who generously devoted her time to teaching me Catalan. In

Catalonia, Ricard Coronado, Neus Nadal, and Laia, Arnau, and Jan Coronado Nadal welcomed me into their homes and treated me like family.

This book never would have been possible without my parents, Beth Greenfeld and Richard Ifft, who first encouraged me to become a reader of history and introduced me to the joys of travel. Their support and encouragement throughout my journey in academia has been far more than I deserved. This book is dedicated to them.

Note on Naming and Coinage

Notaries typically reported sums in the dominant money of account: pence (*denarii*), sous (*solidi*, worth 12 pence), and pounds (*librae*, worth 20 sous). Occasionally, they referred to other currencies, most often Alfonsine *morabatins*, which were worth approximately 10 sous. In the text I have rendered sums in the original currency used by the notaries, but I have converted sums into sous when needed for comparisons or clarity.

When possible, I have translated names of people and places from the Latin of the notarial documents back into the Catalan vernacular, in the hopes of reflecting the language this book's subjects would have spoken in their everyday lives. Where this has proved impossible, I have preserved the Latin.

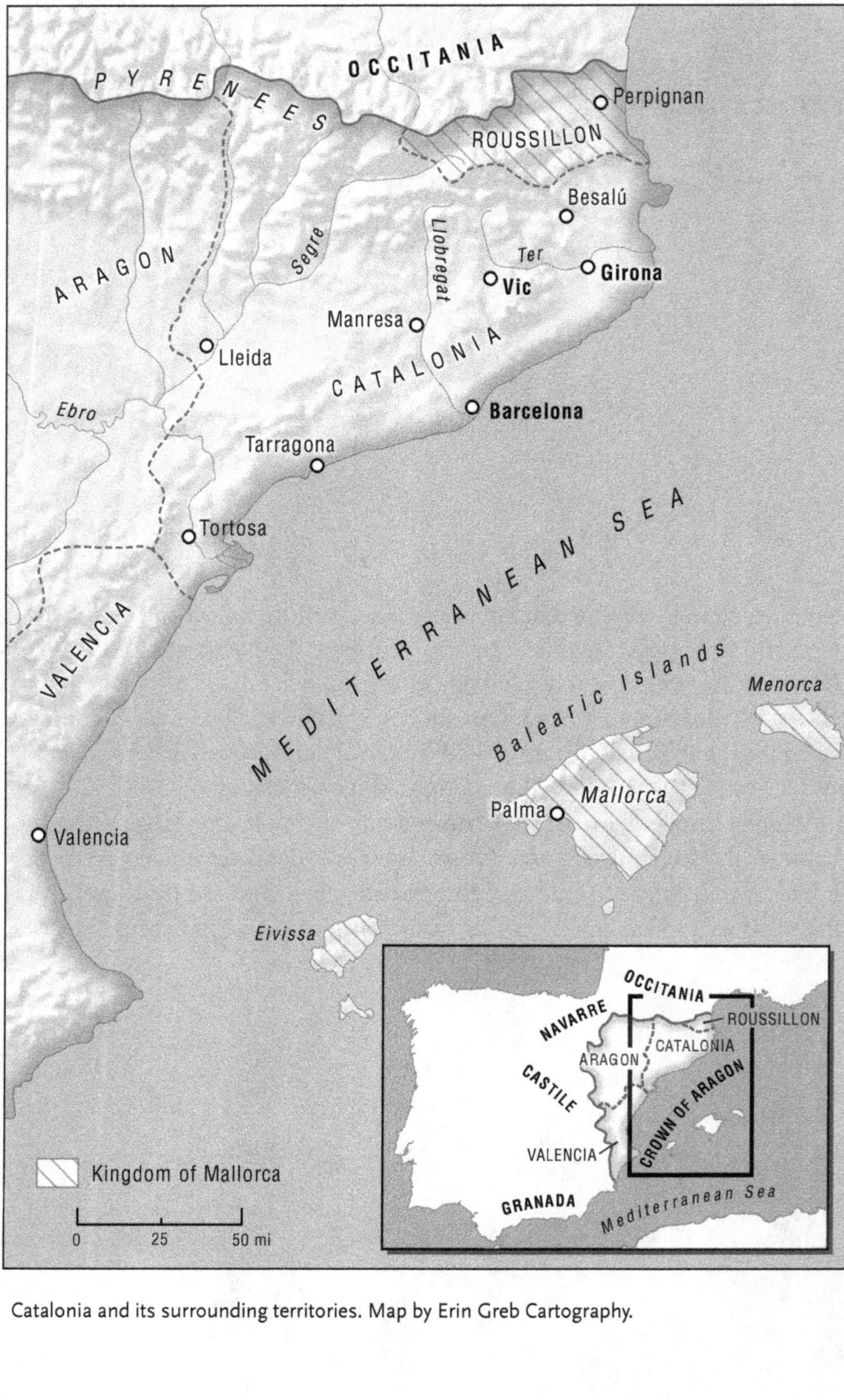

Catalonia and its surrounding territories. Map by Erin Greb Cartography.

INTRODUCTION

"She considers a field and buys it; / with the fruit of her hands she plants a vineyard." Medieval Jews and Christians would have recognized these words as part of a twenty-two-verse description of an ideal wife found at the end of the biblical book of Proverbs—a sacred text shared by the two communities.[1] The "woman of valor" described in Proverbs is wise and pious, but first and foremost, she is deeply invested in her labor both within and beyond the home. She provides food for her household and manages agricultural estates; she spins and sews both to clothe her family and to rake in profits by selling her wares. This book traces the experiences of the Jewish and Christian women who lived and worked in medieval Catalan cities, women who likewise helped support their households "with the fruit of their hands."

The central argument of this book is that religious identity, combined with other factors including gender and socioeconomic status, played a crucial role in determining what kinds of work were open to women. In Catalan cities, Jewish women nearly always played a less visible role than Christian women. This pattern only changed during occasional moments of Jewish communal change and crisis, during which Jewish women briefly took on a more prominent economic role. Women who belonged to the Christian majority, in contrast, experienced more stability: their labor responsibilities were less thoroughly transformed by short-term changes.

Defining Women's Work

Elite men in the Middle Ages often dismissed the meaningful economic contributions women made to their households. Catalan moralist author Francesc Eiximenis (ca. 1330–1409) encouraged women to occupy themselves with tasks such as sewing, spinning, and weaving, but only as a means of avoiding "standing at the windows"—an act he associated with spying on one's neighbors, engaging in idle gossip, and even committing adultery. By concentrating instead on labor, virtuous women successfully avoided such sins.[2] All too frequently, historians have reproduced this idea that women who did not practice a particular trade "kept busy"—not that they worked.

Christine de Pizan (1364–ca. 1430), Eiximenis's younger contemporary in France, offers a valuable corrective to medieval and modern assumptions about precisely what constitutes women's work. According to Christine's Lady Reason, "If you care to pay attention, you will see that all, or at least most, women are so assiduous, careful, and diligent in running their households and providing all things to the best of their ability that it sometimes irritates certain lazy husbands: they think their wives push them too much and prod them to do what they should be doing in the first place."[3] Christine acknowledged women's economic management of their households, and their husbands, as a full-time (albeit often unrecognized) job.

Most scholars of medieval Europe have characterized women's work in this era as low-paid, low-status labor.[4] *The Fruit of Her Hands* complicates this picture by expanding the definition of women's work to encompass the management of household assets as well as waged labor and artisanal production. Studies of women's involvement in skilled, high-status trades have rarely incorporated their management of household resources, while scholarly treatments that address women's control of assets seldom integrate women's managerial responsibilities into larger conversations around women's labor.[5] By placing women's management of financial resources in the broader context of women's work, I highlight the rich and varied spectrum of labor options available to women in medieval Catalan cities. Urban women of different socioeconomic strata ventured into local markets as creditors and debtors, buyers and sellers of real estate, investors in local and international commerce, artisans and tradeswomen, household servants and wet nurses. Taken together, these activities demonstrate that women across social strata performed work that benefited their households and contributed to urban economies.

Families and communities in Catalan cities, I argue, relied on women's managerial labor under certain circumstances, but they also sought to tightly control women's ability to participate in high-status and stereotypically male work. Although the men who shaped legal cultures envisioned men as responsible for the financial well-being of their households, their efforts to safeguard familial wealth sometimes required wives and widows to work to support their families.[6] However, as other scholars have emphasized, a patriarchal "glass ceiling" limited women's ability to engage independently in the most lucrative forms of work.[7] I build on this scholarship by exploring the tensions between the ordinary limitations on women's labor and the reliance on women's potential, if necessary, to support their families through their work in place of the men of the household.

This study assumes women's agency, insofar as it understands the working women of medieval Catalan cities as making choices that they believed would benefit themselves, their families, or their communities.[8] However, the assumption of women's agency does not mean that women fought to undermine patriarchal structures; many women maneuvered within such structures without questioning the gendered norms that shaped their lives. Moreover, although women exercised agency, most did so within a gender system that circumscribed the spectrum of choices available to them—not only as women but also as Christians or Jews and as members of the mercantile, artisan, or laboring classes.

Jews, Christians, and Gender

This study adopts an intersectional approach that analyzes how categories including gender, religious or communal identity, and socioeconomic status combined to shape the social and economic options available to women. Increasingly, feminist medieval scholarship has emphasized the importance of intersectionality and attention to differences among women.[9] This book explores the diverse experiences of women in medieval Catalan cities, with an emphasis on how women's work was shaped by their faith communities: Jewish and Christian women's work followed distinctly different patterns.

The disparities between Jewish and Christian women's work are surprising, given the wealth of scholarship that has emphasized similarities among women of different faiths in the Mediterranean and beyond.[10] Especially in the Iberian Peninsula, the supposed resemblances among Jewish, Christian, and Muslim women have supported the traditional view of the Jews of Sepharad (Spain) as deeply integrated into surrounding Muslim and Christian societies.[11] Increasingly, however, scholars of medieval Iberia have eschewed the utopian implications of the term *convivencia* in favor of an emphasis on its literal meaning, "living together"—a practical coexistence that created a shared culture yet simultaneously relied on the creation and reinforcement of intercommunal boundaries.[12] Contact between Jews and Christians was part of everyday reality in medieval Catalan cities. People of different faiths lived literally side by side, not only in the same cities but at times in the same neighborhoods as well. Jewish quarters in late medieval Iberia were often located in the center of cities; they were neither exclusively Jewish nor the sole site of Jewish residency. Economic interactions required regular contact between Christians and Jews and created interfaith relationships that could be neutral or even friendly in character.[13] Such proximity helped create a shared culture, as Elka Klein has compellingly argued in her work on thirteenth-century Barcelona.[14]

Yet togetherness was a necessity rather than an ideal, and commonalities were constantly contested. Brian Catlos has suggested that the term *conveniencia*, "convenience," more accurately characterizes the interdependent yet hierarchical relationships that Jews, Christians, and Muslims in the Iberian Peninsula developed out of pragmatism.[15] Iberianists have increasingly emphasized the myriad ways in which governing elites and ordinary people—Jewish, Christian, and Muslim—worked to create and reinforce the boundaries between faiths and embraced the construction and maintenance of distinct identities as essential to their community's strength and cohesion.[16] Boundary marking and common culture were not antithetical in medieval Iberia. Concepts, values, and practices shared across communities were even employed in the service of vitriolic religious polemics that aggressively reified interfaith divisions.[17]

By delineating the differences between Jewish and Christian women, this book contributes to the rich scholarship on the complexities of interreligious interaction in the medieval Mediterranean in general and the Iberian Peninsula in particular. Christians, Jews, and Muslims closely resembled one another in their shared use of women's bodies as boundary markers and as meaningful sites upon which to express anxieties about boundary violation. Concerns about sexual boundaries between communities were expressed through fears over the penetration of women's bodies—and thereby also, symbolically, communal borders—by men from outside the community.[18] Here, I explore another way in which women functioned as boundary markers: families and communities expected the laboring bodies of women to conform to the legal and cultural norms that they understood as defining their community. Jews and Christians might have shared many ideas about women and gender, but the male leaders of both communities crafted distinctly gendered norms surrounding women's control of assets and expected women to behave accordingly.

Women's access to financial resources mattered to Jewish communal leaders because it was inextricably linked to Jewish self-governance. Christians and Jews in the medieval world were subject to divergent, albeit overlapping, legal systems—and when Jewish and Christian legal professionals made choices that shaped women's labor in the public sphere, they were influenced by the experience of belonging to a religious minority or majority community. Royal privileges endowed Jewish communal authorities with jurisdiction over most internal affairs; since inheritance, marriage, and divorce were almost by definition internal matters, Jewish communities had more autonomy in the area of family law than in almost any other sphere.[19] Local interpretations of *halakhah*, Jewish law, dictated whether women inherited wealth and whether they could manage their own or their husbands' assets during marriage.

Women's control over financial resources, and therefore also the work options available to them, became an arena for the resistance to acculturation promoted by male rabbinic authorities and carried out by Jewish men and even some women. Rabbinic elites did not actively seek to disempower women, but prevalent gender norms meant that few of the men who belonged to the economic and political elite of local Jewish communities challenged restrictions that limited women's access to wealth. As a result, women's work could serve as a focal point for the construction and maintenance of intercommunal boundaries while only rarely disturbing men's family financial strategies.

While the economic restrictions imposed on Catalan Jewish women had a firm basis in halakhah, a comparison with northern Europe suggests that local factors were paramount. Both quantitative social histories and individual case studies demonstrate that Jewish women in medieval northern Europe worked professionally in credit and trade, sometimes with substantial profits.[20] The contrast between the economic roles played by Jewish women in Ashkenaz (northern Europe) and Sepharad is strikingly mirrored in the two Jewish communities' interpretive use of the ideal wife of Proverbs 31. In Ashkenaz, Rabbi Eleazer ben Judah of Worms (d. 1238) modeled his elegy for his murdered wife, Dolce, on this biblical text. In his idyllic description of his wife, he portrayed her as laboring not only to support her husband while he studied Torah but also to manage a larger household that included both their children and her husband's students. Eleazar emphasized the profits Dolce's work wrought for their household and the Jewish community, rather than the details of her economic endeavors. However, he nevertheless portrayed financial management skills as essential in a good wife—and the "fruit of her hands" as a valued contribution to their household.[21]

While Eleazar's elegy envisioned the economically active wife of Proverbs 31 as a model for the flesh-and-blood women around him, the commentary tradition from the Iberian Peninsula and southern France tended to interpret the figure allegorically, rather than linking her to real women, or to emphasize qualities other than her economic prowess, such as her piety and her obedience to her husband.[22] The lived differences between the Jewish women of Ashkenaz and those of Sepharad mirror the distinct interpretations and applications of halakhic and biblical models for womanhood across communal lines. Local context is therefore crucial to understanding why Jewish women in Catalan cities found their work options more restricted than those of their Christian neighbors or their coreligionists to the north.

Regional Context

Catalonia in the thirteenth and fourteenth centuries was a core territory of the Crown of Aragon, a federative monarchy that encompassed not only much of the northern and eastern Iberian Peninsula but also parts of southern France, Italy, and even Greece. The late thirteenth and early fourteenth centuries saw the Crown of Aragon reach its apogee of economic efflorescence and political power as a Mediterranean empire.[23] The region's economic prosperity, combined with the growing importance of notaries, generated abundant documentation recording the quotidian social and economic lives of the people who lived in Catalonia's urban centers.[24]

Jews as well as Christians in Catalonia benefited from this era of power and prosperity. Jewish presence in the region dated back to the Roman Empire, and in the thirteenth and early fourteenth centuries the Jewish minority was highly visible, self-assured, and growing. While Jews in England and France suffered expulsion, Jews in Catalonia were establishing new communities.[25] Yom Tov Assis even characterized the period of 1213 to 1327 as a "Golden Age" for the Jews of the Crown of Aragon, during which the social and economic stability and vibrancy of the kingdom as a whole facilitated culturally and economically productive achievements among its Jewish subjects.[26] Although Mark Meyerson has questioned the utility of the traditional narrative of a Golden Age followed by decline, he nevertheless emphasizes the security and confidence felt by the Jewish communities of the Crown of Aragon in the thirteenth and early fourteenth centuries.[27]

Moneylending was never the sole form of work practiced within the Jewish communities of the Iberian Peninsula, but it represented a profitable element of some Jewish families' economic portfolio. Julie Mell has recently argued that Jewish involvement in credit has been vastly overemphasized and that only a small elite actually worked as moneylenders.[28] Her work offers an important corrective to assumptions that credit was both an exclusively Jewish business and the sole profession practiced by medieval Jews. However, Mell ultimately overstates her argument and underestimates the importance of credit, at least in the Crown of Aragon, a region she does not discuss. Jewish moneylending, supported and encouraged by royal and baronial authorities, helped new communities establish themselves and provided supplementary income for Jewish families.

For both Jews and Christians, prosperity was punctuated by crisis in the second quarter of the fourteenth century, including famines (especially that of 1333, which one chronicler described as *lo mal any primer*—the First Bad Year) and the Black Death of 1348.[29] The plague reached Barcelona by March 1348, traveling on ships from either Rosselló or Mallorca, and by the beginning of May it had taken enough of a toll to inspire a response in the form of religious processions. Girona saw the arrival of plague in early May, probably also from Rosselló.[30] Within a year, approximately 60 percent of the population of Barcelona and 40 percent of the population of Girona had succumbed to plague.[31] This demographic and public health crisis challenged and traumatized Jewish and Christian communities alike.[32]

Continued social conflicts and crises created demographic and economic challenges in Catalonia in general, and Barcelona in particular, through the rest of the fourteenth and fifteenth centuries.[33] Several Catalan Jewish communities—including that of Barcelona—experienced the most serious threat thus far to their physical safety and security in the wake of the Black Death. Christians, fearing that the plague was either a divine punishment for Jewish sin or the deliberate result of Jewish malice, attacked and murdered Jews in several cities and towns, including both Barcelona and Girona.[34]

The economic affluence and political power of the Crown of Aragon in the late thirteenth and early fourteenth centuries, and the moments of crisis in the second quarter of the fourteenth century, provide an important backdrop for women's work during this period. However, as scholars have long recognized, economic and cultural efflorescence does not necessarily translate into increased opportunities or independence for women.[35] Neither Christian nor Jewish women could take full advantage of economic growth within the Crown of Aragon, with poorer women less able to do so than wealthier ones.

I further argue that Jewish women were disadvantaged by one of the very aspects of Jewish life that inspired Assis to term this period a Golden Age: the self-governing authority enjoyed by the elite male leadership of Jewish communities. Moreover, although the crisis of the Black Death was undoubtedly traumatic for women as well as men of all faiths, it briefly expanded the work options available to Jewish women.

Urban Contexts

This book focuses on three cities of varied size and economic profile: Barcelona, an economic powerhouse and international commercial center; Girona, a regional capital with a substantial textile industry; and Vic, a midsize city with a thriving artisanal community and a market that attracted the inhabitants of the surrounding hinterlands. Comparing these cities allows me to distinguish between regional trends and local ones to craft a richer and more diverse portrait of women's work in medieval Catalan urban culture.

Barcelona was the economic, political, and cultural capital of the region as well as its largest urban center, with a population of around fifty thousand on the eve of the Black Death.[36] The counts of Barcelona had established their control over much of Catalonia by the twelfth century, and in 1137 they became the kings of Aragon through a dynastic marriage. Gradually, Barcelona became the main administrative and political center of not only Catalonia but the Crown of Aragon as a whole.[37] The city expanded dramatically over the course of the thirteenth century, resulting in the building of a new ring of walls that incorporated more recently settled suburbs into the fabric of the city.[38] The late twelfth and early thirteenth centuries also saw Barcelona's transformation into a major center of Mediterranean trade and shipping.[39] Merchant-bankers, who worked in commerce, shipping, and money changing, became increasingly important figures starting in the final quarter of the thirteenth century.[40]

Although Barcelona had resident notaries by the early twelfth century, the city only gained a recognized public notariate in 1258, when King Jaume I of Aragon granted the city a royal privilege that authorized its Christian citizens to elect their own notaries. The city's recognized Jewish inhabitants could also appoint Jewish notaries, who were empowered to craft legally valid contracts in Hebrew for transactions between Jews.[41] Royally appointed notaries worked alongside those appointed by other urban institutions, such as the vicariate or the city councilors, albeit not always without conflict.[42]

The city was home to a long-standing Jewish community, one that probably dated back to the Roman era but was first clearly documented in the sixth century CE.[43] The Jewish quarter, known as the *call*, is documented from the ninth century.[44] By the beginning of the thirteenth century, the Jewish community had around seven hundred or eight hundred inhabitants, making it the largest in the region, and it continued to grow along with the city's Christian population.[45] The growth of the community in the thirteenth century, owing to some extent to the arrival of refugees expelled from France, required its expansion into an additional Jewish quarter partly located outside the city walls.[46] The thirteenth century also saw the increasing involvement of the Jews of Barcelona in moneylending and the consolidation of a new Jewish urban elite.[47]

Girona, about one hundred kilometers to the northeast of Barcelona, functioned as an urban center with a vibrant economic life in its own right yet retained close mercantile ties to Barcelona.[48] Despite the economic success of several prominent Girona merchants, they remained on average less wealthy than their counterparts in Barcelona.[49] The city relied heavily on its textile industry, and merchant-drapers occupied the pinnacle of Girona's social and economic hierarchy.[50] Although we have only limited demographic information before 1360, Girona probably had between eight thousand and ten thousand inhabitants in the early fourteenth century.[51] Girona was also a major site of episcopal power; the bishops of Girona ruled the city and negotiated complex relationships with lay lords, including the count-kings of Barcelona-Aragon and the counts of Empúries.[52]

Girona possessed both an ecclesiastical and a public notariate. The ecclesiastical notariate was somewhat older; it arose from the twelfth-century practice of clerics acting as scribes and was formally authorized in a royal privilege of 1263.[53] The public notariate was under the control of a single family, the Taialà, who received the notariate by royal concession in 1286. Rather unusually, the family was granted the office in perpetuity, not just for the lifetime of the original recipient of the privilege.[54]

The Jewish community of Girona, which dated back to at least the ninth century, was the second largest in the region, after Barcelona, with a population of approximately five hundred Jews in the thirteenth century.[55] A royal privilege of 1258 granted the Jews of Girona the right of self-governance and extended broad (and sometimes arbitrary) powers of taxation to a group of about five officials, the secretaries of the community.[56] The city's *call* was first mentioned in 1160; most Jews lived in this area, partly by preference and partly through the encouragement of Christian authorities. The *call* was not entirely closed off from the city, although gates could block entry to certain streets.[57]

The final city included in this study was both smaller and less central to the regional economy. Vic, the capital of the county of Osona, lies to the west of Girona (about sixty kilometers) and to the north of Barcelona (about seventy kilometers). The bishops of Vic were the great power in the region. They retained political authority, despite challenges from both the count-kings of Barcelona and the Montcada viscounts. For years, jurisdictional authority within the city was geographically divided between the bishops and the Montcada family.[58] The bishops also successfully quashed an urban revolt demanding governance by the citizens in the twelfth century.[59] By the thirteenth century, Vic had become an active center of artisanal production, with a population of about three thousand. The textile, leather, and metal industries were particularly important, with tanned leathers and knives from Vic sold at markets across the Mediterranean.[60] Vic was also home to an ecclesiastical notariate dating back to 1155. The bishops of Vic retained the exclusive right to appoint notaries in their portion of the city until the fourteenth century, when royally appointed notaries began to appropriate jurisdictional authority.[61]

Starting in the mid-thirteenth century, Vic also housed a small but well-documented Jewish community; even with subsequent growth resulting from immigration, the city's Jewish population only reached about one hundred inhabitants.[62] The new Jewish arrivals quickly became embroiled in jurisdictional conflicts between the bishop and the house of Montcada, as many of them resided in an area between the cathedral and the Castell de Montcada, directly along the jurisdictional dividing line of the city.[63] The Jews of Vic, too small of a community to form their own *collecta* (an administrative taxation unit), also maneuvered between the *collectas* of Barcelona and Girona.[64] Unlike Barcelona and Girona, the Jews of Vic did not establish an enclosed Jewish quarter; Jewish residences remained intermingled with those of Christians until at least the fourteenth century.[65]

Sources and Notarial Culture

The contracts crafted by Christian urban notaries—for a clientele that included men and women, Christians and Jews, wealthy merchants and the urban poor—form the heart of this study. From the twelfth century onward, notaries played a central role in medieval Europe as legal professionals who possessed specialized expertise in drawing up economic contracts, court records, and governmental regulations.[66] Notaries were public officials, appointed by royal or municipal governments, who provided legal expertise in contractual forms; even more importantly, they imbued private contracts with public authority.[67] Although all notaries had at least a modicum of literacy in Latin, some simply copied documents from a formulary and filled in their clients' names. More skilled notaries could adapt these formulae to create original documents to meet their clients' specific needs; a few notaries even had university legal training.[68] Increasingly, people of varied social strata, religion, and gender turned to notaries to record aspects of their everyday lives. Scholars have described this phenomenon, seen throughout the western Mediterranean, as the rise of "notarial culture."[69]

Notaries first appeared in Catalonia in the twelfth century, and the first public notariates arose in the second half of that century.[70] By the mid-thirteenth century, ordinary people in Catalonia, as elsewhere in the western Mediterranean, recorded a wide range of contracts with local notaries, including loans, property sales and rentals, wills, and marriage agreements. Starting in the thirteenth century, Catalan notaries began to keep manuals, or registers, with abbreviated copies of every contract. These registers created a record of every transaction that remained in the notary's possession, and they sometimes served as a basis for the official copies of the contract distributed to clients.[71] A fourteenth-century regulation required all notaries to adopt this practice.[72] Notarial registration proved attractive to medieval people; it lowered risk, especially in transactions involving credit, by creating legally enforceable records when money or property changed hands.[73] Notarial documentation might also be mandatory: Jewish moneylenders were legally required to register all loans to Christian debtors with a Christian notary.[74]

Notarial contracts have provided the quantitative and qualitative basis for numerous studies of the social and economic history of ordinary people.[75] As a result, notarial culture has shaped both medieval economies and modern scholarship. However, people experienced and accessed notarial culture in different ways, depending on their gender, religion, and socioeconomic status. Notaries worked with people from across the social spectrum, but first and foremost catered to individuals much like themselves: Christian men, mostly urban dwellers, of middling or elite status.

The norms of notarial culture combined to keep certain people away from the notaries and their transactions off the pages of notarial registers. Many women, both Christian and Jewish, rarely went to the notary unless accompanied by men. Some women may have concluded business transactions without formal documentation. Many Jews preferred to document intra-Jewish business using Hebrew contracts, few of which have survived. The urban poor avoided paying notaries' fees and, in any case, rarely participated in the kinds of transactions that required notarial intervention. Jewish women, impoverished women of all faiths, and poor Jewish men faced an array of intertwined limits on their access to notarial culture.

Much of the work performed by Jewish and Christian women almost certainly occurred outside the confines of notarial culture. The details of these activities often remain invisible to modern scholars, as they generated little documentation. However, as economic life and notarial culture became increasingly interdependent, circumscribed access to notarial culture translated into real limitations on women's ability to participate in many forms of profitable, high-status labor. Christian women were more likely than Jewish women to work successfully within an economy dependent on notaries, but they remained less integrated into notarial culture than men of their own faith and socioeconomic status. Jewish women may have found more opportunities for business within their own community, documented in now-lost Hebrew contracts, but being confined within their own small minority community severely restricted their pool of potential economic partners. Jewish men were far less subject to such constraints.

The three cities that form the focal point of this study were selected in part for their rich documentation prior to 1350. Barcelona has 168 extant registers dating between 1292 and 1350; Girona has 162 registers from between 1311 and 1350; Vic has 325 general registers from between 1250 and 1350, plus 22 notarial manuals devoted exclusively to marriage contracts and 28 *libri iudeorum*, notarial manuals dedicated particularly to transactions involving Jews, from the same period.[76] Despite the substantial number of extant registers, they probably account for only a fraction of the original total.[77] In Barcelona, lost registers pose particular challenges for the study of the city's Jewish community. The small number of Jewish contracts in most registers, combined with a few registers devoted predominantly to transactions involving Jews, suggests that some city notaries specialized unofficially in Jewish business. However, very few of their registers have survived, and some were later bound with the registers of other notaries.[78] In both Vic and Barcelona, the separation of most Jewish contracts into registers dedicated (formally or informally) to Jewish business renders direct comparison of Jewish and Christian economic life difficult. We cannot assume similar survival rates for these documents, and in Barcelona, Jewish contracts are almost certainly underrepresented in the documentary record.

Notaries recorded hundreds of individual transactions in each register, meaning that the several hundred extant registers from these three cities contain thousands of contracts. In order to look broadly across time and place, I adopted a strategy of random sampling. Employing a random number generator, I selected several registers per decade per city; for these, I recorded information about all transactions and determined the proportion of transactions involving women. Using the same method, I selected a larger number of registers per decade per city for which I recorded *only* transactions involving women. The larger sample allowed me to more effectively trace individual women and to identify trends within women's transactions, such as differences by marital status. In total, I consulted 103 registers from Barcelona, 106 from Girona, and 63 from Vic, as well as all 28 of Vic's *libri iudeorum* and 11 of Vic's 22 marriage contract registers. Owing to the smaller number of contracts involving Jews, I consistently recorded all such contracts I found in Barcelona and Girona. In Vic, I randomly selected one *liber iudeorum* per decade from which I recorded all transactions. The thousands of contracts recorded in the consulted registers form the basis of both quantitative analysis and qualitative case studies.

The rich notarial evidence for these three cities remains underutilized. The scholarship on Barcelona's Jewish community is strongest before 1276 and after the Black Death, with something of a lacuna in the late thirteenth and early fourteenth centuries.[79] Most work on Christian women in medieval Barcelona also focuses on the late fourteenth or fifteenth century and relies mostly on the holdings of the Arxiu Històric de Protocols—with little attention to the rich collection of the Arxiu Capitular.[80] The Jewish community of Girona has received extensive scholarly attention, mostly from Catalan scholars, but little thus far has been published in English.[81] Alexandra Guerson and Dana Wessell Lightfoot are in the process of publishing the results of a recent collaborative project on Jewish, Christian, and *conversa* women in Girona, but their scholarship focuses on the fifteenth century.[82] Despite the wealth of sources after 1312, few scholars have considered Christian women in Girona at all, although Christian Guilleré occasionally discusses the importance of marriage alliances in the political and economic strategies of the city's urban elite.[83]

The Jewish community of Vic formed the subject of a monograph published in the early twentieth century, but the overt anti-Semitism of its author, Ramon Corbella i Llobet—who described Jews as particularly suited to moneylending because of their deceitfulness and lack of scruples—inspires suspicion about his conclusions.[84] Fortunately, Catalan scholars have begun to devote further attention to the Jews of Vic; the recently published volume by Irene Llop i Jordana offers thorough coverage of the period up to 1315.[85] The extensive notarial documentation from Vic has not yet been extensively mined for studies of women and gender, although an article by Lluís To Figueras examines women's dowries from Vic as evidence for cloth consumption in thirteenth- and fourteenth-century Catalonia.[86]

Legal evidence enriches the portrait of women's economic life created by notarial documentation. I have drawn on published Jewish and Christian legal codes influential in Catalonia during this period, urban regulations passed by the city council of Barcelona, and *responsa*—queries addressed to rabbis and their legal rulings—from rabbis active in and around Catalonia between 1250 and 1350. The responsa can best be used to glean evidence of what important rabbinic authorities in the region considered appropriate practice. Responsa tend to lack identifying information; real names are normally replaced with a set of standardized biblical names, and place names are often omitted. As a result, responsa rarely allow for fine distinctions between cities or families.

Structure of the Book

This book is divided into three thematic parts: "Family Law," "Notarial Culture," and "Women's Work." The first two sections together offer a multifaceted explanation for both the restrictions experienced by women of all faiths and the wider array of work options available to Christian women than to their Jewish counterparts. Part 1, "Family Law," compares the legal structures and practices surrounding marriage and inheritance among Catalan Christians and Jews. In chapter 1, I posit that Catalan Christian marriage and inheritance practices placed women in a position where they could manage household financial resources, at least under certain circumstances. Legal and social norms positioned men as the preferred managers of financial resources but treated women as valid alternatives in moments of familial or communal need. In contrast, Jewish communities adhered to a set of marriage and inheritance practices that disadvantaged women financially. Chapter 2 argues that rabbinic authorities treated family law and women's control over assets as sites of resistance to acculturation. Through an analysis that incorporates Hebrew and Latin sources, this chapter demonstrates how Jewish communal authorities worked to restrict women's claims to family financial resources and explores the ways in which Jewish families negotiated occasional tensions between communal legal norms and their own economic strategies.

Part 2, "Notarial Culture," presents an intersectional study of how gender and religious identity shaped people's relationship to notarial culture, ultimately arguing that women and Jews, in different ways, had tenuous relationships to notarial culture—and that Jewish women were doubly marginalized. Restrictions stemming from family law and social norms linked to notarial culture combined to narrow the work options for all women, but especially for Jewish women. Chapter 3 explores the push and pull experienced by Christian women, who experienced challenges in negotiating the male spaces associated with notaries but could also develop a lifelong familiarity with notarial culture. In chapter 4, I argue that Jews' understanding of notarial culture as fundamentally Christian shaped their decisions about whether to go to notaries. Jewish women developed a particularly fraught relationship with notarial culture.

Part 3, "Women's Work," delves into the details of what women's work looked like in practice and what opportunities and restrictions shaped the labor performed by women in Catalan cities. Chapter 5 offers an overview of Jewish and Christian women's work as revealed through notarial documentation, which demonstrates that Christian women participated more frequently than Jewish women in a broad range of public economic transactions. Chapter 6 explores in depth the case study of the real estate market, where both Christian and Jewish women played an especially prominent role but Jewish women still faced more restrictions than their Christian counterparts. The final chapter addresses a revealing exception to this pattern: the expansion of Jewish women's role in the credit market during moments of communal change and crisis, as seen through the case studies of Vic in the mid-thirteenth century and Barcelona and Girona in the wake of the Black Death. Communal necessity or crisis forced Jewish communities to adjust their expectations for women's work responsibilities. The challenges posed by life as a minority community required occasional flexibility on women from Jewish communities, yet the changes wrought for women were always temporary.

The conclusion addresses how this book complicates three major narratives: the "Golden Age" of Jews in the thirteenth- and fourteenth-century Crown of Aragon, the contrast between Jewish acculturation in Sepharad and Jewish cultural isolation in Ashkenaz, and the dichotomy between economic self-determination among the women of northern Europe and economic constraints on their counterparts in Mediterranean Europe. The Jewish and Christian women who lived and worked in Catalan cities challenge us to reassess both women's history and Jewish history in the medieval Mediterranean.

I

FAMILY LAW

1

MARRIAGE AND INHERITANCE IN CATALAN CHRISTIAN LEGAL CULTURE

In January 1255, Berenguer Bonell of Vic, his wife Berenguera, and his children Bernat, Ermessenda, Elisenda, and Guillema jointly gave their daughter and sister Martina in marriage to Bernat Osona.[1] By giving Martina in marriage, her parents and siblings also accepted the financial obligation of paying her dowry, the wealth that brides brought to their husbands. The dowry typically represented a substantial share of a family's assets, which some families took years to pay in full. The marriage contract therefore set up a complicated relationship of credit and debt. The bride and her family might remain indebted to her husband for years, but the dowry also represented a debt that the husband owed to his wife or her heirs when death ultimately dissolved the marriage. Marriages were not only social relationships but economic ones. Marriages also impacted far more people than just the bride and groom; they tied together two families as well as two individuals.

The marriage contracts drawn up for Martina and her sisters Elisenda and Guillema reveal Catalan Christians' legal assumptions about women's claims over the property of both their fathers and their husbands. Berenguer's daughters gradually disappeared from their sisters' marriage contracts. Although Elisenda had given her sister Martina in marriage, Martina's name does not appear in Elisenda's 1262 marriage contract.[2] In turn, neither Elisenda nor Martina played a formal role when their last sister, Guillema, married in 1267.[3] By that time, however, a new woman in the family joined in giving Guillema in marriage: Bernat's wife, also named Guillema. The presence, and absence, of

Berenguer's daughters, wife, and daughter-in-law reflects the extent to which these women were thought to have a stake in the family's financial strategies.

The Christian majority in Catalonia operated within a legal culture, shaped from a blend of Roman law and local customary law, that fostered women's control over financial resources—but only within certain limits. Christian women could claim the right to inherit alongside their brothers, but upon marriage, they typically relinquished any additional claims over their parents' estate and transferred their inherited wealth into the hands of their husbands. Christian wives and widows enjoyed some managerial authority over their husbands' property but could make only tenuous ownership claims. The constellation of Christian marriage and inheritance practices in thirteenth- and fourteenth-century Catalonia together formed a system that enabled some women to both possess and control assets, but nevertheless assumed that most wealth would be managed by men.

Over the course of this chapter, I will trace the gendered structures that governed Christian women's access to financial resources. The wider argument of the chapter is that the legal culture of Catalan Christians treated women's control over family assets, under certain circumstances, as essential to household solvency and urban wealth. Women's managerial authority over money and property was only promoted insofar as it served family financial strategies, not as an end in itself. However, the contrast with Catalan Jewish legal culture—which forms the subject of chapter 2—illuminates Christian women's advantages relative to their Jewish counterparts.

I begin with a discussion of the *capítols matrimonials*, the set of contracts that together structured the economic exchanges crucial to marriages and that form a major source base for this chapter. Subsequently, I examine the legal norms that dictated whether and how women owned and managed property, starting with dowry and inheritance, the property transfers that were most explicitly discussed in the *capítols matrimonials* and that for women were fundamentally interlinked. I then turn to how the legal understanding of the dowry and other marital gifts as debts enabled married women to play a role in managing the conjugal estate. Finally, I discuss the circumstances under which widows could wield authority over their late husbands' property.

Getting Married in Medieval Catalonia: The Anatomy of a Marriage Contract

When Elisenda, daughter of Berenguer de Mans, and Jaume de Montcada of Barcelona married on September 23, 1307, the notary Bernat de Vilarrubía recorded a set of contracts—together known as the *capítols matrimonials*—that defined the new couple's economic relationship with their families and with each other.[4] Ultimately, a marriage was created only with the exchange of words of consent—increasingly done before a church and in the presence of a priest.[5] However, especially among the wealthy, marriages were predicated upon interfamilial agreements centered on exchanges of money and property.

In this case, the *capítols matrimonials* comprised six separate contracts, drawn up over the course of two weeks. First, Jaume's father, Esteve de Montcada of Barcelona, granted his son a large dwelling, described as a *hospicium*, which could include a multistory domestic space as well as workshops and storefronts.[6] This property represented part of Jaume's eventual inheritance, and the grant not only provided the young couple with a place of residence but also ensured that Jaume could credibly commit to eventually repaying his wife's dowry and providing her with an additional marital gift out of his own estate. Esteve subsequently confirmed to Elisenda that the property could indeed serve as a pledge for the return of her assets. Berenguer de Mans, in turn, granted his daughter 12,000 sous to be used as her dowry.

The couple signed their dowry contract only after both Jaume and Elisenda had established their independent claims over financial resources. Elisenda granted Jaume the 12,000 sous she had inherited from her father as her dowry, while Jaume promised to make his bride a gift of 6,000 sous out of his own goods, payable at the dissolution of the marriage. Jaume also confirmed that he had received 4,000 sous of Elisenda's dowry from her and her father. Two days later, in the fifth contract, Jaume released Elisenda from any further claims related to her dowry.[7] On October 7, two weeks later, Jaume confirmed that he had received Elisenda's cash dowry in its entirety, as well as jewels, textiles, and other valuable objects that she had moved into their new shared household.[8]

These contracts illuminate the complex web of social and financial institutions surrounding marriage. When Catalan couples got married, they typically established new households rather than living with either set of parents; the creation of a new conjugal home required them to gather and pool assets from both their families.[9] Marriage contracts simultaneously reflected and shaped young women's claims to the property of their fathers and husbands. The following sections will trace how couples obtained and used these funds—and how the exchange of assets in marriage contracts structured women's relationship to financial resources throughout their lives.

Dowry and Inheritance in Medieval Europe

Most Catalan Christian women received the bulk of their inheritance in the form of the dowry, which by the thirteenth century had become the most important type of marital gift throughout Mediterranean Europe as well as parts of northern Europe.[10] Daughters received the dowry (Latin *dos* or Catalan *exovar*), which could include cash, real estate, and movable goods, from their birth families and transferred it to their husbands. Under normal circumstances, a husband retained managerial authority over his wife's dowry for the duration of the marriage. However, the wife maintained ownership of her dowry; she could reclaim it in widowhood or even sue her still-living husband for its return in the case of mismanagement or insolvency.[11] Wives who predeceased their husbands could dispose of the dowry in their wills. Their children, if they had them, usually inherited, but wives could also leave legacies to family members or make charitable bequests.[12]

Over the last several decades, scholars have debated whether the dowry should be considered a form of women's inheritance or, alternatively, a means of disinheriting daughters and limiting their authority over both their fathers' and their husbands' estates. Diane Owen Hughes argued that the advent of the dowry system diminished wives' claims over their husbands' property and effectively disinherited daughters.[13] Hughes's portrayal of the dowry system is compelling but broad and synthetic, encompassing evidence from the thirteenth through the fifteenth centuries in Catalonia, southern France, and Italy.

Subsequent scholarship has complicated Hughes's synthesis. The negative effects of the dowry system were probably most felt in Italy—and there, most particularly in Florence—and worsened over the course of the later Middle Ages. Unsurprisingly, as a result, scholarship focused on late medieval and early modern Florence has for the most part confirmed Hughes's negative portrayal of the dowry system as a force for women's disinheritance and dispossession, or at least as a system that worked to concentrate family property in the hands of men.[14]

Even in Italy, however, the dowry system did not necessarily disinherit girls, especially outside Florence. In twelfth- and thirteenth-century Genoa, nearly half of all testators with sons and daughters bequeathed girls an equal share of family wealth—a surprisingly strong tendency toward equal treatment.[15] Dowry inflation among patrician families in Renaissance Venice provided substantial inheritances for women from the wealthiest families. Owing to the wealth that they brought into their marriages, wives also gained a significant voice in their husbands' financial decisions.[16] Daughters and sons in late medieval Venice inherited equally from their mothers, and fathers often voluntarily chose to give their daughters bequests beyond the dowry.[17]

In thirteenth- and fourteenth-century southern France and Catalonia, the dowry system remained compatible with traditions affirming women's inheritance rights. Women in fourteenth-century Manosque tended to receive portions equal to those granted to their brothers, whether in the form of dowry or as bequests in their parents' wills. While dowered daughters could legally be excluded from further inheritance, in practice they often received large supplementary bequests.[18] Brides in thirteenth-century Barcelona and Perpignan received ample dowries, which represented substantial shares of the family patrimony.[19] Arguably, Catalan dowry culture resembled that of northern Europe, challenging easy distinctions between the north and the Mediterranean. Families in England also treated the dowry as part or all of daughters' expected inheritance, while families in early modern France remained committed to providing for daughters and sons nearly equally.[20]

The evidence from Barcelona, Girona, and Vic supports an understanding of the dowry as a form of women's inheritance, albeit one that limited women's practical control over their inherited wealth. The *capítols matrimonials* relied on the legal fiction that property passed through women's hands: in the 1307 marriage between Jaume de Montcada and Elisenda de Mans, for example, the contracts portray Elisenda as receiving her dowry from her father, Berenguer, before transferring it to her new husband. In reality, the documentary double transfer of ownership disguised the direct transfer of resources from a woman's father to her husband; Elisenda never controlled her dowry wealth as an unmarried woman. However, as Natalie Zemon Davis has argued, constructed fictions in archival documents reveal a great deal about contemporary mentalities.[21] The legal fiction of these grants reflected the presumption that young women owned their inherited wealth, even if they never managed it.

Practicing Partible Inheritance in Medieval Catalonia

Upon her marriage to the cobbler Pere de Puig on November 17, 1311, Bonanata, daughter of the miller Arnau de Garriga of Girona, released her father from any debt "on account of my paternal inheritance and *legítima*."[22] Many *capítols matrimonials* contained a similar clause or contract in which brides released their parents from any inheritance claims beyond their dowries.[23] Bonanata could licitly assert her right to receive a portion of her father's estate because of the pervasiveness of partible inheritance in late medieval Catalonia. The tradition of partible inheritance stemmed from Visigothic law, which remained influential in the thirteenth and fourteenth centuries.[24] Visigothic codes dictated that the majority of the parental estate—four-fifths of the father's property and three-quarters of the mother's dowry wealth—should be divided equally among all children, through either shared inheritance or equal division of the estate. Further, Visigothic law affirmed the principle of gender-egalitarian inheritance, assigning equal rights to sons and daughters.[25] Parents could favor a single heir—usually a son—with a larger portion, up to one-third of the value of the estate.[26] In practice, not all parents treated their sons and daughters as equivalent heirs; as early as the eleventh century, many Catalan peasant families selected a single child, usually the eldest male, as the heir invested with the family patrimony.[27]

Beginning in the thirteenth century, the Catalan-Aragonese monarchs increasingly emphasized the legal principles of the *ius commune*, a fusion of Roman and canon law influential throughout western Europe.[28] Roman law granted testators freedom to divide their property as they wished but guaranteed all children, with the exception of emancipated sons and married daughters, a small legacy and divided the estate equally among all eligible heirs in the case of intestacy.[29] The *ius commune* also introduced the concept of the *heres universalis*, or universal heir, who took on all legal responsibilities of the deceased and became liable for his or her debts.[30] Although some Catalan Christian families demonstrated a preference for a single primary heir even before the *ius commune* gained a significant foothold, the Roman-style *heres* and the increased freedom of testators under the *ius commune* bolstered this increasingly common practice.[31]

Catalan customary law, which in most cities took precedence over both Visigothic law and the *ius commune*, developed its own rules for inheritance.[32] Urban customary law typically allowed testators to select a single primary heir but required parents to provide all their legitimate sons and daughters with the *legítima*, an equal share of one-third of the estate, which for daughters could come in the form of the dowry.[33] In cases of intestacy, the estate would be divided equally among the children of the deceased. In the absence of children, grandchildren or other descendants would inherit, followed by parents or other ascendants, and finally siblings—regardless of gender.[34] Daughters could receive inheritance portions beyond their dowries, referred to as their *paraphernalia*. Husbands had no managerial authority over their wives' paraphernal goods (as opposed to the dowry), and women could dispose of these goods as they wished, without their husbands' consent.[35]

Among some sectors of society in medieval Catalonia, Visigothic partible inheritance traditions gradually gave way to primogeniture. Beginning in the thirteenth century, patrician families in Barcelona named a single child as heir in order to concentrate financial resources in the hands of a single, normally male, representative of the family.[36] A similar process, dating back to the tenth century, can be seen among rural Catalan families. Egalitarian partible inheritance traditions among these groups were gradually replaced with practices that limited daughters' inheritance rights: naming a single child as heir; providing one child, always a son, with an increased portion; providing smaller portions to daughters than sons; and excluding dowered daughters.[37]

In contrast, testators belonging to the urban mercantile and artisanal classes of the Christian community of Perpignan apparently preferred partible inheritance to primogeniture. Out of thirty-two testators with multiple children, only nine privileged a single male heir. Although some parents preferred sons over daughters, or limited the rights of married daughters, many mothers and fathers distributed their property nearly equally among all their daughters and sons.[38] Daughters also received substantial dowries, which represented a significant portion of the patrimony.[39] In other words, although partible inheritance as practiced in thirteenth-century Catalan cities may not have been fully egalitarian, it nevertheless assured daughters of a substantial share of their parents' wealth.

The case of Berenguer Bonell and his daughters highlights how Catalan legal culture upheld daughters' and sons' theoretical inheritance claims as equally valid—as well as how many families ultimately treated daughters differently from sons. At moments when a contractual commitment could dramatically transform the composition of the patrimony, broad groups of potential heirs actively participated in or consented to transactions. The assumption of joint inheritance granted both sons and daughters at least a theoretical voice in their parents' business dealings; in-laws, siblings, parents, and occasionally even aunts and uncles or cousins might become involved, depending on family circumstances. Hence groups of relatives gathered to give brides in marriage and accept responsibility for their dowries, as well as to sell family-owned real estate.[40] Both dowry contracts and real estate sales suggest that partible inheritance traditions proved most pervasive in the market town of Vic and weakest in the commercial powerhouse of Barcelona. The distinction may support Stephen Bensch's contention that the move toward single heirship among the Barcelona patriciate stemmed from economic considerations.[41] Diversifying investments was crucial to success in the bustling Mediterranean maritime economy of Barcelona—but in the smaller town of

Vic, families might have considered these investment strategies less feasible or less essential. Alternatively, change simply may have come more slowly to smaller and more provincial cities: partible inheritance traditions were in decline in Vic by 1350.[42]

Although families respected unmarried women's potential inheritance claims, in practice few women remained integrated into the management of family property after they had married and received dowries. Although a son might jointly manage property alongside his parents for as long as they lived, most daughters disappeared from their parents' financial transactions after marriage. To return to the example of the Bonell family, Martina and Elisenda ceased to participate in family transactions after their marriages, while their brother Bernat not only continued to act alongside his father but even involved his wife in family business.

The young women who participated in or consented to their parents' or siblings' financial dealings typically did so precisely at the moment when they would have been least equipped to make informed financial decisions. Several contracts specified that the young women involved had not yet attained legal majority; minor girls—and boys—would have had little experience in managing financial resources. In 1286, Ponç de Cirera of Vic, his wife Bartomeua, and their children Jaume, Beatriu, and Elisenda sold a plot of land, and all three children renounced their right to contest the sale on the grounds of being legal minors.[43] The notary omitted the children's precise ages, but at the oldest they would have been in their late teens.[44] Unmarried teenage daughters almost never managed property independently and probably had little sense of whether a sale would help or hinder their own financial prospects. Ponç's children may have formally participated in the transaction, but we cannot assume that they offered informed consent.

Parental promises to obtain consent from very young children underline the distinction between respecting potential heirs' theoretical inheritance claims and expecting them to participate actively in family economic strategies. When Maria, wife of Guillem Oliver of Barcelona, sold property on her husband's behalf in 1319, she promised to obtain the consent of her daughter and son, who at the time were only nine and seven years old.[45] Even more dramatically, in 1318, the silversmith Miquel Arnau of Barcelona and his son Bartomeu agreed to obtain consent from their two-year-old daughter and half-sister Miqueleta when they leased out houses with an attached workshop.[46] Clearly, daughters' theoretical claims over family property did not necessarily translate into managerial authority over their parents' estates.

In practice, daughters rarely comanaged inherited wealth. Documents that trace inheritance payments and testamentary legacies provide valuable insight into how joint inheritance functioned in practice. While most scholars have relied on testaments as evidence for inheritance practices, Thomas Kuehn points out that this focus excludes those who died intestate—often as a deliberate strategic decision—and only considers inheritance strategies as desired by the deceased, not as actually practiced by their heirs.[47] Even when a testament existed, heirs spent years, even decades, dealing with the aftermath of inheritance—administering the estate of the deceased, dividing an inheritance among siblings, returning dowries to widows, and disbursing legacies to friends, relatives, and charitable causes. The contracts that heirs drew up in relation to these activities reveal how they understood and evaluated overlapping claims to an estate, sometimes beyond the dictates of the testament, and sometimes in the absence of any testament at all.

Brothers and sisters often inherited jointly through intestacy, and parents who preferred this option may have deliberately avoided or delayed crafting a will. Intestacy often produced groups of two or more joint universal heirs (*heredes universales*), who acted together to manage and sell inherited property.[48] Nor did intestate succession and other joint heirship strategies necessarily exclude married daughters.[49] A contract from 1340 described Constança, wife of Pere Bell-lloc of Barcelona, and her brother Nicolau Pascual as "universal heirs via intestacy" of their father Ramon Pascual, a swordsmith of Barcelona.[50] Marriage, in other words, did not automatically invalidate daughters' claims to the family patrimony. Heiress sisters who relinquished future inheritance claims did so by contract, not by default. In 1287, for example, Elisenda, daughter of Ferrer Cassard of Vic, made her brother Guillem, a cleric, a grant of all her real property after she married.[51] Married daughters also in some cases continued to act alongside still-living parents; in 1323, Miquela, widow of Pere de Mans of Vic, her son Ramon, and her married daughter Berenguera, wife of Ramon Arnau of Barcelona, together sold a market stall in Vic.[52]

Yet even in cases of joint or partible inheritance, the responsibility of paying legacies and dividing the estate often fell to a single male heir. Men acting alone made almost half of inheritance payments in Vic, and over half in both Barcelona and Girona, whereas family groups acting together made about 13 percent of inheritance payments in Vic and under 6 percent in the two larger cities (see table 1).[53] Much like the evidence from dowry contracts and property sales, inheritance payments indicate that partible inheritance

TABLE 1 Inheritance payments among Christians

	Barcelona, 1292–1350		Girona, 1311–1350		Vic, 1250–1350	
	Donors	Recipients	Donors	Recipients	Donors	Recipients
Single male	66 (52.8%)	71 (56.8%)	43 (61.4%)	43 (61.4%)	97 (47.3%)	111 (54.1%)
Single female	27 (21.6%)	36 (28.8%)	15 (21.4%)	19 (27.1%)	40 (19.5%)	56 (27.3%)
Married couple	6 (4.8%)	3 (2.4%)	5 (7.1%)	4 (5.7%)	30 (14.6%)	18 (8.8%)
Female group (relatives)	1 (0.8%)	1 (0.8%)	1 (1.4%)	0 (0%)	0 (0%)	4 (2%)
Male group (relatives)	2 (1.6%)	1 (0.8%)	0 (0%)	1 (1.4%)	3 (1.5%)	7 (3.4%)
Male group (non-relatives)	19 (15.2%)	4 (3.2%)	2 (2.9%)	0 (0%)	11 (5.4%)	2 (1%)
Male/ female group (relatives)	4 (3.2%)	9 (7.2%)	3 (4.3%)	3 (4.3%)	24 (11.7%)	7 (3.4%)
Illegible	0 (0%)	0 (0%)	1 (1.4%)	0 (0%)	0 (0%)	0 (0%)
Total no. of inheritance payments	125		70		205	

remained more popular in Vic than in Barcelona or Girona, where single male heirs accepted primary responsibility for managing inherited estates. The seemingly greater preference for primary male heirs in Girona compared to Barcelona actually reflects a distinction in who took responsibility for making inheritance payments: in Barcelona, testators often appointed executors to carry out their wishes and pay legacies.[54] The executors could be the principal heirs of the deceased but could also be other relatives or friends. Although men in Genoa often charged their widows with this responsibility, the dying in Barcelona often selected a group of male friends and family members.[55]

An analysis of the recipients of inheritance payments also demonstrates the prioritization of men as heirs and the limits of partible inheritance. Family members rarely received inheritances jointly, and men received inheritance payments around twice as often as women in all three cities (see table 1).[56] The small number of women recipients of inheritances confirms that most daughters received the bulk of their inherited wealth at marriage, in the form of the dowry, and exerted no subsequent claims to their parents' estates. Nor did women often manage inherited resources jointly with their siblings, at least not in the long term. In most families, siblings divided their parents' estates rather than managing them together. Property rental contracts confirm the evidence provided by inheritance payments: although family groups often sold property in tandem, they less frequently leased out property together.[57] Siblings worked together to transform indivisible jointly owned real property into more fungible cash, but they avoided long-term joint management of rental properties.

Very few parents named daughters as sole universal heirs, and most heiress daughters either had no siblings or only sisters. In other words, families rarely gave daughters preferential treatment over sons. However, a few parents made different choices. In 1261, for example, Joan, son of Bernat de Sorigueres, acknowledged that his sister Berenguera de Sorigueres and her husband Pere had disbursed his inheritance.[58] Berenguera's control of family funds, combined with the fact that her husband had adopted her family surname, suggests that she had inherited the bulk of the patrimonial estate. Some daughters who received such preferential treatment may have been privileged as children of a prior marriage, but in other cases the rationale behind selecting a daughter as heiress is less apparent. A 1275 contract identified Simona, Bernat, and Benvinguda as children of both Ramon de Cudina of Vic and his wife Ramona, but it stated that both parents had named Simona alone as their universal heiress.[59] Some families may have privileged the eldest child regardless of gender. In other cases, mothers selected a single daughter as universal heiress, perhaps on the assumption that their husbands would provide more substantial legacies to the other children. Blanca, daughter of Martí Ferrer and Bonanata and wife of Nicolau de Villar of Girona, acted as her mother's universal heiress in 1341 when she paid her sister Caterina a legacy of 40 sous left by their late mother.[60]

Heiress daughters incurred the same financial responsibilities as male heirs: paying their parents' debts, disbursing legacies and charitable donations, and distributing the inheritances of their siblings. Francesca, wife of Jaume de Torre of Girona and universal heiress of her father, the notary Arnau de Mans, paid the dowry and inheritance legacy of her sister Caterina, wife of the merchant Bernat Bertrand, in April 1345.[61] In an intriguing reversal of the dowry system, some heiresses even received dowries from their husbands, who moved into their homes and sometimes adopted their surnames. In 1326, for example, Elisenda, daughter and universal heiress of Berenguer de Quintana of Sant Julià de Vilatorta (a village near Vic), received from her groom Ferrer d'Olmeda 1,000 sous, which he described as "for my dowry" (*pro mea dote*).[62]

Creating a Conjugal Estate: Women's Wealth in Medieval Catalonia

A newly married couple formed a household by blending the husband's and wife's assets into a new conjugal estate. The exchange of marital gifts brought most of women's wealth under the control of their husbands—but also endowed them with some measure of authority over their husbands' assets. The structures surrounding marital property allowed women, within limits, to manage or comanage household financial resources.

Wives relinquished management of their dowries to their husbands but retained ownership throughout their married lives and in widowhood. The assets women received as a dowry formed the basis of their current and future financial security, especially for women from prosperous families. Substantial dowries attracted husbands capable of appropriately supporting their wives and children. Dowry wealth also ensured women's financial stability in widowhood; wealthy widows received income from rental properties they had received as a dowry and invested cash dowries in profitable commercial ventures.

Dowry size in thirteenth- and fourteenth-century Catalan cities remained stable, with little evidence of the extreme dowry inflation that Dante criticized in fourteenth-century Florence.[63] However, the wealth brides brought into marriage varied based on both local norms and family socioeconomic status. Median dowry values were higher in larger, wealthier cities; the median dowry in Barcelona was 1,200 sous, compared with 720 sous in Girona and 600 sous in Vic (see table 2).[64] Brides from working-class families brought dowries well below the average; Guillema ça Ribes, an inhabitant of Vic, married Berenguer ça Vall with a dowry of only 60 sous in 1303.[65] Given that the notary referred to Guillema and Berenguer as "residents," not citizens, of Vic, both were probably laborers who had recently moved to Vic from the surrounding hinterlands in search of work.[66] Urban elites, in turn, brought dowries far above the average; a dowry of 25,000 sous sealed a marriage alliance between two wealthy urban mercantile families in Barcelona

TABLE 2 Value of Christian cash dowries

	Barcelona, 1292–1350	Girona, 1311–1350	Vic, 1250–1350
Total no. of pure cash dowries	111	111	418
Minimum value in sous of Barcelona	150	170	60
Maximum value in sous of Barcelona	25,000	12,000	9,000
Median value in sous of Barcelona	1,200	720	600
Average value in sous of Barcelona	3,988	1,960	900

in 1334.[67] Depending on the liquidity of the bride's family, the dowry could be paid relatively quickly or over the course of years.[68]

For some brides, dowry wealth also included real estate. Scholars have often used the prevalence of real property dowries to evaluate whether families, and particularly fathers, respected daughters' claims over the family patrimony. Hughes argued that the turn toward cash dowries in the western Mediterranean exacerbated daughters' disinheritance by cutting off their access to the most economically and symbolically significant portion of the patrimony.[69] However, empirical evidence has weakened Hughes's claims that cash fully supplanted real estate in the dowries of Mediterranean brides. Over one-third of brides marrying in fourteenth-century Manosque brought dowries that included real estate; real estate holdings appeared in about half of the dowries in thirteenth-century Perpignan.[70] Families in late medieval Venice also provided their daughters with real estate holdings to use as dowries, and husbands earmarked specific pieces of their own real property as guarantees for dowry repayment.[71] Recent scholarship has also challenged the assumption that Mediterranean families valued real property more highly than wealth in the form of cash or movable goods, which were often included in dowry wealth.[72]

Brides in Catalan cities regularly brought dowries that included real estate. Real property appeared in 14 percent of dowries from Girona, slightly under one-quarter of dowries from Barcelona, and over one-third of dowries in Vic (see table 3). In both Barcelona and Girona, however, dowries including real property declined over the course of the fourteenth century. The casualties of the Black Death in Marseille concentrated family resources in fewer hands, with the result that more brides married with dowries including real estate holdings.[73] In Barcelona and Girona, in contrast, the Black

TABLE 3 Christian marriage contracts with dowries including real estate

	Barcelona, 1292–1350		Girona, 1311–1350		Vic, 1250–1350	
	Total no. of dowry contracts	Propertied dowry contracts	Total no. of dowry contracts	Propertied dowry contracts	Total no. of dowry contracts	Propertied dowry contracts
1250–1275	—	—	—	—	81	26 (32.1%)
1276–1300	12	6 (50%)	—	—	208	68 (32.7%)
1301–1325	82	18 (22%)	6	1 (16.7%)	153	53 (34.6%)
1326–1347	43	9 (20.9%)	118	17 (14.4%)	117	43 (36.8%)
1348–1350	8	1 (12.5%)	5	0 (0%)	93	44 (47.3%)
Total	145	34 (23.4%)	129	18 (14%)	652	234 (35.9%)

Death failed to arrest the downward trend: brides marrying between 1348 and 1350 were even less likely to receive real property as a dowry than young women in the preceding decade were. However, the trend against real estate dowries does not necessarily mean that women lost control over real property: in those same years, women selling and leasing out real estate holdings appeared in slightly higher numbers.[74] Families—including brides—may have preferred to keep inherited real property separate from the dowry.

The evidence from Vic presents a different picture. The proportion of dowries including real estate slowly but consistently climbed from 1250 onward, and the Black Death brought a particularly dramatic jump: slightly over one-third of dowries between 1326 and 1347 included real estate, compared with nearly half of dowries between 1348 and 1350. During these same decades, women's joint landholding alongside family members declined, but women increasingly managed rental properties independently.[75] Although a decline in partible inheritance traditions may have weakened women's claims over real property, women who did own real estate managed it with less intervention from their husbands and male relatives. A slight trend toward dowry inflation may have encouraged cash-poor but land-rich families in Vic to incorporate real property into their daughters' dowries. The phenomenon of landowning families with little liquid wealth may have been more common in Vic than in Barcelona or Girona, necessitating the higher percentage of real estate dowries in Vic. The change in the wake of the Black Death also suggests that as demographic decline concentrated assets in the hands of fewer survivors, women more often inherited landed wealth.

Although the dowry had become the primary marital gift by the thirteenth century, husbands also contributed to the future wealth of their wives and the current solvency of the household with their own gift: the *sponsalicium*. This gift had gradually replaced a more sizable contribution; under Visigothic law, a wife received a tenth (*decimum*) of her husband's estate. Although some Barcelona grooms continued to promise the Visigothic *decimum* as late as the mid-twelfth century, marriage contracts increasingly stipulated that husbands could replace real property pledged as *decimum* with fixed sums in cash.[76] With the rise of the dowry system, the husband's gift—varyingly referred to as the *sponsalicium, donatio propter nuptias,* and "addition" (Latin *augmentum* or Catalan *escreix*)—diminished in value.[77] Catalan law fixed the *sponsalicium* at half the value of the dowry, and some husbands provided more meager sums.[78] Moreover, while some grooms increased the value of their contribution to account for wealth received in the form of non-estimated real estate (real estate holdings without a formal appraised value), others only provided half the value of their brides' cash dowries.[79] A widow enjoyed management rights over the *sponsalicium* during her lifetime, but upon her death, it automatically passed to the couple's children or, if they had none, to her husband's heirs.[80]

Theoretically, the exchange of marital gifts strictly defined the boundaries between the property owned by a wife and that owned by her husband. In practice, however, wives' and husbands' overlapping rights of ownership and management created a shared conjugal estate. Occasionally, couples even eschewed the dowry system in favor of shared property or *mig per mig* marriages, in which married couples pooled all their resources into a shared conjugal fund, to be divided upon the death of the first spouse between the surviving spouse and the deceased's heirs.[81] Similar community property marriages prevailed under custom in neighboring Castile as well as in some northern European cities.[82] Jesús Lalinde Abadia argued that in Catalonia, only the poorest women, those who could not afford to provide dowries, married under the *mig per mig* system.[83] However, evidence from thirteenth-century Perpignan and fifteenth-century Valencia indicates that some middling-status families also entered *mig per mig* marriages.[84] My sample yielded no *mig per mig* contracts from Barcelona, but one from Girona and nineteen from Vic.[85] However, most of the couples who married under the *mig per mig* system in these cities came from the lower strata of society.[86] The disparity between Vic on the one hand and Barcelona and Girona on the other could indicate that the surviving notarial registers in the latter two cities disproportionately record the dowries of better-off families. Despite *mig per mig* brides' formal ownership rights over the entire conjugal estate, the documentary record provides no direct evidence that they played a more active role in jointly managing property than women who married with a standard dowry.

Although the dowry system placed most of women's wealth under the control of their husbands, women nevertheless functioned as managers of household wealth under certain circumstances. In some cases, separation of marital property placed women in control of wealth, as they could and did independently administer their inherited *paraphernalia*. Contracts sometimes specified when women drew on their *paraphernalia* to extend loans or invest in commercial ventures. In 1300, for example, Guillema, wife of the tanner Pere de Vila of Barcelona, loaned the cobbler Pere Ulric 7.5 pounds, which she had taken from the *paraphernalia* she inherited from her parents.[87] In contracts where married women sold inherited property without obtaining their husbands' consent, these holdings may have come from their *paraphernalia*, although the contracts do not always specify all the relevant details about the property in question. In 1333, Bartomeua, wife of Berenguer de Vic of Barcelona, sold two plots of land that she had inherited from her late father, Guillem Ermengaud. Her husband was present in the city at the time of the sale, and he remained heavily involved in his wife's economic endeavors—in a subsequent contract, she appointed him as her agent to transfer corporeal possession of the property. However, he did not formally consent to the sale, suggesting that the property came from her *paraphernalia* rather than from the dowry ostensibly under his control.[88]

When wives managed household financial resources, they often did so by exploiting the blurred boundaries between the wealth of wives and that of husbands. The tension between wives' ownership rights and husbands' managerial rights also gave wives a lien over the entire conjugal estate, which could endow women with extensive authority over their husbands' property as well as their own. Wives retained ownership over both dowry and *sponsalicium*, but husbands had the right and responsibility to manage the estate in its entirety.[89] However, husbands obligated their entire estates for the repayment of the dowry and *sponsalicium*. As a result, both spouses could technically claim authority over any part of the estate. The move toward cash dowries further muddled the strict separation of goods, as fungible cash was more easily integrated into the larger conjugal estate than was real property.[90]

The integration of the wife's dowry and *sponsalicium* into a shared family estate created a system that promoted husbands' and wives' cooperation in the management of household resources. Wives' ownership claims could allow them to exercise managerial authority within certain limits. The gendered structure of the conjugal estate operated on the assumption that husbands could manage their wives' property in an effective and financially responsible manner. If they failed to do so—for example, if a man's indebtedness threatened the security of his wife's assets as well as his own—wives could recover their dowries.[91] Court records even indicate that a wife's claim that her husband had incurred debts beyond his means could enable her to legally reclaim her dowry.[92] Although dowry recovery suits imply an adversarial relationship between husband and wife, couples in these suits may have colluded to protect family assets from creditors.[93] In more ordinary circumstances, the practice of obtaining wives' consent to transactions gave them a supporting managerial role in family financial strategies.

Notarial contracts involving married couples reveal the strategies that husbands, wives, and the people with whom they did business adopted to ensure the legal validity of their business transactions. In both Catalonia and southern France, wives regularly renounced the Velleian senatus consult, a

Roman legal decree that permitted the nullification of women's transactions if they had participated under compulsion.[94] In some documents, wives also renounced the *si qua mulier*, an addition to the senatus consult from Justinian's *Corpus Iuris Civilis*, which invalidated any grants that women had made to their husbands.[95] Medieval experts in Roman law interpreted the senatus consult to mean that a wife's marital property was protected from the demands of her husband's creditors; by renouncing the senatus consult in a debt contract, a wife obligated her dowry and *sponsalicium* for the loan and waived her right to sequester her dowry from creditors. Both Rebecca Winer and Marie Kelleher argue that the practice of renouncing the Velleian senatus consult diminished women's authority over their marital property.[96]

However, creditors' preference that their debtors' wives renounce the senatus consult made husbands' transactions subject to their wives' approval. Although some husbands may have coerced their wives into granting permission, women did not necessarily give approval automatically, nor did they participate in every transaction. Indeed, had wives' renunciation become purely formulaic, we would expect it to appear in nearly every transaction involving a married man. In reality, wives participated more selectively in their husbands' business dealings; Margarida, wife of the elite Girona notary Bernat Taialà, acted alongside her husband in six of the thirteen loans he received from Jewish creditors between 1331 and 1345.[97] She separately renounced the senatus consult in each of these six loans.[98] Nothing clearly differentiated the loans Bernat received alongside Margarida from those he took out independently—but her dotal assets could only be used to secure the debts that she cosigned and for which she renounced the senatus consult. The pattern of wives' physical presence and act of renunciation—combined with their absence from some of the debts incurred by their husbands—suggests that wives avoided lending support to some transactions, or that couples crafted economic strategies centered on wives' selective participation.

In some cases, the absence of renouncing wives may attest to husbands' creditworthiness or to a prior relationship of trust between creditor and debtor. Some men, in contrast, may have faced difficulty in obtaining credit, or received less favorable terms, if they acted without their wives' consent. However, the absence of wives could also indicate that women deliberately limited the risk to their property by participating in some, but not all, of their husbands' debts. Given the extensive evidence that women in the medieval Iberian Peninsula acted decisively to protect their assets, we should not assume that wives always acquiesced to their husbands.[99] Some women undoubtedly took their formulaic assent seriously and used it to gain a greater voice in the management of household resources. Legal professionals and notaries may not have sought to empower women, but they built a system in which women's public participation in family businesses ensured the validity of transactions.

Dividing the Conjugal Estate: Widows' Claims

Although some married women managed financial resources independently or alongside their husbands, widowhood brought many women independent control over substantial assets for the first time in their lives. At minimum, a widow could demand the return of her dowry and *sponsalicium* from her husband's heirs or executors.[100] Despite widows' apparent independence, widowhood placed many women in a vulnerable position. Widows in lower socioeconomic strata rarely had dowries large enough to support themselves, and any widow, regardless of wealth, might experience difficulties in recovering her dowry from her husband's recalcitrant heirs.[101] However, the set of legal practices that arose around widowhood provided women, especially wealthy women, with broad economic authority over not only their own property but also the entire conjugal estate.

Widows who did not seek to remarry immediately could exert authority over their husbands' assets by strategically delaying in collecting their dowries. The right of *tenuta*, enshrined in both royal privileges and local customary law, allowed widows to control their late husbands' estates while they left the dowry and *sponsalicium* uncollected.[102] When a widow took advantage of this custom, she not only helped secure her financial stability but also played an essential economic role as administrator of the family estate.

Widows utilized the *tenuta* as justification for selling and leasing out property as well as collecting on debts owed to their late husbands. In 1336, for example, Maria, widow of Jaume Marquet of Barcelona, along with her mother Geralda, widow of Ramon Vinader, collected on 500 pounds owed to the late Jaume from a commercial investment. Geralda acted as the guardian of Jaume and Maria's minor children, while Maria identified herself as "holding and possessing all the goods of my late husband, on account of my dowry and *sponsalicium* and other rights, in accordance with the written custom of Barcelona."[103] Occasionally, women even transformed their proprietary rights over their husbands' property into quasi-official political appointments; in 1328, Saura, widow of Guillem de Malla, the royal vicar and bailiff in the city of Vic, claimed to "hold, possess, and administer" the goods of her husband when she collected on debts owed to the court of the bailiff.[104] The royal court in the Crown of Aragon typically upheld women's claims to control their late husbands' estates—even against adult sons.[105]

Dying fathers of minor children often named their soon-to-be widows as the children's legal guardians (the term *tutrix* was used for younger children, while the term *curatrix* was employed for a daughter over twelve or a son over fourteen). Widows who served as guardians of their minor children adopted a broad range of economic responsibilities through their new roles as managers of their children's wealth. According to the legal and social norms of Catalan Christian communities, widowed mothers were the ideal guardians, the individuals most invested in the personal and financial well-being of their children. Widowed mothers even assumed guardianship automatically if their husbands died intestate.[106] Legal strictures prevented women under twenty-five from serving as guardians; youth could explain why the late Jaume Marquet selected his mother-in-law Geralda rather than his wife Maria as guardian of their children.[107] He may have assumed that the two women would work together and that Maria would act as a *de facto* coguardian.

Widowed guardians from wealthy families could aspire to levels of commercial success unavailable to most women. A few examples illustrate the options available to widows in control of vast estates. In 1330, Valença, widow of Pere Guitart of Barcelona, made two separate investments in a commercial partnership between a Barcelona merchant and a Mallorca merchant: 30 pounds on her own behalf, and 175 pounds in her capacity as guardian.[108] Her contemporary Blanca, widow of Berenguer Albanell of Barcelona, became a real estate magnate and built valuable social and economic alliances by marrying her daughter Blanqueta to the vice-admiral Galceran Marquet.[109] The only woman who established a formal commercial partnership (*societas*) in the documentation under study—Sobirana, widow of the draper Guillem d'Abadia of Girona—wielded her authority as guardian of her minor children to continue her late husband's business, in cooperation with fellow draper Bernat Massot, from 1338 to 1343.[110] In Vic, Francesca, widow of the jurist Francesc d'Alda and guardian of their minor children, played a prominent role both before and after the Black Death in collecting debts and leasing out rental properties.[111]

However, women's power as guardians had real limitations. Widows with little prior experience in managing financial resources had to rely on agents to discharge their responsibilities.[112] Guardians who struggled to maintain the solvency and the liquidity of the estate sold off real estate holdings so they could disburse legacies and pay debts in cash.[113] Inventories drawn up by widowed guardians allowed both courts and family members to closely monitor how successfully they administered their wards' property.[114]

Widows could also be deprived of guardianship, and even custody, of their children if they remarried.[115] The late Arnau Capbou of Barcelona had refrained from naming his widow Maria guardian of their minor daughter Antigona, instead selecting his brother Pere. In 1319, Pere transferred Antigona into the care of her mother, along with Guillema, a baptized, enslaved Black woman responsible for Antigona's daily care.[116] However, Pere retained managerial authority over Antigona's inherited wealth, and he specified that Maria could only care for her daughter on the condition that she live "chastely and honestly, and also without a husband." When widowed guardians did remarry, they usually yielded their position as guardians to others; in 1308, for example, Sibil·la, widow of Ramon de Copons of Barcelona, remarried and named her brother as substitute guardian for her minor children.[117]

However, some remarried widows managed to retain custody, and occasionally even guardianship, of their children from previous marriages.[118] Caterina, widow of Guillem Verdaguer and then wife of Ramon Jorba, retained custody of her daughter Constança from her first marriage even though she relinquished guardianship. In a 1338 contract, she and her husband received a maintenance allowance for Constança from her legal guardian Sibil·la, wife of Pere Celler.[119] Alamanda, wife of the gilder Jaume Rubí of Vic, continued to openly serve as the guardian of Resplenda, her minor daughter with her first husband, Jaume Huguet. Her second husband even assisted in managing Resplenda's property as Alamanda's agent.[120] In this case, the Black Death may have required more legal flexibility than usual; by 1350, Resplenda might have had no other close relatives willing or able to serve as guardian.

Inheritance payments highlight widows' importance as managers of their late husbands' estates in their capacity as holders of *tenuta*, guardians of their minor children, testamentary executors, or some combination of the three. In all three cities, women made about 20 percent of inheritance payments, and most of these women were widows in control of their husbands' property (see table 1).[121] When men did not name executors, their widows took a leading role in disbursing inheritances to their children and stepchildren. In 1346, for example, Joan Albert, son and universal heir of Ramon Albert of Girona, released his stepmother Blanca from further inheritance claims; she had presumably controlled her late husband's estate until transferring it to her stepson.[122] Male executors sometimes found that widows had established control over the deceased's property and turned to them to disburse sums earmarked for the funeral.[123] Only a few men officially named their wives as executors; the few women who took on this role may have had prior experience in financial management. Sibil·la, widow of the scribe Bernat Moner of Girona, borrowed money alongside her husband and leased property independently during her marriage before serving as his executor in 1332.[124]

Conclusions

The marriage and inheritance practices that prevailed in thirteenth- and fourteenth-century Catalan cities made Christian women's management of financial resources possible. Partible inheritance traditions affirmed women's claims over their parents' assets, while the dowry system as practiced in medieval Catalonia granted women authority over their husbands' estates as both wives and widows. Although ultimately only a minority of women went before the notaries to conduct business, these practices provided the essential foundation for women's work as managers of estates.

The legal culture surrounding marriage and inheritance in medieval Catalonia does not reflect any particular desire to promote women's economic rights. Rather, Catalan Christians understood women's economic rights as protecting the solvency of the household at large. If men failed to manage household wealth appropriately, or died before their sons could assume managerial responsibilities, wives and widows ensured that family-owned assets could be safely passed to the next generation. Endowing daughters with near-equal shares of their parents' estate helped ensure that they could attract husbands who might become important social and economic allies. Women played an essential role in preserving wealth and transmitting it to the next generation—their children, who would continue their husbands' lineages and cement alliances with their birth families.

The following chapter will turn to Catalonia's Jewish communities, which upheld a far more restrictive understanding of women's claims over the wealth accumulated by their fathers and husbands. Far from resembling one another, these two religious communities adhered to separate gendered legal norms surrounding both marriage and inheritance. A comparison of these two distinct legal cultures helps explain why Christian women played a more prominent role as managers of financial resources than their Jewish counterparts.

2

GENDER, ACCULTURATION, AND RESISTANCE IN CATALAN JEWISH FAMILY LAW

On August 15, 1325, two elite Jewish men—Bonjueu Cresques of Girona and Bonjueu Saltell of Barcelona—turned to a Christian public notary of Girona, Pere Massanet, to record a set of four interrelated contracts.[1] With these contracts, they formalized the financial arrangements that would bind their two families together through the marriage of Bonjueu Cresques's daughter Reina and Bonjueu Saltell's son Saltell Gracià. The choice to employ a Christian notary to draw up Latin contracts demonstrates these two Jewish families' familiarity with the legal practices of Catalan Christians. Yet the content of the contracts—and the subsequent history of the new couple—indicate that these Jewish elites also endeavored to preserve a set of distinctive Jewish legal customs. These customs would leave Reina with less control over financial resources than most Catalan Christian women of comparable status enjoyed.

Marriage brought Saltell Gracià, a boy of about fifteen, newfound independence and personal control over material assets. Bonjueu emancipated his son and made him a grant of half a substantial urban dwelling in the Call Major of Barcelona.[2] Saltell also received a substantial dowry from his new bride: 1,000 morabatins, or around 10,000 sous, comparable to the dowries brought by members of the upper echelons of Girona's Christian urban elite.[3] Through marriage, Saltell established a connection to a prominent Jewish family of Girona, the city that would become his new home. His father-in-law, Bonjueu Cresques, was a successful moneylender and, by 1328, one of the secretaries of the *aljama* (self-governing Jewish community) of Girona, a position in the Jewish community's governing council that was typically reserved for the members of a few elite families.[4] With his new control over financial resources and ties to the city's political and economic elite, Saltell in 1325 found himself poised at the brink of a successful career.

Subsequent documentation confirms that Saltell fulfilled the promise of his youth. He extended only a few loans, but they were often for very large sums.[5] Jews practiced a variety of trades beyond moneylending; the size of the loans he made indicates that Saltell had found wealth and success in some other business less well documented by notarial evidence. In 1346, Saltell took his father-in-law's place as a secretary of the *aljama*.[6] He extended two substantial loans to the prominent Christian Bernat de Taialà in 1348 and 1349, suggesting that he and Bernat, leading figures in the city's Jewish and Christian communities, maintained a cordial relationship.[7]

For Saltell's new wife, Reina, marriage wrought important changes in her personal status but failed to alter her control—or lack thereof—over financial resources. As discussed in the previous chapter, Christian brides of comparable social status could receive inheritances beyond their dowries and often expected to exert some control over family finances. Reina, in contrast, relinquished all additional inheritance claims when she married, and she gained no visible authority over the estate that her new husband built with her wealth. Still perhaps as young as thirteen, Reina confirmed that she had received her dowry and released her father, Bonjueu Cresques, from any additional claims she might have over his goods and those of her late mother, Bonafilla, on account of her paternal and maternal inheritance portion and *legítima*.[8] She even went so far as to renounce any future claims if her father died intestate.

Many Christian brides signed similar contracts—but most of them forfeited future claims in favor of siblings, including sisters who had not yet received dowries and brothers who expected to inherit the bulk of the family estate. Based on the extant notarial evidence, however, Reina had no siblings. Bonjueu may have had minor children who later died, or he may have still nurtured hopes in 1325 that he could produce a male heir; he had remarried by 1334.[9] But it is possible that Bonjueu seriously considered leaving most of his estate to more distant male kin rather than his own daughter. A thousand morabatins was an impressive dowry, but it probably represented a mere fraction of Bonjueu's total estate, especially given that he remained active in the credit market for twenty-five years after his daughter's marriage. Reina may have received enough money to comfortably support herself in widowhood, but upon her marriage, she relinquished claims over even greater wealth.

Nor did she exercise authority over her husband's estate, at least not in the public sphere. After her marriage, Reina disappeared entirely from the written record. The continued social, economic, and political relationship between her father and husband raises the possibility that Reina played a crucial role behind the scenes as an invisible link between the two men. But the very invisibility of such a role relegates it to the realm of speculation. At no point in her married life did she consent to, or participate in, a transaction made by her husband. The extant evidence does not even permit a definitive declaration of whether she was living or dead.

Reina's tenuous claims to both her father's and her husband's wealth stemmed from Jewish legal traditions, which differed from those of the surrounding Catalan Christian community. This chapter begins with an overview of the Jewish legal norms that governed women's access to financial resources as daughters, wives, and widows. Subsequently, I explore the interplay and negotiation between Jewish and Christian legal practices that occurred when Jewish families engaged with Latinate notarial culture. With few exceptions, I argue, Jewish families preserved Jewish customs even while adapting to Christian legal norms—and did not necessarily see the combination as contradictory. Finally, I turn to how Catalonia's most prominent Jewish leaders resisted adaptations that employed Christian legal norms to expand the economic options available to women.

Women and Wealth in Jewish Legal Culture

Medieval Jewish communities enjoyed the right to govern themselves in accordance with Jewish law, and rabbinic authorities and community leaders jealously guarded that right. The sphere of family law, in particular, fell under the jurisdiction of Jewish courts. Some Jews took family law cases to the royal courts of the kings of Aragon, but Christian monarchs often turned to respected members of the rabbinic elite for advice rooted in halakhah (Jewish law).[10] The halakhah that governed inheritance, marriage, widowhood, and divorce, therefore, had real implications for Catalan Jewish women's access to financial resources.

Jewish families and communities in the medieval and early modern Mediterranean shaped hybrid legal cultures that selectively combined elements of both Jewish law and local Christian practice. Ivan Marcus, in his work on Ashkenaz, coined the term "inward acculturation" to refer to the process by which medieval Jews adopted certain elements of the dominant culture and rejected others in order to shape a uniquely Jewish communal identity.[11] Paradoxically, as Marcus and others have argued, Jews in the Mediterranean and beyond even utilized non-Jewish thought and practice to affirm difference and polemicize against non-Jews.[12]

Scholarship on women and family in medieval Mediterranean Jewish communities has focused primarily on how Jewish family law was shaped by adaptations and accommodations of local non-Jewish practices. In early modern Italy, Jewish communities developed a set of practices around inheritance and dowry that blended Jewish and Christian legal customs and created a shared set of legal norms for a diverse Jewish community.[13] Jewish women in late medieval Venetian Crete adapted language about cruelty and abuse drawn from canon law to convince local Christian courts to force their husbands into divorce.[14] Jews under Muslim rule in the Middle East and North Africa frequently had recourse to Muslim courts; local Jewish divorce practices were in part shaped in response to fears about Jewish women's reliance on the Muslim court system and potential conversion to Islam.[15] Examples of this phenomenon have also been found in the medieval Crown of Aragon. Christian practices promoting the guardianship of widowed mothers may have influenced some Jewish families in Perpignan to grant widows with minor children more control over family finances.[16] Some Catalan Jewish marriage and inheritance practices have also been linked to the customs of the surrounding Christian community.[17]

While some Jewish individuals, families, and communities employed Christian and Muslim legal norms to bring their own economic strategies to fruition, I argue that studies of selective acculturation in family law have paid insufficient attention to the element of *selectiveness*. Adherence to the legal norms of one's own faith also represented a deliberate choice. Jewish communities in the Iberian Peninsula and beyond worked to maintain a distinct Jewish identity and to strengthen boundaries between different faith groups, with the result that legal divergences between majority and minority structured Jewish women's lives.[18] The bodies of Jewish women often functioned as boundary markers in premodern multifaith societies; their hoped-for sexual inviolability represented the desired security of the Jewish community's conceptual and physical borders—and the violation of their bodies signaled the community's weakness.[19] I contend that Jewish women functioned as boundary markers in other ways as well: in Catalan Jewish communities, the restricted public economic roles and responsibilities of Jewish women became an arena in which Jews performed difference.

The following two sections will trace how leading rabbinic authorities in thirteenth- and fourteenth-century Catalonia constructed women's claims over both family patrimony and conjugal property. The *Mishneh Torah*, a twelfth-century legal code authored by Maimonides—a Jew born in Muslim-ruled al-Andalus who spent most of his life in Egypt—had, by the thirteenth century, become an influential source of consolidated legal knowledge for Jews in the Crown of Aragon.[20] Catalan rabbis had to reckon with and respond to the *Mishneh Torah* even if they disagreed with certain positions, given that it was the sole example of a code that presented the entirety of the law in a consolidated and organized fashion.[21] The codified legal norms for marriage and inheritance presented in the *Mishneh Torah* therefore helped shape the gendered structures of property ownership and management among Catalan Jews and often directly reflected relatively uncontroversial norms derived from the Talmud.

The chapter also draws on responsa, legal queries addressed to rabbinic authorities and their rulings, to illuminate local practices promoted by rabbis in and around Catalonia. The figures most responsible for developing a distinctive Catalan rabbinic tradition were Rabbi Jonah ben Abraham Girondi (d. 1263) and his cousin Rabbi Moses ben Nahman, also known as Nahmanides (d. 1270).[22] However, few responsa authored by these two rabbis have survived. Their student Rabbi Solomon ibn Adret (d. 1310) not only became a crucial figure in the development of a Catalan school of halakhic interpretation but also provides the richest picture of Catalan Jewish legal culture, thanks to the sheer volume of his surviving responsa. Ibn Adret was unusually prolific and his writings especially well preserved: over three thousand responsa authored by ibn Adret have been preserved, collected, and published.[23] The sheer quantity of ibn Adret's written work, combined with his influence in Catalonia during and after his lifetime, makes him particularly valuable to any study of Catalan Jewish legal culture. I have also incorporated responsa from some of the slightly later luminaries of the Catalan rabbinic tradition, such as Rabbi Nissim ben Reuven Girondi (d. 1376) and Rabbi Isaac ben Sheshet Perfet (d. 1408), as well as the writings of Rabbi Yom Tov ben Avraham Ishbili (d. 1320), who originally hailed from Seville and ended his life in Saragossa but studied with ibn Adret.

Women and Girls in Jewish Inheritance Law

Jewish inheritance law took as its central principle the fundamental inequality of men and women as heirs. In explicating the order of inheritance, Maimonides treated this gender-based norm as second only to the basic principle that granted children primacy over other relatives as heirs. He stated, "This is the order of inheritance: when a person dies, his children inherit, and they receive priority over everyone else, and males [sons] receive priority over females [daughters]. In every case, the female does not inherit with the male."[24] In other words, women should never be treated as heirs equivalent to men with the same relationship to the deceased. Daughters would inherit only in the absence of sons; fathers could inherit from their children, but mothers could not; husbands would inherit automatically from their wives, yet wives could not inherit from their husbands.[25] Maimonides also circumscribed parents' ability to bypass inheritance laws; a dying man could not licitly make a will disinheriting his sons in favor of his daughters.[26] Catalan Jews did not usually flout gender-based inheritance divisions. Some parents chose the route of partible inheritance, which divided property between all sons and daughters, but neither Jewish fathers nor mothers privileged daughters over sons, a practice occasionally witnessed among Catalan Christians.[27]

Women did not entirely lack inheritance rights; the principle of priority based on family relationship ensured that women could inherit under certain circumstances. Daughters without brothers legally took precedence over more distant relatives, and fathers could not licitly disinherit their daughters in favor of alternative heirs.[28] Maimonides also provided a theoretical example of a case in which a granddaughter could inherit more wealth than a grandson. If a man died with two sons, both had predeceased him, and one left three sons while the other left a single daughter, the granddaughter would inherit half her grandfather's wealth and the other half would be divided between the three grandsons, because the two sets of children would have equal inheritance claims stemming from their fathers.[29] Similarly, because the principle based on order of descent took precedence over the principle of gender, a granddaughter descended from a son would inherit in lieu of a grandson descended from a daughter.[30] Nevertheless, women and men had fundamentally unequal inheritance rights under halakhah.

Overall, Catalan rabbis maintained this constellation of gendered inheritance practices. Solomon ibn Adret never even entertained the possibility of a daughter inheriting equivalently with a son.[31] While some Jewish families employed premortem grants to transfer property to wives and daughters without challenging inheritance laws, ibn Adret treated such stratagems with skepticism. One woman maintained that she had received property transmitted as a gift from her mother, who had in turn received it from her husband (the claimant's father). When her brothers contested her ownership, ibn Adret took their challenge seriously.[32]

However, ibn Adret consistently affirmed daughters' inheritance rights insofar as they conformed to Jewish law. In one case, he confirmed that a childless man's living sister maintained her inheritance rights against the claims of a nephew born of a deceased sister.[33] Daughters undoubtedly inherited in the absence of sons.[34] Rabbinic ordinances in neighboring Castile even slightly expanded women's inheritance rights, granting mothers the right to inherit the dowries of their daughters, and daughters and sons to inherit equally from their mothers.[35] Rabbi Isaac ben Sheshet Perfet, active in the late fourteenth and fifteenth centuries, permitted a mother to inherit from her son if he had no other heirs.[36] However, while communal ordinances provided new possibilities for women to inherit from one another or in the absence of alternate heirs, most of the family patrimony remained within the male lineage.

Fathers' financial obligations to their daughters centered on the provision of maintenance and concluded after they had provided their daughters with appropriate dowries and transferred them into the financial care of husbands. Intriguingly, Maimonides presented the requirement to provide for daughters not as a duty a man owed to his children but as one of the obligations a husband owed to his wife. A wife was entitled to expect maintenance for her daughters until they married, from either her husband or his heirs.[37] Maimonides specified that the basic maintenance of minor daughters took precedence over the inheritance of sons—perhaps reflecting a concern that brothers inheriting a smaller estate might fail to provide for their sisters without a clearly defined legal responsibility to do so.[38]

However, Maimonides also specified that daughters with brothers could make no claims on their fathers' estates beyond sustenance and—in the case of a wealthy family—an appropriate dowry, valued by Maimonides at one-tenth of the estate.[39] The wealth provided to daughters beyond their maintenance would usually be far less than that received by their brothers as inheritance. Assuming, for example, a wealthy family with two sons and two daughters, each daughter would receive one-tenth of their father's estate, and each son would receive two-fifths of the estate—a share four times the size of what their sisters received.

Jewish Wives and Widows in the Conjugal Estate

Jewish brides contributed essential financial resources to their new households through the dowries they brought into their marriages. Nevertheless, Jewish law denied wives managerial authority over their own property during their married lives and invalidated most of their claims to their husbands' estates. Widows expected to recover their dowries and receive any additional wealth gifted by their husbands in the marriage contract (*ketubah*) but held no authority over the rest of the estate. According to Jewish law, the central gift that created a marriage was the husband's grant of money to his wife, which represented one of several ways in which men could "acquire" wives, the others being the signing of a contract and sexual intercourse.[40] In practice, Jewish marriages in medieval Catalonia involved the transfer of three different types of marital gifts, all detailed in the *ketubah*. The term *ketubah* referred not only to the marriage contract but also to the husband's mandatory gift to his wife, traditionally valued at 200 *zuzim* for a previously unmarried woman or 100 *zuzim* for a widow or divorcée.[41] When translated into contemporary currency, however, this sum was quite modest: 200 *zuzim* was worth a mere 25 sous.[42] Typically, therefore, husbands also promised their wives an additional marital gift of more significant value, referred to as the *tosefet ketubah*, or supplementary *ketubah*.[43] A new bride also brought her husband a dowry (*nedunya*), typically paid on her behalf by her parents or brothers.[44]

Elka Klein argued that Catalan Jews developed a marriage system that blended their own legal traditions with those of their Christian neighbors. The dowry gradually became the primary marital gift, while the combined *ketubah* and *tosefet ketubah* resembled the Catalan husband's gift (*sponsalicium*).[45] However, although the dowry-based marriage system practiced by Jews in Catalonia resembled that of their Christian neighbors, the dowry also had deep roots in Talmudic tradition.[46] While the development of the dowry in Jewish culture might reflect Roman legal influence from Late Antiquity, the Jewish dowry system in medieval Catalonia did not necessarily reflect contemporary Christian influence.[47] Jewish couples in the medieval Islamic world married under a very similar system of marital gifts, in which the groom provided both the minimal *ketubah* and a more substantial supplement, while the bride contributed a dowry.[48]

Moreover, the husband's gift in Catalan Jewish practice usually represented a much smaller contribution than the Christian *sponsalicium*. Even with the addition of the *tosefet ketubah*, Catalan Jewish grooms on average provided smaller sums relative to the dowry than Christian grooms, for whom the *sponsalicium* was normally set at half the value of the dowry. Based on eleven extant Catalan Jewish marriage contracts from the thirteenth and fourteenth centuries, the average dowry for Jewish brides was approximately 2,900 sous of Barcelona.[49] These contracts suggest that many grooms (as seen in the four Hebrew *ketubot*) provided a standardized sum of 200 sous for the *tosefet ketubah*—a sum far outstripped in value by the dowry. Four of the seven notarial contracts failed to specify the *tosefet ketubah* at all; of the remaining three, only one adopted the Christian practice of providing a husband's gift worth half the value of the dowry.[50] The other two grooms provided supplementary gifts worth slightly less than one-quarter of their wives' dowries.[51] In total, the average *tosefet ketubah* (when specified at all) comes to 614 sous—about one-fifth the value of the average dowry.

Despite the significant financial contribution Jewish wives made to their households via their dowries, rabbinic authorities granted them little managerial authority over shared household assets. The responsibilities of husbands to their wives, and wives to their husbands, reflected a legal ideal within Jewish communities in which husbands functioned as the exclusive managers of the conjugal estate.[52] Husbands enjoyed not only the right to profit from their wives' property but also the ownership over wages she earned and objects she found during the course of their marriage.[53] In turn, he incurred a series of obligations centered on financially supporting his wife and their children. Husbands accepted the responsibility to provide food, clothing, and shelter to their wives as well as to incur expenses for medical care in case of illness, burial in case of death, and ransom in case of captivity. They undertook to provide general maintenance for their wives not only during their lifetimes but even after death, so long as their wives remained within their estates and did not remarry.[54] Husbands' obligations to their wives also incorporated responsibilities toward their shared children; men committed to provide for their daughters until marriage, and to grant their sons an inheritance.[55]

Although widows could receive maintenance if they remained unmarried within the estates of their late husbands, under local interpretations of halakhah, they could not claim managerial authority over their husbands' estates—unlike their Christian neighbors.[56] Nor, strictly speaking, did halakhah allow husbands to name wives as their heirs, although premortem writs of donation allowed men to circumvent this policy if they wished to do so.[57] Bonadona, widow of Astrug Caravida of Girona, referred to a Hebrew writ of this type when collecting on loans owed to her late husband.[58] Rabbi Yom Tov ben Avraham Ishbili considered a case in which a man had divided his assets equally among his widow and sons for the duration of her lifetime.[59] Alternatively, widows could recover their dowries and use them to support themselves financially, although families and communities might have preferred widows with adult sons to instead receive maintenance from the family estate.[60]

Selective Adaptations: Jewish Family Law in Latin Notarial Culture

Relatively few Jews turned to the notaries to record contracts related to inheritance, marriage, or divorce. Jewish scribes, whom the kings of Aragon understood as parallel figures to Christian notaries, served their communities by drawing up a range of contracts between Jews, including real estate sales, loans, and commercial investments as well as wills, marriage contracts (*ketubah*, plural *ketubot*), and bills of divorce (*get*, plural *gittin*).[61] Hebrew contracts had a crucial function in Jewish marriage law, as they created relationships rather than merely recording them. The writing of the *ketubah* brought a valid marriage into being, while the writing and delivery of a *get* brought a marriage to its permanent legal conclusion.[62] Hence even those Jews who sought out Latinate notarial contracts used them to supplement, rather than replace, Hebrew writs.[63] The contract that recorded the financial arrangements surrounding the marriage between Reina Cresques and Saltell Gracià, for example, stated that Bonjueu had transferred wealth to his son and that the sum of the dowry had already been specified in Hebrew contracts.[64] When they sought to safeguard their investments through Latin contracts, they had to adapt to the alternative legal expectations of Christian notaries—but they still maintained distinctive economic structures.

The small number of notarial contracts related to Jewish inheritance, marriage, and divorce indicates that most Jews preferred to conduct their family affairs without the intrusion of the notaries. At least some Jews saw the notariate as yet another Christian intrusion into their lives and avoided engaging with notarial culture whenever possible.[65] However, Jewish culture and society were far from monolithic, and some Jews turned to the notaries to craft hybrid contracts that drew on both halakhah and the norms of notarial culture. These contracts could help secure Jewish families' assets if they needed to pursue their rights in Christian courts. By law, Christian courts in the Crown of Aragon had to accept Hebrew writs as valid documentary evidence, and some Jews provided copies of Hebrew contracts when doing business with Christians.[66] Latin contracts, however, eased the process of proving claims before Christian authorities. Starting in the eleventh century, Christian notaries collaborated with Hebrew scribes to craft authenticated translated documents, many of which affirmed uncontested Jewish ownership of property.[67] Latin notarial contracts provided an added layer of defense, ensuring that Jews could effectively protect their assets and control their distribution if they went before a Christian court.

Jews who sought to dispose of property in a manner not justified by halakhah, or to prove ownership in unusual cases, may have found it especially prudent to obtain Latin as well as Hebrew contractual evidence.[68] Other Jews worked with Christian notaries to craft parallel Latin contracts at the behest of Christians—for example, when selling property to Christians concerned about relying on contracts in an unfamiliar language and script.[69] Although most Jews who sought out notarial contracts did not actively seek to circumvent Jewish family law practices in favor of Christian ones, all such contracts required negotiation between Christian and Jewish legal norms.[70] Jewish families made different choices about whether and how to adapt to the expectations of Christian notaries, who made assumptions rooted in their own legal culture about Jewish women's authority over family assets. A few Jewish families responded by taking a more expansive view of their daughters' and wives' claims over family property, counter to the wishes of many local rabbinic authorities. Most others, in contrast, employed Christian legal norms to reaffirm family financial strategies fully compatible with halakhic norms—and even to reinforce the exclusion of women from the patrimony.

Jewish Daughters and Family Property in Latinate Notarial Contracts

Catalan Jewish parents with both sons and daughters almost always excluded married daughters from any inheritance beyond their dowries. The 1267 will of Goig, wife of David Canviador of Vic, provides an especially striking example of how even Jewish women left the bulk of their wealth to the men, not the women, of their family.[71] Goig worked as one of Vic's most successful moneylenders and had significant assets at her disposal. Yet despite her own economic self-sufficiency, she did not substantially contribute to her daughters' financial well-being. She named her husband as her universal heir, in accordance with Jewish law, and granted her four sons legacies ranging between 500 and 1,500 sous. In contrast, she excluded her married daughter Astrugona entirely, although she promised that Astrugona's daughter would receive a legacy of 200 sous upon her marriage. She left her unmarried daughter Reina only 100 sous, a rather meager contribution to her future dowry. Goig's clear prioritization of her husband and sons reflects the general preference among Catalan Jews to promote the inheritance rights of men over those of women. Notably, while the rabbinic elites working to shape legal norms were all men, property-owning mothers were apparently no more likely than fathers to distribute wealth to daughters.

In certain exceptional cases, however, Jewish parents ignored legal strictures on daughters' inheritance rights in order to protect the financial futures of unmarried girls. Astrug Gracià of Tarragona, for example, bequeathed property he held in the *call* of Barcelona to both his son Issach and his daughter Mireta, who held it jointly.[72] However, the notary did not identify the children as joint universal heirs, suggesting that Mireta did not necessarily receive a share of the estate equal to her brother's, as opposed to a legacy intended to provide her with an appropriate dowry. Moreover, the records provide no evidence that Mireta ever actively managed property; her guardian sold off her inherited real estate while she was still a minor. Even Mireta's situation was rare. The notarial documentation refers to dozens of Jewish men, but only a handful of Jewish women, as their fathers' heirs.

Jewish men and women consistently assumed that married daughters had relinquished any additional rights of inheritance. Only one married Jewish woman appeared alongside her brother as a coheir, and she probably inherited prior to her marriage. Astrug Vidal Maimó and his sister Preciosa, wife of Jucef Llobell of Vic, jointly issued a grant in 1336 as their father's heirs.[73] However, Vidal had died a decade before, and his widow Astrugona had served for several years as the guardian of their minor children; both Astrug and Preciosa were probably under the age of fourteen and unmarried when their father died.[74] Preciosa first appears as a married woman in 1334, more than eight years after her father's death.[75]

Even fathers who treated their married daughters as economically capable actors prioritized their sons as heirs. Prior to his death in 1348, Vidal Bonafeu of Barcelona entrusted the guardianship of his minor son Roven to both his widow Dolça (Roven's mother) and his daughter Astruga (Roven's sister), the wife of wealthy Barcelona Jew Massot Avengena.[76] Clearly, Vidal considered both his wife and his daughter to be competent managers of financial resources who would be able to effectively manage his son's inheritance. Often, Jewish fathers selected male relatives or community leaders to act as guardians in lieu of, or alongside, widowed mothers, owing perhaps to concerns about whether women could successfully transition into new roles as managers of substantial estates.[77] Vidal's son-in-law Massot, a community leader with close ties to the royal family, was exactly the sort of man often called upon to serve as guardian for fatherless Jewish children.[78] However, although Massot acted on behalf of his wife and mother-in-law as their legal agent, he had no formal status as guardian.[79] While Vidal may have appointed Astruga as guardian on the assumption that her husband would assist in managing Roven's wealth, he did not hesitate in naming only his wife and daughter as formal guardians. Despite his apparent respect for Astruga's abilities, however, he prioritized transmitting his wealth to his son: there is no indication that he granted her an inheritance beyond her dowry.

Jewish parents typically excluded married women with living brothers from inheritance and only rarely treated unmarried daughters as equivalent coheirs with their brothers. Christian families, on the other hand, often treated unmarried daughters as coheirs and made provisions for daughters who had already married. Jewish brides also had less access to family-owned real property than their Christian counterparts. Nearly one-third of Christian brides' dowries included real estate holdings (see table 3). In contrast, all of the extant Hebrew *ketubot* and notarial Jewish marriage contracts expressed the value of the dowry exclusively in terms of cash, although several responsa refer to Jewish women who had dowries including real property.[80]

Some Jewish parents refrained from permanently endowing their daughters with real property but used real estate holdings as pledges for unpaid dowries. If the property served as a pledge, rather than as part of the dowry, families reserved the right to repossess it in exchange for cash. Vidal de Camprodon and his wife Goig, a Jewish couple in Vic, transferred property in the *call* of Barcelona to their son-in-law Issach, a Jew of Barcelona, as security for their daughter's dowry.[81] In 1288, Bonmacip of Vic appointed an agent to evict tenants from houses he owned in the *call* of Barcelona; these tenants had rented the property from Jucef Darahi, the soon-to-be ex-husband of his daughter Reina.[82] Jucef, like Issach, probably controlled this property as a pledge for the eventual full payment of his wife's dowry. Strikingly, in both of these cases Jewish families transferred control of property they owned in another city to a son-in-law who lived there. They may have used these pledges primarily as a means of delegating management responsibilities for distant property holdings to sons-in-law who lived nearby and could act as convenient agents. The goal was not to permanently transfer real property to their daughters.

Although Jewish daughters without brothers were entitled under halakhah to inherit all their parents' assets, Jewish families treated heiress daughters very differently from the sons who stood to inherit their parents' wealth. Bonjueu Cresques of Girona, with whom this chapter began, employed Latinate Christian norms to reinforce Jewish restrictions on daughters' inheritance. The contract in which Reina relinquished her inheritance rights at the moment of marriage had no parallel under Jewish law. If she had brothers, the contract would have served no purpose in a Jewish court but could have prevented her from pursuing a claim under Catalan customary law.[83] If she had sisters, the contract denied her any inheritance beyond her dowry and designated the remainder of the estate for the younger daughters of the family. If she had no siblings, which seems plausible given their absence from the documentary record, Bonjueu sacrificed his daughter's inheritance rights solely for the sake of potential unborn children, or out of a desire to keep most of his property within the male lineage of his family.

Most Jewish fathers with only daughters as their presumptive heirs took particular care to protect their married daughters' assets, and they remained active participants in safeguarding their daughters' dowries from unworthy husbands.[84] In the late 1280s, Bonmacip of Vic supported his daughter's divorce, which enabled her to move from her husband's home city of Barcelona—where very few Jewish women took an active role in managing household financial resources—back home to Vic, where Jewish women played an unusually prominent role in the credit market (see chapter 7).[85] Reina's second husband, Astrug Caravida of Girona, relocated to Vic, where Reina continued to manage her dotal and extradotal inherited assets during her marriage, probably with her parents' support.[86] Other Jewish parents relied on intrafamilial endogamy to keep heiresses' resources within their own male lineage: Bonafilla, daughter and heiress of Astrug Bedoç of Girona, married her uncle, Cresques Jucef.[87] This particular practice had biblical roots; Moses granted the daughters of Zelophehad the right to inherit from their father in the absence of male heirs but mandated that they marry men of their own tribe.[88]

Jewish Women and the Conjugal Estate in Latin Notarial Contracts

Halakhah as interpreted by most Catalan rabbis granted Jewish wives and widows no particular authority over the conjugal estate. Engagement with notarial culture occasionally allowed Jewish women to exert authority over the property of their husbands, living and dead, but they remained less enmeshed in the management of conjugal property than their Christian counterparts. Christian wives regularly acted alongside their husbands as joint debtors, tenants, buyers and sellers of property, and investors. This joint activity reflected a legal culture that treated married couples as comanagers of a shared conjugal estate, albeit with distinctly gendered roles. Jewish couples acted together much less frequently and often only under unusual circumstances.

Jewish women borrowed money alongside their husbands much less frequently than Christian women and thus lacked the opportunity to exert control over the dissipation of household resources by granting or withholding consent to debts. Direct comparisons between Jewish and Christian

TABLE 4 Sales on credit to Christians and Jews in Girona, 1311–1350

	Christian debtors		Jewish debtors	
	No.	**% of total**	**No.**	**% of total**
Individual men	255	72.4	313	83.9
Individual women	11	3.1	12	3.2
All-male groups	48	13.6	28	7.5
All-female groups	0	0	2	0.5
Married couples	33	9.4	10	2.7
Other mixed-gender groups	5	1.4	8	2.1
Total	352		373	

Note: Percentage totals only reach 99.9% due to rounding.

borrowing practices are difficult, as the notarial registers contain few examples of Jewish debtors. Most Jews in need of credit probably borrowed from other Jews using Hebrew contracts or private oral agreements. One such oral contract (a loan described as having been made *sine carta*) between Jews eventually generated supplementary notarial documentation, as the creditors and debtor turned to a notary to record the loan's repayment.[89] However, while Jews rarely borrowed cash from Christians, they regularly purchased goods from Christian merchants on credit. This practice was especially well documented in Girona, where Jews as well as Christians bought high-value textiles on credit from the city's merchant-drapers. Sales on credit therefore permit a closer comparison of Christians and Jews. Christian married couples acted together in about 10 percent of sales on credit made to Christians, whereas Jewish couples acted in tandem in less than 3 percent of sales on credit made to Jews (see table 4).

Wealth disparities and perceptions of creditworthiness may account for the few cases in which Jewish couples did act together when borrowing. Six of the ten sales on credit made to Jewish married couples involved families who rarely appear in the notarial documentation. They may have come from less wealthy sectors of Girona's Jewish community. Abraham Issach, who twice bought cloth on credit alongside his wife Oravida, referred to himself as a butcher, a much-needed profession in Catalan Jewish communities but not as high-paid or high-status as other work.[90] Such a profession also required relatively little contact with Christians, as he would have sold kosher meat to a primarily Jewish clientele. Wealthier Jewish men, especially those with business connections in the Christian community willing to vouch for their creditworthiness, had the luxury of assuring merchants that their wives' involvement would be unnecessary. While wives' consent did not always translate into meaningful managerial authority, the absence of a culture in which wives approved their husbands' transactions may have left Jewish women with less of a voice in the disposition of conjugal property than their Christian counterparts.

Jewish husbands occasionally relied on their wives to act as their legal agents when they traveled out of town, but they empowered their wives in this manner less often and less fully than Christian men.[91] Jewish law offered a form of legal agency, and women could licitly serve as agents. In practice, however, all the Jewish women who acted as their husbands' agents attributed their authority to Latin notarial contracts. Agency contracts under Jewish law were oral agreements that drew legal force from the presence of witnesses; these Latin written documents may have supplemented oral agency contracts accomplished in accordance with halakhah.[92] Regardless of contractual form, Jewish women played a more circumscribed role as legal agents than Christian women. While Christian men often granted their wives generalized authority over the conjugal estate, Jewish husbands instead empowered their wives only to accomplish certain specific tasks. In an agency contract from 1327, Vidal Massana of Vic carefully delineated his wife Bonadona's responsibilities by conceding to her only the right to collect on debts owed to him within the bounds of the city and vicariate of Vic.[93]

A small number of Catalan Jewish women enjoyed both greater economic self-sufficiency and greater control over conjugal wealth. In Vic, where Jewish women in general and Jewish wives in particular played a uniquely prominent role in the credit market, husbands and wives acted together to release debtors from further claims. The two Jewish women most active in the credit market of Vic during the second quarter of the fourteenth century—Goig, wife of Salomó Vidal, and Tolsana, wife of Astrug Jucef—each extended only a single joint loan with her husband. However, Goig and Salomó jointly released debtors on eight occasions, while Astrug and Tolsana together confirmed that five debtors had fulfilled their obligations.[94] The prevalence of joint debt repayment contracts suggests that even though Jewish couples in Vic did not visibly work together, they understood their lending as part of a family business, perhaps rooted in the shared capital of the conjugal estate.

In the rare cases where Jewish daughters inherited wealth beyond their dowries, they faced greater challenges than Christian women in managing these assets effectively and independently. Under Catalan customary law, wives retained managerial authority over their extradotal assets (*paraphernalia*).[95]

The Talmud divided wives' property into two different categories: *nikhsei tzon barzel*, essentially the dowry, and *nikhsei melog*. The *ketubah* specified the value of all *tzon barzel* property, which the husband could treat as his own until the dissolution of the marriage through death or divorce, at which point the widow or divorcée could claim full reimbursement. *Melog* assets, comparable to *paraphernalia*, remained the wife's property during her married life, but her husband enjoyed the right to retain any profit derived from these assets.[96] In other words, halakhah guaranteed husbands more authority over their wives' extradotal wealth than Catalan customary law. This divergence could explain why Jewish women so infrequently managed their *paraphernalia* or *melog* property independently.

Jewish women who received substantial inheritances beyond their dowries often formally relinquished managerial authority to their husbands. Bonadona, wife of Vidal Bonet of Mallorca, inherited from her father, Bramon de Torroella of Girona, and collected on a single debt owed to him in 1326.[97] Soon after, however, she named her husband as agent and disappeared from the documentary record; he managed the entirety of her inheritance on her behalf for the next decade.[98] When Jewish wives did control their paraphernal goods, they did so only sporadically. In 1318, Jueva, wife of Fabib Maimó of Barcelona, sold raw silk from her *paraphernalia* to a Jewish couple who worked in the silk industry.[99] However, beyond the two contracts related to this sale, Jueva did not publicly manage assets in the extant documentation.

Widowhood allowed Jewish women to participate more actively in the management of family financial resources, but most Jewish widows nevertheless exercised less economic authority than Christian widows. Some of the most economically successful Jewish widows benefited from the selective adoption of Christian customs. Although Jewish husbands could not licitly name their wives as heirs, some men circumvented such prohibitions while still adhering to halakhic norms by using extratestamentary bequests. Astrug Caravida of Girona made his wife Bonadona his heir by granting her all his goods and the debts owed to him in a Hebrew writ drawn up prior to his death in 1334.[100] The couple also had two daughters, both married by the time their father died, whom Astrug effectively disinherited in violation of halakhah.[101] Although Astrug had employed a Hebrew contract to entrust his estate to his wife, his choice may reflect an awareness of Christian expectations that widows could control their late husbands' estates. At the same time, however, he was empowered to make this choice and expect it to be upheld by the fact that his daughters, like most Jewish girls, might have been unfamiliar with the procedures of either Jewish or Christian courts.[102]

While Jewish husbands occasionally left their wealth to their wives, those who made this choice nearly always disinherited daughters rather than sons.

While Astrug maneuvered within halakhic norms to treat his wife as his heir, a few Jewish widows relied explicitly on Christian custom, without referencing halakhah, to exercise control over their late husbands' estates. Christian widows enjoyed the right of *tenuta*, which allowed a widow to administer her late husband's property for at least a year if she delayed in collecting her dowry and *sponsalicium*.[103] In the wake of the Black Death, when an unprecedented number of Jewish widows controlled their late husbands' estates (see chapter 7), several stated in notarial debt collection contracts that they held and administered their husbands' goods "on account of their dowry and *sponsalicium*," in accordance with the written custom of Barcelona.[104] While Christian widows regularly appealed to this right throughout the fourteenth century, Jewish widows only employed this Christian legal custom during a moment of communal crisis, brought on by the demographic losses of both the Black Death and the subsequent massacres of Jews in Barcelona.[105] Only the crisis wrought by these tragedies, and the subsequent instability of Barcelona's Jewish community, enabled and encouraged Jewish widows to make a claim rooted exclusively in Christian custom.

A few Jewish men and women selectively adopted Christian notaries' assumptions about women's managerial authority in order to bring their family's economic strategies to fruition or in cases of necessity. However, adherence to halakhic restrictions on women's control over assets remained the norm. Male rabbinic elites, moreover, proved unwilling to accept women's property claims when they were grounded in Christian practice. Women's claims over family property, especially wives' and widows' control over the conjugal estate, became a site for the resistance to acculturation. Catalan rabbinic authorities challenged women and their families who made claims rooted in the customs of their Christian neighbors.

Tensions: Acculturation and Resistance in Rabbinic Texts

Solomon ibn Adret vociferously condemned Jews' use of non-Jewish courts for affairs internal to the community and expressed his fear that use of Christian courts led inevitably to the broader adoption of non-Jewish culture.[106] Rena Lauer rightly questions whether the stringent stance ibn Adret took reflected everyday practice, pointing out that many Jews—ibn Adret included—employed Christian courts for internal Jewish business when needed.[107] Rabbinic resistance to acculturation, just like acculturation itself, was selective. When it came to women's control over assets, Catalan rabbis implicitly and explicitly challenged the adoption of non-Jewish customs.

Rabbinic elites worked to maintain and reinforce a range of Jewish practices that limited women's authority over household wealth. Although some Jewish parents chose to treat minor daughters and sons as joint heirs, such questions only occasionally came before the rabbis. Brothers were perhaps reluctant to employ rabbinic law to disinherit their sisters. The need for substantial dowries to marry their sisters to men of appropriate status may have placed brothers from wealthy families in a position where they expected to provide their sisters with significant shares of their parents' estates regardless of halakhic dictates.[108] After all, such marriages, which built essential social and economic alliances, benefited them as well.[109] However, men had fewer qualms about challenging the inheritance claims of more distant women relatives; in one responsum of Solomon ibn Adret, a nephew challenged his aunt's claim to his uncle's property (her brother's).[110] His student Yom Tov ben Avraham Ishbili discusses a case in which a group of heirs even challenged their own mother's claims to control a portion of her late husband's estate for the duration of her lifetime.[111] Although in both these cases Ishbili and ibn Adret ultimately affirmed women's inheritance claims as justified by halakhah, the existence of these disputes indicates that men thought it worth the effort to pursue even tenuous inheritance claims against the women of their families.

Wives' and widows' control over the conjugal estate proved more contentious, as rabbis sought to combat Jewish families' selective adoption of Christian practices. The responsa of the prolific ibn Adret provide the best examples of rabbinic resistance to Jewish women's use of Christian legal culture to protect their assets. One query provided ibn Adret with an opportunity to explicitly assert the illegitimacy of Jewish women's use of Christian courts. A man identified pseudonymously as Reuven owed money to a Christian creditor.[112] His wife went before a Christian court to reclaim her dowry on account of her husband's bankruptcy. Christian women made dowry restitution claims with some frequency; as they lacked justification under Jewish law, Jewish women could only make claims like this if they turned to Christian courts.[113] While her actions successfully protected both Reuven's estate and her dowry from the claims of Reuven's Christian creditor, a Jewish creditor—identified as Simeon—challenged their actions on the basis of halakhah. He claimed that since the wife had no right under Jewish law to collect her dowry, Reuven could not use his wife's dowry recovery suit to justify defaulting on the debt owed to Simeon.

Ibn Adret enthusiastically sided with Simeon, affirming the legal principle that a wife could never collect her dowry, *ketubah*, and *tosefet ketubah* while the marriage lasted. He even overtly challenged a Provençal rabbinic authority who held a contrary opinion, flatly stating that he disagreed with Rabbi Isaac ben Abba Mari (d. 1193), who had argued that a wife could collect her dowry, albeit not her *ketubah* or *tosefet ketubah*, before her husband's death. The contrast between the two could indicate divergences between Provençal and Catalan schools of halakhic interpretation.[114] Ibn Adret's response was blunt, concise, and firm, beginning with the clear statement that "her collection was not in accordance with the law, and what she collected was not to be collected." Although he denied women the right to appeal to a Christian legal practice that would give them more control over their assets, his goal was not merely to benefit men at women's expense. Arguably, Reuven shouldered the greatest financial burden, as he now had to repay a substantial loan but could no longer claim managerial rights over his wife's dowry in a Christian court. While in practice ibn Adret's ruling worked to limit wives' control over assets, his primary goal was to prevent Jews from pursuing Jewish family law cases in Christian courts, especially when such cases involved Jews selectively adopting Christian legal norms.[115]

Ibn Adret explicitly permitted Jews to employ notarial contracts, even in family law cases, but remained vigilant in challenging Jews who embraced Christian legal practices alongside Latin legal formulae.[116] A family property dispute allowed ibn Adret to criticize a married couple who adhered to a concept of conjugal property rooted in Christian, rather than Jewish, legal culture. Another pseudonymous Reuven and his wife had jointly purchased houses, and their names appeared together as cobuyers on the bill of sale.[117] After his death, his widow collected her dowry and marriage portion in accordance with the written text of her *ketubah*. Subsequently, however, the widow clashed with Reuven's heirs over the question of who owned the houses. Such disputes between widows and heirs were hardly uncommon.[118] This particular dispute, however, reveals not only contested claims to property but also divergent concepts of how property ownership worked.

According to the heirs, the property had belonged entirely to Reuven and therefore should now belong exclusively to them. The widow counterclaimed that she owned the houses, on the basis of two separate justifications. First, she argued that the use of her name on the contract presumed joint ownership over the property. Second, she claimed that she and her husband had purchased the houses using funds drawn from her extradotal inheritance, making them legally hers.[119]

Although ibn Adret refrained from making a final ruling on the grounds that he could not establish the truth of all parties' claims, he rejected outright one half of the widow's two-pronged strategy: her right to make a claim on the grounds of the text of the bill of sale. Ibn Adret firmly rejected the declaration of shared ownership, stating, "Even if the contract was written in the wife's name, she did not buy [the houses]." Participation, in other words, did not imply possession; ibn Adret cited a Talmudic passage to prove this point.[120] Halakhah and Catalan notarial culture diverged on this matter: among Catalan Christians, participation in the purchase or exploitation of land represented an essential form of proof of control over property.[121] The nature of conjugal property supported such an assumption: owing to the mingling of cash resources, and the wife's far-reaching claims over her husband's estate, joint ownership of the property would seem plausible.

Strikingly, ibn Adret validated the widow's claim if she could prove her second assertion: that the couple had purchased the houses with assets that represented part of her inheritance. Reuven's heirs relied on legal claims drawn from a halakhic understanding of family property, which explicitly denied the validity of claims drawn from a Catalan Christian understanding of joint property ownership. Despite the language of joint purchase in the bill of sale, they argued, the property belonged to Reuven alone. The widow, in contrast, hedged her bets by employing both concepts of property ownership: she first described the property as jointly owned by her and her husband, and then subsequently, as individually owned by her alone. Her choice to pursue both strategies could reflect her awareness of the fact that she had a stronger case under Christian law than under halakhah, where her claim would depend on her ability to prove that the cash to purchase the houses belonged to her. Ibn Adret, however, insisted on the exclusive validity of the halakhic understanding of family property and of women's property rights. His response indicates a careful effort to reject Jewish families' use of Christian legal norms while still respecting women's economic rights when justified under halakhah.

Ibn Adret's student, Rabbi Yom Tov ben Avraham Ishbili, treated widows attempting to recover their dowries from their late husbands' estates with slightly more generosity, but he still carefully circumscribed women's property rights in accordance with the boundaries of halakhah. In a case where a widow claimed to have jointly purchased land alongside her husband, Ishbili suggested, as a compromise, that she retain half the property as her share of the purchase and claim her dowry from the other half.[122] This solution ultimately left the widow in control of the purchased property—but only if she agreed to treat half of it as repayment for her dowry. The land, for Ishbili, could not have been co-owned in its entirety by husband and wife but divided into halves, one of which now belonged to the widow and one of which now belonged to her late husband's heirs. Ishbili took her claim seriously but insisted that it entitled her only to half of a shared whole. A Christian court, in contrast, might have treated the husband's and wife's rights as overlapping and thus accepted her claim to control the property in its entirety.

In another case, Ishbili carefully maneuvered between the halakhic mandate that permitted a widow to collect her dowry from any part of her late husband's estate and an effort to avoid granting the widow broader managerial authority over household assets. A widow, Ishbili ruled, could sell off property belonging to her late husband. However, he treated such sales as valid only insofar as they contributed directly to the widow's recovery of her dowry and *ketubah*.[123] Once again, Ishbili's solution revealed a greater willingness to accommodate the economic needs of widows than some of the rulings of ibn Adret did, but he nevertheless carefully delineated widows' claims in a manner that closed off the more expansive avenues through which Christian widows exercised authority over their late husbands' estates.

Women's authority over household financial resources became a crucial site for the resistance to acculturation, though not necessarily because rabbinic authorities actively set out to disadvantage or disempower women. Rabbis willingly sided with women against men if they made appeals rooted in halakhah. However, the disempowerment of women under the prevailing gender system rendered the sphere of women's control of assets an eminently winnable battle in the war against acculturation.

Resistance to acculturation, like acculturation itself, remained selective. Rabbis were very aware that their authority depended on the willingness of communal elites to accept their guidance.[124] Even in the arena of family law, certain practices went largely unchallenged despite their lack of halakhic justification, such as the emancipation of teenage sons or the privileging of a single son as universal heir. Rabbis' awareness that practices privileging boys and men formed a more central part of family economic strategies than practices benefiting daughters, wives, and widows may have allowed them to safely assume that relatively few families would contest efforts to promote a more restrictive understanding of women's access to wealth. Indeed, the families who negotiated between Jewish and Christian legal norms to entrust their daughters and wives with authority over family assets did not actively seek to empower women or to resemble their Christian neighbors. Rather, they promoted women's control over wealth as part of larger family economic strategies. Women represented a useful tool in the maintenance of intercommunal boundaries precisely because of their own powerlessness.

Conclusions

Jewish law, in comparison with Catalan customary law, narrowed the economic options available to daughters, wives, and widows. The inheritance and marriage practices rooted in halakhah and promoted by Catalan rabbis denied daughters with brothers the right to inherit and severely restricted wives' and widows' control over conjugal property. Jewish women sometimes exerted control over family assets, often with the support of their husbands or male relatives, by relying selectively on a combination of Jewish and Christian legal norms. Rabbinic authorities, however, worked to resist Jewish families' use of Christian courts and Christian legal culture in areas governed by halakhah. Women's control of assets became a particularly significant site of resistance to selective acculturation—largely because the restrictions on women's access to wealth would have seemed palatable to male Jewish elites.

Jewish women did not necessarily seek to flout Jewish law and accrue greater authority over financial resources even when they did employ Christian legal norms. Many women had never previously managed financial resources and did not necessarily desire to do so, at least insofar as they remained in financial comfort. Nevertheless, these restrictions narrowed the options available to those Jewish women who sought to engage in profitable labor managing financial resources. The halakhic restrictions on women's control of wealth are essential to understanding why Jewish women worked less often and in fewer economic sectors than either Christian women or Jewish men.

II

NOTARIAL CULTURE

3

CHRISTIAN WOMEN IN NOTARIAL CULTURE

On June 12, 1336, a Christian married couple acknowledged that they owed a debt to a widowed Jewish woman.[1] The loan was for a small sum, 25 sous—probably just enough to support the couple financially for a few weeks.[2] The creditor, Bonadona, was the widow of Astrug Caravida, a Jew of the city of Girona, and a woman who possessed a level of wealth and financial independence unattainable for most women (and many men), whether Jewish or Christian. She had not only recovered a substantial dowry upon her husband's death but also received from the late Astrug a sizable grant, which included all the debts owed to him. The debtors—Bonanata, daughter of the late Pere Joan, and her husband Pere—were a peasant couple who lived in the small rural parish of Sant Vicenç de Canet d'Adri, settling a debt originally incurred by Bonanata's parents.

This chapter and the following one seek to explore how gender, combined with other factors, shaped Bonadona's and Bonanata's experiences of notarial culture. In what ways did these women have similar experiences in a physical and conceptual space dominated by men? In what ways did their experiences diverge as a result of their differences in religion, socioeconomic position, and marital status? Even when women did business with other women (a relatively infrequent occurrence), obtaining a notarial contract involved interacting with men, including both strange and familiar faces. Bonadona, Bonanata, and Pere signed two contracts: an acknowledgment of the debt and a renegotiation of the terms of repayment. Jaume Transfort, a public notary in the city of Girona, drew up the contract, made copies for his clients and for his own records, and through his authority rendered the loan legally enforceable. Each notarial contract required two witnesses. These contracts had two different pairs of witnesses—four men in total. The act of witnessing could reveal social ties between witnesses and participants.[3] In these contracts, however, the connections between the witnesses and the contracting parties remain opaque. One witness, the canon Guillem Vives, had witnessed another contract that same day; another, the draper Bonanat de Llemena, relied regularly on Transfort and other notaries for his business but had no visible connections to either the creditor or the debtors. The other two witnesses, like the debtors, came from villages outside Girona, but neither village was close to Canet d'Adri.[4] In total, this transaction brought together eight people—seven of them Christian, and six of them men—many of whom had no obvious connection to one another outside these contracts.

The growing reliance on notaries as legal experts and public officials created a rich documentary record that has proved invaluable for social historians of the western Mediterranean. The diverse clientele that sought out the services of the notaries to record quotidian economic transactions participated in a system that generated thousands of documents illuminating the everyday lives of ordinary people. Yet the individuals who populate the pages of notarial registers experienced the notariate in different ways. Gender, religious identity, and social status all shaped how people approached notarial culture. Witnesses like the wealthy draper Bonanat de Llemena and notaries like Jaume Transfort had the comfort of knowing that the laws and practices that governed notarial culture had been created by and for men very much like themselves, and that most of the people who came and went through the doors of the notary's office were also men, members of their faith community, and property-owning citizens. However, the main participants in this particular loan had a more complex and fraught relationship with notarial culture. Notaries worked within and helped shape a legal system interconnected with broader structures of inequality, and they catered primarily to a male, Christian, and at least moderately wealthy clientele. Bonadona, as a Jewish woman (although a wealthy one), Bonanata, as a peasant woman (although a Christian), and even Pere, as a peasant (although a Christian man), existed on the margins of notarial culture.

The central argument of this section is that women like Bonadona and Bonanata experienced notarial culture in fundamentally different ways—both from one another and from men of their own religious identity and social stature. This chapter and the following one employ intersectional understandings of identity to explore how Christian and Jewish women of different social strata accessed—or failed to access—notarial culture in Catalan cities. Some aspects of women's experience of notarial culture remain in the realm of speculation: notarial registers extensively document economics, but not emotions. Notarial contracts nevertheless illuminate some of the gendered dynamics that help explain why even women who controlled financial resources appear less regularly than men in notarial documentation. The documents we find in archives are not neutral representations of facts but rather constructed objects that shape how historians understand the past.[5] Notarial contracts do not merely reveal the economies of medieval cities but helped shape them.

This chapter focuses on the complex interplay of factors that both embedded Christian women within urban notarial culture and kept them on its margins. What was it like to go to a notary in medieval Catalan cities? How might women's experience of notarial culture have differed from that of men? When did women go to the notary, and when are they conspicuous by their absence? Despite the legal, economic, and familial circumstances that required some women to participate in notarial culture, the pages of notarial registers nevertheless tell the story of an urban economy and society that included women but was dominated by men. Notarial culture itself contributed to this phenomenon.

Experiencing Notarial Culture

The notaries' own records, combined with urban regulations for the notariate, allow us to re-create the everyday experience of recording a contract with a notary. In the twelfth century, professional notaries gradually replaced priests and monks as the creators of written records. Counts, kings, and eventually urban municipal governments appropriated the jurisdictional authority of validating contracts and imbued the notaries who crafted these contracts with their own public authority.[6] In the Crown of Aragon, the king, local lay and ecclesiastical lords, and municipal governments all asserted the power to authorize notaries.[7]

Both royal and urban regulations mandated that notaries be men of free status, of a certain minimum age, and of good reputation. They had to live within the jurisdiction in which they received their appointment, and notaries appointed in secular jurisdictions could not have taken holy orders.[8] Prior to their appointment, notaries also had to demonstrate competence in fulfilling their professional obligations, either by taking an exam or by serving an apprenticeship.[9] At minimum, the everyday work of the notary required Latin literacy and familiarity with a set of basic templates; most loan contracts, for example, used a simple format in which little changed other than names, dates, and sums of money. However, notaries were also called upon to craft more complex contracts, which would require knowledge of the legal norms of both the Romano-canonical tradition and Catalan customary law. Wills, dowry contracts, and real estate sales all necessitated lengthier and more complicated documents that reflected the idiosyncratic wishes of clients. Although few notaries received formal legal training at the university level, most developed the skills they needed to meet their clients' expectations through apprenticeships.[10]

Only Christians could receive the formal designation of notary public, although the kings of Aragon also appointed Jewish and Muslim notaries, who were charged with crafting and authorizing documents produced for members of their own communities.[11] While notaries varied in income and social status, the profession could undoubtedly bring wealth and power to its practitioners.[12] In Girona, the notaries who served on the city council belonged to the *mà major*, the uppermost echelon of the non-noble urban elite.[13]

Notaries drew up a wide range of contracts but played an especially important role in facilitating credit, investment, and real estate transactions; creating relationships of legal agency; and recording the transmission of family wealth through marriage and inheritance. Many notarial contracts created long-term formal relationships between people. Loans tied together borrower and lender until the debt was repaid; business partnership and rental contracts created financial relationships between individuals that could last a year or more; and marriage contracts, at least in theory, created a lifelong personal and economic bond. Other contracts provided proof of ownership for high-value property, including real estate, ships, livestock, or slaves.[14] Those transactions that did not require notarial contracts typically involved immediate exchanges of goods for cash—and normally brought lower profits.

In all three cities, notaries recorded more credit contracts than any other type of transaction. Wealth in the medieval western Mediterranean largely existed in the form of household objects, clothing, or real estate, not stores of coins. The economy therefore depended on an effective credit system, as cash flowed quickly in and out of even the wealthier medieval urban households, and that credit system depended on notaries.[15]

Notaries worked in many different places and spaces across Catalan cities and their hinterlands. Like most craftsmen, notaries designated a room in their own homes as an office or workshop and conducted business there.[16]

TABLE 5 Types of notarial contracts in general sample

	Barcelona, 1292–1350	Girona, 1311–1350	Vic, 1250–1350
Mutuum[1]			
New loans	183	266	620
Repayments	288	263	553
Other	10	91	118
Subtotal	481	620	1291
Commenda[2]			
New contracts	282	240	436
Repayments	66	12	29
Subtotal	348	252	465
Sales on credit			
New contracts	54	701	269
Repayments	15	6	13
Subtotal	69	707	282
Real estate			
Rentals	135	142	453
Sales	184	154	451
Other	8	2	14
Subtotal	327	298	918
Procurator[3]			
Appointments	316	100	290
Quitclaims	13	1	1
Subtotal	329	101	291
Inheritance	112	71	131
Dowry			
Contracts	37	22	1
Debts	5	11	8
Quitclaims	32	61	72
Returns	13	5	15
Subtotal	87	99	96
Arbitrations	77	11	30
Donationes inter vivos[4]	36	59	74
Apprenticeship contracts	6	8	63
Service contracts	25	50	28
Slave contracts	18	2	5
Societas contracts[5]	15	7	11
Salary payments	14	1	2
Ship contracts	9	3	0
Testaments	5	43	1
Inventories	5	0	0
Guardianship contracts	7	3	0
Sales of goods	5	12	12

(continued)

TABLE 5 Types of notarial contracts in general sample (*continued*)

	Barcelona, 1292–1350	Girona, 1311–1350	Vic, 1250–1350
Sales of livestock	3	5	16
Annuity contracts[6]	16	11	0
Other[7]	130	95	140
Total	2124	2458	3856

[1]The most common form of loan contract; it is usually simple and brief.

[2]A type of contract employed for both deposits and commercial investments. They were typically designed to divide profits between investor and recipient.

[3]The contractual form in which a person appointed a legal agent, either for general business or to accomplish a specific task.

[4]Literally "grant between the living"; the *donatio inter vivos* often represented a premortem inheritance transfer.

[5]A contractual form of business partnership, which delineated the investments made by all parties and the way in which the profits would be divided.

[6]This category includes both the *censal*, a perpetual annuity, and the *violarium*, an annuity given for a limited amount of time (for example, the lifetime of the recipient). Neither was extensively represented in the documentation, but both became increasingly significant as a form of credit in the later fourteenth and fifteenth centuries.

[7]Includes a variety of contract types not discussed in this study, including ecclesiastical contracts and those related to feudal obligations, as well as some too damaged to properly identify.

Some notaries also set up portable tables in public urban areas frequented by members of the local mercantile elite—for example, the Plaça de Sant Jaume in Barcelona.[17] Notaries may have sought out similar public spaces when they plied their trade in neighboring villages. In Italy and southern France, notaries regularly drafted contracts in private homes.[18] The notaries of Barcelona, Girona, and Vic may have done the same, but they rarely specified any information about where the contract was concluded, except perhaps to identify the city or town.[19]

Whether they worked in an office, a public square, or a series of private homes throughout a neighborhood, notaries created around them a space that brought clients together. Witnesses repeat across contracts concluded on the same day; the cleric Guillem Simó, for example, witnessed several transactions in Girona on May 30, 1326, suggesting that he spent the day not far from the notary Pere Massanet.[20] Parties involved in one contract would witness another on the same day and before the same notary, as when Ramon Albert of Girona witnessed a real estate contract while waiting for a notary to record his *commenda*-deposit contract.[21] The clients of urban notaries clustered together to conduct commercial and family business—and perhaps even to make new connections with future economic partners.[22]

Notaries provided their clients with official copies of contracts, written in relatively clear script on high-value parchment. Inventories indicate that ordinary people preserved these copies in chests for safekeeping and understood these physical objects as constituting part of their household valuables. Geralda, widow of the lawyer Ramon Vinader and guardian of her minor grandchildren, had an inventory drawn up of the goods belonging to her wards in 1335.[23] The inventory listed several notarial contracts, identified by content, date, and the name of the authorizing notary. Most provided proof of either property ownership or debts owed to the children. Evidently, Geralda recognized the value of these material demonstrations of less tangible assets and their importance to her wards' estate.

Parchment contracts like the ones described in Geralda's inventory account for only a small fraction of the notarial contracts that have survived from medieval Europe. Notaries also recorded slightly abbreviated copies for their own records. From at least the thirteenth century onward, notaries kept these copies in registers, designated volumes usually comprising one hundred folios or more, each of which contained hundreds of individual contracts. The records kept in registers could serve as a basis for the composition of official copies.[24] Whereas notaries utilized high-quality, durable parchment for client copies, they turned to more affordable paper for the registers that remained in their possession.[25] By the fourteenth century, the common practice of keeping registers had become enshrined in law in Catalonia.[26] Notarial registers therefore provide an essential window onto who went to the notaries and why, and they hint at how people of different social strata, gender, and religious identity experienced their interactions with notaries and fellow clients.

When Jaume Transfort recorded the credit contracts between the Jewish creditor Bonadona and her Christian debtors, Bonanata and Pere, he drafted a total of five individual contracts on the same pages (fig. 1). Altogether, these contracts identify twenty-two separate people who sought out the notary to conduct business on June 12, 1336.[27] Out of these twenty-two people, twenty were men, eight of whom can be clearly identified as members of the city's commercial elite. Another two of the men were clerics.

The notariate catered primarily to people with money and property. Men and women with wealth to manage had the greatest need for notarial services. Impoverished peasants and the urban poor rarely participated in exchanges of sufficient value to justify notarial intervention; as Sharon Farmer has noted, the tendency for medieval source material to emphasize transfers of wealth poses significant challenges for the study of people who lacked it.[28] Even when making more substantial exchanges—for example, concluding

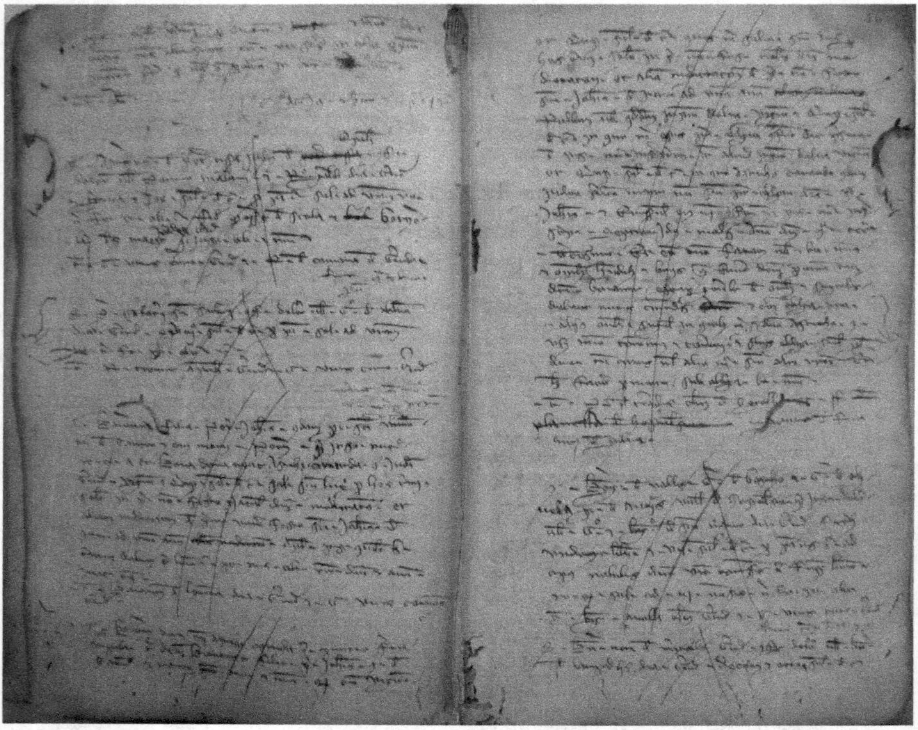

FIG. 1. Sample page from a register of the notary Jaume Transfort of Girona. Arxiu Històric de Girona, secció Girona, Gi-4, vol. 12, fols. 55v–56r.

dowry contracts—those with fewer resources at their disposal may not have considered notaries' fees worth the benefits of registration. Notaries charged fees on a sliding scale, depending on both the type of contract and the value of assets involved.[29] Fees for most basic contracts were low—perhaps 2 sous for an agency contract or a simple loan—but even small fees may have discouraged the urban and rural poor from relying on notaries.[30]

Gender and Notarial Culture

The same snapshot of the clientele of the Girona notary Jaume Transfort portrays a male-dominated space clustered around the notary, whether in an office or a market square, or roving around a neighborhood. Bonadona and her debtor Bonanata, the only women who worked with Transfort on that day, would have encountered many men, some strangers, including both the witnesses for their own transaction and perhaps also the men who concluded contracts before and after them. Although Bonadona, as a Jewish woman, had her own complicated relationship with notarial culture (see chapter 4), after her husband's death in 1334 she had regularly used the services of the city's Christian notaries. Bonanata, on the other hand, had far less familiarity with notarial culture. She may never have gone to the Girona notaries before and might never again. Only her responsibility for a debt incurred by her parents spurred her to travel to the city of Girona (about fourteen kilometers away from home), seek out a Jewish creditor, and conclude a contract before an urban notary.

Notarial documentation clearly demonstrates that some women in medieval Catalan cities engaged in work that profited their households and that this work required their participation in notarial culture. However, it is crucial not to overstate women's involvement in the economic system made visible to us through notarial documentation. A researcher can easily read several pages of a notarial register without coming across a single woman. There is no economic sector in which women operated on a level equal to men. Women were less likely than men to act independently; many of the women whose names were recorded on the pages of notarial registers played only a supporting role in the business of their husbands or fathers. Those women who carried out business on their own initiative were more reliant than men on support from family members.

In the context of a patriarchal gender system, it is impossible to isolate a single reason why women were disadvantaged relative to men of their own social stature. However, I argue that notarial culture itself contributed to an economic system that circumscribed women's ability to engage in the kinds of work made visible through notarial documentation. The pages of notarial registers portray notarial culture as deeply masculine. Even when notaries did business in public squares or in their clients' homes, the social norms and legal requirements of notarial contracts ensured that men dominated the space around the notary.

The notariate was a public institution, but not a neutral one. Public notaries were deeply invested in the political project of creating and reinforcing urban identity. Notaries verbally mapped the city through written references to urban space and place, and they crafted geographies that attempted to impose a uniform understanding of urban space and a shared urban identity, as defined by the city's governing elite.[31] These efforts to impose a common urban identity centered primarily on men of the elite and middling classes, whose wives and daughters remained merely incidental. Barcelona citizenship petitions highlight the marginal position of women in ideologies of civic identity. The Barcelona city government conferred citizenship on people from a broad range of social strata, all of whom chose the city as their primary place of residence. Nearly all petitioners for citizenship, however, were men. The presence of wives and children in male petitioners' urban households signaled their residence and strengthened their citizenship petitions, but most women claimed citizenship only through their husbands and fathers, not through independent petitions.[32]

As an institution working to create and reinforce urban identity, the notariate also primarily concerned itself with the needs of men. The pages of notarial registers portray notaries as in the constant process of creating around them a male-dominated space, sometimes in their own offices, sometimes in city streets or market squares, and sometimes even in their clients' own homes. The gendering of physical space effectively works to reinforce prevailing gender hierarchies; as Linda McDowell has theorized, "the mapping of a place or location onto gender identities has been a key part of the establishment and maintenance of women's positions and is reflected in both the materiality and the symbolic representation of women's lives."[33]

Medieval cities and villages did not have sharp boundaries between public and private space. Workshops or storefronts often formed part of private homes, and domestic and economic life were deeply intertwined. Yet family members and urban governments alike nevertheless associated certain spaces with women and other spaces with men, and they policed the behavior of women who transgressed boundaries between male and female space.[34] Women expected to walk through city streets and pass in and out of shops and workplaces, whether conducting business, assisting their husbands, or shopping. Yet they also expected to dress and behave in certain ways when they moved through these male urban spaces. The notary's office or table certainly functioned as masculine space in this sense. Even if notaries accommodated women clients by meeting them in their homes, the process of crafting a contract crowded women's domestic space with men, including some who may have been tangential or unfamiliar figures in women's lives.

If women associated the experience of crafting notarial contracts with negotiating a male-dominated space, they may have hestitated to turn to the notaries to conduct business. Alternatively (or additionally), men may have discouraged their wives, mothers, and daughters from work that required interaction with unfamiliar men or sought to accompany them when they went to the notary. Intersections of gender and socioeconomic status further complicated women's experiences of the notaries. Wealthy urban women were far more likely to develop some familiarity with notarial culture. A peasant woman like Bonanata, in contrast, only infrequently required the services of notaries and therefore may have found the experience particularly daunting—especially if their circumstances required Bonanata and her husband to travel into the city from its hinterlands.

Women's relationship with notarial culture was complicated and multifaceted; some women experienced pressures both to avoid notarial culture and to obtain notarial documentation. Social expectations, family needs, and economic considerations did not always coincide. Women navigating notarial culture were therefore always in the minority but never entirely absent. The offices, tables, and domestic gatherings created around notaries can also be thought of as representing what Barbara Hanawalt termed "ambiguous spaces" in her discussion of medieval English taverns. Women worked in taverns as both brewers and servers, but they found their virtue called into question when they occupied that space in either a professional or social capacity.[35] Similarly, women's work as managers of household resources brought them into contact with notaries, but concerns over reputation and the transgressing of boundaries—whether their own or those of family members—shaped or circumscribed the choices women made about whether and how they engaged with notarial culture.

Notarial documents do not describe women's dress or behavior when they sought out notarial contracts. However, notarial contracts hint at the strategies women adopted to mediate or minimize their presence in the masculine space surrounding the notary—usually by relying on men to accompany or replace them. We cannot say definitively whether such strategies represent women's own choices, and thus a form of agency, or whether women were pressured to adopt these strategies by their husbands, fathers, or adult sons. Regardless, women's reliance on men to navigate notarial culture had the potential to weaken their authority over assets. Notarial culture functioned to both reproduce and reinforce a gender system that never fully excluded women from urban economic life but consistently left them less able than men of their own status to securely engage in profitable forms of work.

Women in Notarial Culture: Negotiating Male Space

The norms of Catalan legal culture required many Christian women, especially those from prosperous families, to develop some familiarity with the notariate. However, most women experienced notarial culture only or primarily through the mediation of their husbands and male relatives, who accompanied them for most notarial transactions. Medieval women negotiating ambiguous or male-gendered space employed a range of strategies to ensure their own comfort and legitimize their presence. In medieval England, women traveling sought out male companions for their own safety, while women in urban public spaces adjusted their dress and behavior to minimize their contact with male space.[36] Women merchants in Ghent used the gendered partitioning of market spaces to emphasize the legitimacy of their presence in spaces open to women.[37] Catalan women usually developed familiarity with notarial culture by participating in transactions alongside men—and many continued to rely on male support throughout their lives when they conducted business with notarial contracts.

Some young women first experienced notarial culture as accessories to the economic strategies of their parents. Girls in their teens went with their parents to consent to property sales or other transactions that could affect their inheritance. In 1260, for example, Ramon de Coll and his wife Guillema sold a rural estate alongside their children Pere and Elisenda.[38] Archival documents record fiction as well as fact, and it is difficult to definitively prove that minors like Pere and Elisenda were physically present for sales.[39] However, notaries adopted a variety of verbal strategies that distinguished between present and absent participants. Notaries sometimes included the word "absent" after a party's name or relegated absent minor children to a position deep within the contract, when their parent promised to obtain consent, rather than in the opening list of sellers. Even if the seller list conflated absent and present parties, the experience of having to consent to a sale (albeit with little real authority) may have helped familiarize children and teens with notarial culture.

Many young women first experienced notarial culture when they participated in the financial arrangements surrounding their marriages. The signing of the *capítols matrimonials*—especially the dowry contract—formed an essential element of marriage for most Catalan couples.[40] Even before a valid marriage took place, the signing of the *capítols matrimonials* created a new financial relationship between the bride, the groom, and their families. Blanca, daughter of Jaume Cardona of Barcelona, never married her fiancée Arnau de Serrià, who died prematurely—but she still had to negotiate with her would-be father-in-law for the return of her dowry, as she and her parents and grandmother had already paid 4,000 of the promised 14,000 sous.[41]

However, women normally did not act alone when they signed the set of documents that would permanently alter their personal and financial futures.

Whereas most grooms signed the *capítols matrimonials* without the visible participation of their families, brides are usually portrayed in contracts as appearing in the company of at least one family member (most often the father).[42] The experience of signing the *capítols matrimonials* familiarized many women with notarial culture at the precise moment that they gained a newfound authority over financial resources. However, the presence of their husbands and fathers simultaneously reinforced the association of notarial culture with male space. Recent brides would have recalled their first experience of notarial culture as one mediated by their fathers and their future husbands. Moreover, despite the legal fiction of brides' participation in the transfer of the dowry, notarial *capítols matrimonials* ultimately documented a process that limited women's managerial authority over the property they owned. The signing of the *capítols matrimonials* brought women into contact with notarial culture only to affirm that many of them would not need to work with a notary again, at least not for years to come.

Similarly, while women went to the office of the notary to consent to or participate in their husbands' transactions, these moments of engagement with notarial culture only highlighted their own marginal relationship to the notariate. Whether a woman acted independently or with others, a notary would nearly always identify her in relation to her husband (living or dead) or father.[43] A man, in contrast, would sometimes be identified in relation to his father, but he would often be identified by profession or neighborhood. This notarial practice emphasizes the fact that women often accessed notarial culture via their husbands and fathers.

Other notarial practices imply that notaries understood women as accessories to contracts rather than as central participants, especially when they acted alongside their husbands. In contracts where husbands and wives jointly incurred debts, notaries sometimes left a blank space in lieu of the woman's name; men who were primary parties to a contract were almost never left nameless in this manner. In June 1340, for example, the stonemason Pere Novell of Girona incurred a debt alongside his wife, but the notary never filled in her name, Berenguera, which we only know from other contracts in which she acted jointly with her husband (fig. 2).[44] Berenguera's namelessness suggests that her identity did not matter a great deal to the notary, who made no apparent effort to confirm the name with her or her husband. The blank space substituted for Berenguera could suggest she was never physically present at all, despite accepting responsibility for the debt, or merely that her presence was seen as unimportant.

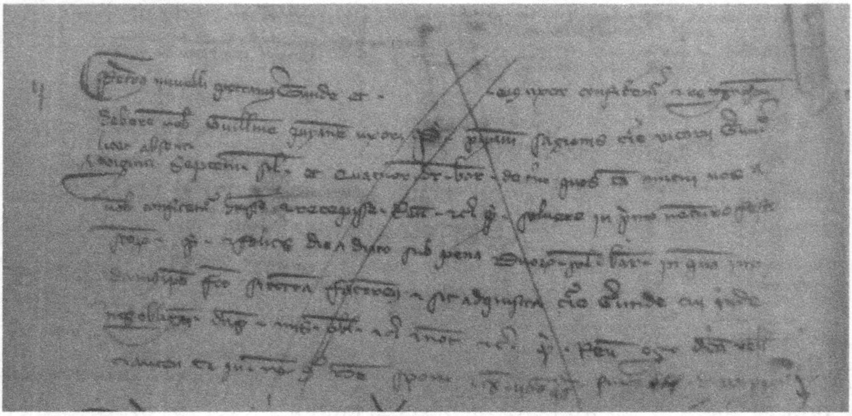

FIG. 2. Contract for debt incurred by Pere Novell and his wife Berenguera of Girona. Arxiu Històric de Girona, secció Girona, Gi-4, vol. 4, fol. 82v.

Even wives who participated fully in their husbands' business dealings might disappear from follow-up contracts. In 1335, for example, the tavern-keeper Pere Domenech of Girona and his wife Brunissenda jointly purchased an urban dwelling. Although the initial contract portrayed Brunissenda as a co-buyer and new co-owner of the property, the later contract (in which Pere paid for the property) omitted any mention of his wife.[45] Notaries and their male clients treated wives as less essential than their husbands to notarial transactions and notarial culture. These experiences may have further reinforced women's impression of notarial culture as a masculine province, accessible to them mostly through the mediation of their husbands or male relatives.

Women often involved their husbands or male relatives in their transactions even when doing business with financial resources that they appeared to own independently. Their efforts to ensure the physical presence of a trusted male figure may reflect an understanding of notarial culture as best accessed in the company of men. In 1263, for example, Brunissenda, daughter of Perpinyà and Ramona de Segalers, went with her husband Bonanat Benencasa before a public notary in Vic to sell a market stall (fig. 3).[46] The notary consistently placed Brunissenda's name before her husband's and identified her first as her parents' daughter. These unusual documentary practices functioned to identify the wife as the owner of inherited property. In the second contract, confirming the sale, the notary nearly forgot to include Bonanat at all, only belatedly inserting his name above the line. The construction of this contract suggests that the property belonged to Brunissenda; Bonanat played a far too peripheral role for a man who jointly owned

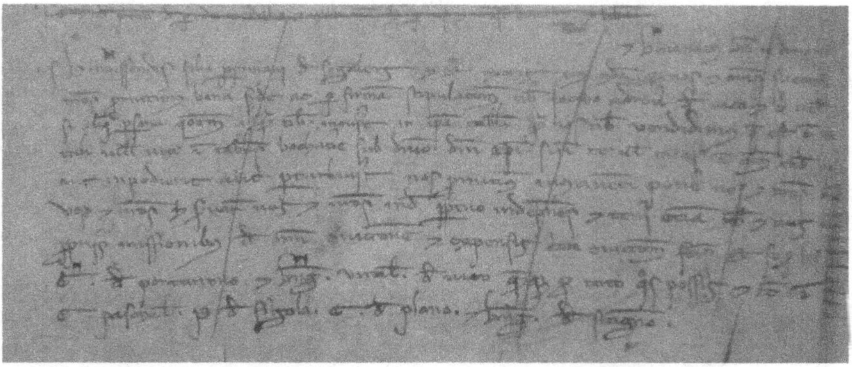

FIG. 3. Contract for sale of market stall by Brunissenda, wife of Bonanat Benencasa of Vic. Arxiu Biblioteca Episcopal de Vic, Arxiu de la Curia Fumada, vol. 10, fol. 141v.

the property or held it as his wife's dowry. Rather, he apparently participated only to help Brunissenda negotiate the male space of the notary's office. His involvement, however, had real economic implications: it potentially created a presumption of joint ownership and therefore strengthened his claim to the cash they received for the sale.

Women Out of Notarial Culture: Avoiding Male Space

While some women relied on their husbands or male relatives to accompany them to the notary's office, others remained absent entirely. By appointing legal agents to conduct transactions on their behalf, women avoided future appearances in the notary's office. Notarial contracts did specify why people appointed agents rather than handling their business in person. However, women acting independently appointed agents at rates out of proportion to their actual involvement in business.[47] When women handed the reins of their business to an agent, they almost always appointed men.[48] Some of the women who appointed agents probably did so to avoid travel; in 1319, for example, Margarida, wife of Bernat d'Artèries of Barcelona, tasked the cleric Bernat Dalinar with transferring possession of an enslaved person she had sold to a woman in Mallorca.[49] Others, however, appointed agents to accomplish seemingly mundane business, like Ramona, wife of Brunet de Bell-mirall of Girona, who empowered her husband to collect debts owed to her.[50] Some of these women could have been too busy or too ill to accomplish their business in person. However, the disproportionately high rates

TABLE 6 Christian women in notarial transactions in medieval Catalan cities, 1250–1350

Contracts	Barcelona	Girona	Vic
Loans (creditors)			
Total no. of contracts	163	157	617
With independent women	10 (6.1%)	16 (10.2%)	20 (3.2%)
With mixed-gender groups	2 (1.2%)	1 (0.6%)	20 (3.2%)
Loans (debtors)			
Total no. of contracts	165	259	615
With independent women	11 (6.7%)	9 (3.5%)	24 (3.9%)
With mixed-gender groups	10 (6.1%)	82 (31.7%)	136 (22.1%)
Real estate (sellers)			
Total no. of contracts	164	154	451
With independent women	20 (12.2%)	8 (5.2%)	29 (6.4%)
With mixed-gender groups	29 (17.7%)	63 (40.9%)	229 (50.8%)
Real estate (buyers)			
Total no. of contracts	164	154	451
With independent women	8 (4.9%)	8 (5.2%)	9 (2.0%)
With mixed-gender groups	9 (5.5%)	36 (23.4%)	76 (16.9%)
Real estate (landlords)			
Total no. of contracts	116	142	453
With independent women	14 (12.1%)	7 (4.9%)	35 (7.7%)
With mixed-gender groups	6 (5.2%)	22 (15.5%)	82 (18.1%)
Real estate (tenants)			
Total no. of contracts	116	142	453
With independent women	9 (7.8%)	11 (7.7%)	14 (3.1%)
With mixed-gender groups	14 (12.1%)	19 (13.4%)	75 (16.6%)

of women appointing agents suggest that at least some may have done so to avoid further notarial business. Although reliance on agents may have saved women discomfort, it also left last-minute decisions about their money and property in the hands of others.

Other women simply absented themselves from business that required notarial intervention, leaving the management of financial resources to their husbands or male relatives. Christian women acting independently participated in at most 12 percent of contracts, depending on the economic sector (see table 6). Women also made economic choices that, at least in practice, functioned to minimize their reliance on notaries. For example, women sold property more often than they purchased it or leased it out as landlords. The disparity between women's property ownership and women's property management suggests that access to financial resources alone did not shape how women controlled their assets. Women may have sold off properties received through inheritance or in payment of the *sponsalicium* rather than commit to the work of managing them.[51] Such decisions did not necessarily promote long-term financial stability. Women sellers received an immediate cash infusion but lost the regular income they could earn from rental properties.

The small number of women who appear on the pages of notarial registers both reflected and reinforced the gendered character of notarial culture. Legal norms reserved the profession of notary and the act of witnessing for men, and women did most of their business with men rather than with other women. All these factors exacerbated gender disparities in the group of people who gathered to conclude notarial contracts; a woman who went to the notary independently could easily find herself alone with at least four other men. The experience of being the only woman present, or one of only two or three in a large crowd of men, may have discouraged women from regularly relying on notaries or led their families to pressure them to avoid notarial business.

Conclusions

Catalan Christian legal culture in the thirteenth and fourteenth centuries imposed some restrictions on women's control over financial resources but simultaneously created opportunities for women to participate in the work of managing household assets. The inheritance and marriage practices that structured women's access to money and property cannot fully explain why relatively few women populate the pages of Catalonia's notarial registers—nor why even fewer appeared as independent actors. Although legal norms asserted women's control over assets under certain circumstances, the masculine character of notarial culture may have discouraged women from embracing managerial responsibilities or led men to dissuade their wives, mothers, sisters, and daughters from managing wealth independently.

Some women, especially those of elite and middling status, found themselves called upon to go the notary's office alongside their fathers, brothers, and husbands. Ultimately, these brief moments of partial integration into notarial culture only highlighted the ways in which the notary's place of business functioned as a male space—even when it overlapped with domestic space. However, most Christian women of lower social strata did not even attain this level of familiarity with notarial culture. Families who did not own real property, or who lacked the collateral or capacity for repayment to obtain substantial loans, did not participate in the types of notarial transactions that required the consent of daughters and wives. Lower-income families also relied less heavily on notaries when contracting marriage. Average and median dowry values suggest that the middling and wealthier classes are disproportionately represented in extant notarial dowry contracts. Women of lower status, who had much smaller dowries or entered common property marriages, did not have this kind of experience of notarial culture—and appear less regularly in the pages of notarial registers than either high-status women or low-status men.

The gendered dynamics of notarial culture made it more difficult for even property-owning women to manage their assets and deprived lower-income women of notarial protection for what assets they had. The increasing economic importance of the notariate therefore posed significant challenges to women's economic self-sufficiency in medieval Catalonia. Notarial documentation shaped, as well as recorded, gendered economic structures.

4

JEWS, NOTARIES, AND THE CHRISTIAN CITY

After her husband's death, Bonadona, the widow of Astrug Caravida of Girona, found herself better positioned to work as a creditor than most women and men in her city's Jewish community. Professional moneylenders typically came from the wealthiest sector of the Jewish community—a group to which Bonadona and her late husband belonged.[1] Prior to his death, Astrug bypassed the restriction on wives inheriting from their husbands with a premortem Hebrew writ, which transferred to Bonadona all his goods and all the debts owed to him.[2] Astrug made an unusual choice in granting his wife so much of his wealth, but an acceptable one, according to local interpretations of halakhah; Ishbili affirmed the validity of such gifts and the incontrovertible rights of the wives who received them.[3] Her *de facto* inheritance from Astrug left Bonadona in control of a quite substantial estate. Astrug had extended over a hundred loans between 1321 and 1334, several for sums of over a thousand sous.[4]

Few Jewish widows received such consideration from their husbands, and Bonadona probably would not have found herself in such a financially advantageous position if she had had sons. But Astrug and Bonadona had only daughters, who had already married and received dowries before their father's death.[5] Given the wealth at her disposal, Bonadona seemed poised at the brink of a career as a prominent moneylender. However, the extant records portray her as far less successful than her husband: between 1334 and

1340, she collected on twenty-one loans made by her husband and extended only nine new ones.[6] Her career was far briefer and far less profitable than that of her late husband.

Jewish widows in Girona and Barcelona never achieved the level of success enjoyed by their late husbands.[7] Even with her meager nine new loans, Bonadona stands out as one of the most prominent Jewish woman creditors in Girona.[8] However, her failure to establish a lending career comparable to that of Astrug did not stem from a lack of access to financial resources. Nor did it reflect incompetence: in her energetic efforts to secure her daughter's divorce without sacrificing her financial security, Bonadona demonstrated both legal savviness and financial acumen.[9] Since neither illiquidity nor inability can explain Bonadona's at best moderate success as a moneylender, why did she play such a minor role in the public business of credit, in comparison with men of comparable status?

I argue that Bonadona's limited involvement in the notarial credit market in widowhood, despite her access to wealth and her expertise in both law and business, reflected the dual marginalization of Jewish women in a fundamentally male and Christian notarial culture. No formal restrictions barred Jewish women from turning to the city notaries, either as women or as Jews. However, the understanding of notarial culture as dominated by Christian men may have discouraged Jewish women from regularly taking advantage of the services provided by urban notaries. Jewish men also probably preferred women in their families and communities to avoid the male-dominated, Christian spaces that notaries created around them—in offices, at tables, and perhaps even in Jewish homes.

The complicated relationship Jewish women had with notarial culture, both as women and as Jews, helps explain why they went to notaries far less often than either Christian women or Jewish men, as well as why even the wealthiest and most financially independent Jewish women remained marginal figures in the sectors of the economy most reliant on notarial intervention. This chapter will begin with a discussion of how notarial culture was marked as Christian, followed by an overview of Jews' relationship to notarial culture as seen through the registers of Barcelona, Girona, and Vic. Finally, I will turn to Jewish women's experiences of notarial culture. I argue that discomfort with male, Christian notarial culture—either women's own discomfort or that of their families—posed unique challenges for their economic self-sufficiency, different from those experienced by either their male coreligionists or by women of the dominant Christian faith.

Notarial Culture and Christian Space in Catalan Cities

The crafting of urban identity in thirteenth- and fourteenth-century cities relied not only on discourses of masculinity but also on the marginalization of Jews. Jews often lived at the geographical centers of cities in Catalonia and elsewhere in Europe, in Jewish quarters located adjacent to the cathedral or in mixed neighborhoods.[10] Yet despite living physically in the center of Catalan cities, Jews existed on the metaphorical margins. Cities in the Crown of Aragon excluded Jews from urban citizenship, albeit granting them certain privileges as residents, and exercised only limited jurisdictional authority over the Jews in their midst.[11] By their own preference and that of the Catalan-Aragonese monarchs, Jews lived in self-governing communities subject only to royal authority.[12]

Clerical and lay urban elites across Europe employed space and place to define urban public spaces as Christian and to reaffirm the exclusion of Jews from Christian urban society. Sculptural programs on the exteriors of churches featured anti-Jewish polemics of varying subtlety, which served as visual reminders for both Jews and Christians of Jews' subordinate status.[13] Religious processions, organized by both ecclesiastical professionals and lay confraternities, worked to Christianize city streets and consolidate urban religious identity through the perceived holy power of sacred images and relics.[14] A 1322 ordinance issued by the bailiff of Barcelona physically excluded Jews from Christian city streets on the feast of Corpus Christi, when they would be fined 20 sous for leaving the *call* or their homes (presumably, if their homes were outside the Jewish quarter).[15] In the later fourteenth and fifteenth centuries, anti-Jewish public preaching in western Mediterranean cities would denigrate Jews as Christ-killers and usurers.[16] Even basics of ritual and social life, such as attendance at mass, by their very nature reinforced Christian cohesion and excluded those who belonged to the city's Jewish community.[17] The Jews of Barcelona were constantly reminded of their subordination and exclusion from Christian ritual by a 1303 city ordinance that mandated that they hide from or kneel before a priest en route to give communion.[18]

Even though Jewish quarters in medieval Catalonia were neither closed off nor isolated, the delineation of certain streets as Jewish space allowed Christians to reaffirm the exclusion of Jews from most of the Christian city. The ritual stoning of the walls of the Jewish quarter of Girona during Holy Week, a regular occurrence in the early fourteenth century, worked to maintain boundaries between religious groups.[19] The symbolic significance of the

Jewish quarter and its walls reveals the importance of space and place in the Christianization of medieval cities. The massacre of Jews in Valencia in 1391 may have represented an effort to reincorporate the city's Jewish quarter into the fabric of the Christian city.[20] Starting in the thirteenth century, regulations mandated that Jews distinguish themselves by wearing brightly colored badges or cloaks, with the aim of ensuring that Jews who ventured into Christian space nevertheless remained identifiable as outsiders.[21] The Barcelona urban governing council repeatedly issued such regulations over the course of the fourteenth century, which specified that Jews wear either a red and yellow cape or affix a yellow circle (*rota*) on their outer layer of clothing.[22]

Notaries often worked in areas that functioned as Christian public space. Clients frequently found notaries either in offices that formed extensions of Christian domestic space or in public areas closely associated with the urban governing councils that formally excluded Jews from their ranks.[23] When Jews approached notaries, the dominant presence of Christians inevitably reminded them of their status as members of a marginalized minority community. On June 12, 1336, when Bonadona, widow of Astrug Caravida of Girona, agreed on terms with her Christian debtors, Bonadona was one of only four Jews and the only Jewish woman in a crowd of twenty-three people, including the notary Jaume Transfort, represented on the pages of the register.[24] Although Jews could licitly serve as witnesses to notarial documents, Jewish men rarely witnessed contracts between Christians, and Jewish women never acted as witnesses. Most contracts involving both Christians and Jews had at least one Christian as witness, and no Jew witnessed any of the contracts drawn up by Jaume Transfort on June 12, 1336.

Even when personal exemptions and spotty enforcement allowed Jews to avoid wearing distinguishing markers, they nevertheless remained aware of their minority status when in crowds of Christians.[25] Notarial culture required Jews to display their Jewish identities both verbally and textually in written contracts. Jews were distinguished in the pages of Catalan notarial registers not only by their often distinct names but also by the word "Jew" (*judeus*), used as a descriptor. Christian identity functioned as an unmarked category: the notaries never explicitly identified people as Christians.[26] Jews, in contrast, were consistently identified as Jews, often in lieu of other types of identity markers, such as profession or neighborhood of residence, which were commonly employed to distinguish Christians.[27] In most cases, notaries described Jews using only their religion and city of residence (e.g., "Mosse de Scola, Jew of Girona") and rarely included other identifying markers. In the few cases in which notaries included Jews' professions, they usually did so because this piece of information was relevant to the transaction. For example, a 1314 contract from Barcelona identified a married couple as "Samuel Xaham, Jew of Barcelona, silkweaver and dyer, and his wife Miriam, a dyer" when they purchased raw silk for use in their trade.[28] Notaries rarely employed the feminine *judea*; instead, they identified most Jewish women as such only via the Jewish identity of their fathers and husbands ("Bonadona, wife of the late Astrug Caravida, Jew of Girona").[29]

Jews, notaries, and royal authorities alike understood the blend of Roman law and Catalan customary law that shaped notarial contracts as "Christian law." A royal privilege of 1271 granted the Jews of Girona, Besalú, and the communities under their jurisdiction the right to draw up marriage contracts using "Christian or Hebrew charters."[30] Kings and notaries did not always identify notarial contracts as "Christian"; this particular privilege deliberately employed the term in order to contrast Latin, Romano-Catalan notarial contracts with Hebrew-Aramaic ones drawn up in accordance with halakhah.[31] Nevertheless, the description of Latin notarial contracts as "Christian" reflects a general understanding that these documents stemmed from a language and legal system identified with Christian culture. On the rare occasions when Jewish clients asked notaries to engage with Jewish law, the notaries betrayed a lack of understanding of this divergent legal tradition, seen through mistranslations of Hebrew terms and misuse of Jewish legal concepts.[32] Jewish clients themselves took responsibility for explaining relevant points of halakhah to Christian notaries.[33]

In some Catalan cities, including Vic, notaries relegated transactions involving Jews to their own separate registers. These *libri iudeorum*, literally "books of the Jews," treated the religious identity of participants as fundamental to the categorization of contracts, and they textually segregated Jews and their business from the wider Christian community. The cover of one *liber iudeorum* from Vic suggests that some notaries closely identified the real Jews who passed through their offices with the anti-Jewish caricatures that had become increasingly popular in late medieval visual culture.[34] The cover features a drawing of a man depicted with the same hooked nose, long beard, and pointed hat utilized in numerous thirteenth- and fourteenth-century images hostile to Jews (fig. 4).[35] He is labeled with the name "Salomó Vidal"—a real Jew of Vic who worked professionally as a creditor, as did his wife Goig.[36]

As modern viewers, we cannot entirely determine to what extent the image drew on Salomó's likeness and to what extent it represents a maliciously exaggerated caricature. Pamela Patton has read Salomó's visage as "monstrous" and the image as a distorted mockery of Jewish usurers.[37] The physiognomic

FIG. 4. Drawing on the cover of a *liber iudeorum* from Vic. Arxiu Biblioteca Episcopal de Vic, Arxiu de la Curia Fumada, vol. 4603.

markers that distinguished Salomó resemble the ones found in a more overtly antagonistic caricature from a thirteenth-century English Exchequer Receipt Roll.[38] However, while that image hammered home its hostility toward Jews by associating them with demonic forces, the Vic drawing includes only an isolated, labeled Jewish figure that probably functioned in part simply to identify the register as a *liber iudeorum*.[39] Regardless, the drawing suggests that Christian notaries perceived Jews entering Christian space as being physically distinct from their Christian clientele and easily recognizable as Jews.

Jews in and out of the Notary's Office

Although Jews (especially Jewish men) used the services of the notaries with some regularity, they never became fully integrated into Catalan notarial culture. Some Catalan Jews even experienced the notariate as an unwanted

Christian intrusion into their lives.[40] Many Jews chose to rely on Jewish scribes authorized to draw up Hebrew contracts, rather than Christian notaries, when seeking documentation for intra-Jewish business and family law contracts.[41] The notariate never formally excluded Jewish clients; refraining from relying on notaries was largely a matter of personal choice, whereas choosing to turn to a notary was at times a necessity and reflective of Jews' subordinate status. The relationship between Jews and notaries could nevertheless involve cordial cross-cultural interaction; Jewish clients, Jewish scribes, and Christian notaries collaborated to translate contracts.[42] However, even this practice of working together to create translated documents emphasizes Jews' and Christians' shared awareness that the minority Jewish community existed at the intersection of two distinct legal cultures, only one of which represented the ruling authority.

In all three cities, most notarial contracts involving Jews recorded credit arrangements with Christian debtors.[43] The preponderance of credit contracts in the notarial documentation of Jewish life does not prove that all or even most Jews worked full-time as creditors (see chapter 5). Jews practiced a diverse array of professions, and many moneylenders worked only part-time in credit as a means of supplementing incomes from other sources.[44] Credit transactions disproportionately dominate the notarial portrait of Jewish business life because Jewish creditors were legally obligated to obtain notarial registration for all loans to Christians.[45] Moreover, Jewish creditors benefited from notarial registration of loans; notarial documentation could provide added security in the event that a debtor resisted repaying.[46] The hash marks drawn through most notarial loans suggest that Jewish creditors almost always managed to either receive repayments or renegotiate credit arrangements. For both legal and practical reasons, therefore, Jews relied more heavily on the notaries when making loans to Christians than when conducting other types of business.

Jews also turned to the notaries to record written contracts when conducting other types of business with Christians, in the event that formal documentation proved necessary. As members of a marginalized minority, Jews could not impose their legal culture on Christians, instead maneuvering within Romano-Catalan legal culture. Rabbinic authorities fully accepted that local legal norms governed any business relationships with non-Jews, in accordance with the Talmudic principle of *dina de-malkhuta dina* ("the law of the land is the law").[47] As professionals within the Christian legal system, the notaries provided essential services that enabled Jews to conduct profitable business transactions with members of the Christian majority.

However, Jews' apparent reluctance to rely on the services of the notaries for intracommunal and intrafamilial business highlights the Jewish community's complicated and fraught relationship with notarial culture. Family law fell under the exclusive jurisdiction of rabbis and Jewish communal leaders, and few Jews turned to the notaries to record contracts related to inheritance, marriage, or divorce.[48] Intra-Jewish business transactions could also be completed with Hebrew contracts, without the intervention of Christian notaries, with the result that intra-Jewish business probably remains underrepresented in the notarial evidence.

Occasionally, however, Jews sought Latin notarial documentation for intracommunal business. Especially in property transfers, such contracts could facilitate future trade with Christians; Christian property buyers often sought proof of ownership from Jewish sellers and may have preferred notarial contracts to Hebrew *shetarot* (contracts), even though the latter were legally valid in Christian courts.[49] Astruga of Vic, ex-wife of Bonastrug des Mestre, probably obtained notarial documentation for her divorce arrangements in part to protect a grant she made to her son in the form of outstanding loans worth 1,700 sous.[50] With Latin contracts in hand, her son could more easily collect on debts originally owed to his mother by Christian borrowers. Yet even when Jews relied on notaries to protect their assets, their actions reflect an awareness of their own status as members of a minority community. Their dependence on the Christian legal system demanded that they reinscribe their marginality by placing their Jewish bodies in Christian space and adhering to Christian legal norms.

On the Margins of the Margins: Jewish Women and Christian Notaries

Jews' experiences of going to the notaries to record loans, other contracts involving Christians, and occasionally business with other Jews would have reinforced their understanding of notarial culture as fundamentally male and Christian. Notaries' offices would have been filled with Christian men and their tables surrounded by them. Occasionally, circumstances may have required notaries to go to Jewish homes. In Marseille, notaries passed through the Jewish quarter to record property transfers.[51] Jewish wills from the Crown of Aragon do not specify that the notary came to the testator's home, but when the testator was described as ill, it seems probable that the notary went to his client.[52] However, notaries brought people with them: concluding a notarial contract at home could require Jewish women to bring groups of Christian men into their domestic space. In notarial contracts between Christians and Jews, at least one if not both witnesses were Christian men. When Jewish women recorded Latin notarial wills, which required at least seven witnesses, over half were Christians.[53] It is unclear whether these Christian men had a prior relationship with the dying Jewish women whose last wishes they witnessed.

However, just as some wealthy Christian women learned to negotiate male space successfully, wealthy Jewish men developed a familiarity with Christian legal norms and negotiated Christian notarial culture to their own advantage. Lower-income Jewish men and Jewish women of all social strata were much less likely to experience even this limited integration into Christian notarial culture. Most Jewish men and women who used the services of the notaries came from wealthy families and worked at least part-time in areas like credit, which necessitated regular trips to the notary's office. In contrast, lower-income Jews, who typically did not extend loans, buy property, or engage in other types of business that required notarial intervention, had little experience of the notary's office.[54] In the occasional moments when the Jewish poor entered the office of the notary, they would have been less well equipped than their wealthier counterparts to maneuver within a Christian space and an unfamiliar legal culture. Similarly, halakhic limitations on women's control of assets left few Jewish women with wealth to manage before they entered widowhood, even among the wealthiest sector of the Jewish population. As a result, most Jewish women had less familiarity with notarial culture than men of their own social stature did. They also experienced a unique form of double marginalization: engagement with notarial culture required Jewish women to navigate both Christian space and male space.

Even among the elite, Jewish women experienced greater challenges than either Jewish men or Christian women of comparable social rank in negotiating male, Christian notarial culture. Whereas young Christian women developed an early familiarity with notarial contracts as participants in their parents' transactions and as brides, most Jewish girls neither consented to their parents' business deals nor signed notarial *capítols matrimonials*. Given Jewish daughters' limited inheritance rights, few families felt it necessary to obtain consent from their daughters or sisters. Jewish couples usually formed marriages with Hebrew-Aramaic contracts and without recourse to notaries. After marriage, Jewish women had less authority than their Christian counterparts over the conjugal estate, and they only rarely controlled property independently. This constellation of marriage and inheritance practices not only restricted Jewish women's access to financial resources but also ensured that most Jewish women had no experience of Christian notarial culture until widowhood, if at all.

Jewish women who suddenly found themselves in control of financial resources—whether as heiresses or as widows—suddenly had to navigate within a legal culture, and in some cases a physical space, that may have been not only unfamiliar but uncomfortable, as it reinforced their marginalization both as women and as Jews. When Bonadona, widow of Astrug Caravida, arrived in the office of the notary Jaume Transfort on June 12, 1336, she found herself in the company of only three other Jews and only one other woman—and no other woman of her own faith.[55]

In the Crown of Aragon and beyond, gender and religious identity intertwined to shape the social roles available to men and women. Jewish minority communities expressed anxiety about the physical inviolability of women's bodies, which functioned as boundary markers between religious communities. Sexual intercourse between Jewish women and Christian men posed a metaphorical threat to the security of Jewish communities. The ability to prevent and police sexual contact between Jewish women and non-Jewish men demonstrated the strength possessed even by subordinate, minority Jewish communities.[56] Jews in the Crown of Aragon never normalized social and economic contact between Jewish women and Christian men; such interaction posed a threat to the community writ large.

These communal anxieties, perhaps shared by women themselves as well as their husbands and sons, could explain why, when Jewish women found themselves in control of assets, they were even more likely than Christian women to adopt strategies that allowed them to avoid or mediate their presence in the male, Christian spaces around city notaries. Astruga, widow of Jucef de Beziers of Barcelona, undoubtedly had myriad reasons to return to her home city of Girona after she was widowed—but one may have been that her family connections would allow her to manage assets while only rarely working directly with Christian notaries. Astruga returned to Girona in September 1348, following the deaths of both her husband and her father.[57] Both men had probably died either in the Black Death, which had swept through both cities by May 1348, or in the subsequent anti-Jewish violence, which was especially destructive in Barcelona.[58]

These family tragedies left Astruga a wealthy woman. She not only recovered her dowry from her late husband's estate but also inherited from her father, as his sole heiress, and from an uncle, as a coheiress alongside her surviving uncles and cousins.[59] However, Astruga almost never went to the notary independently; she either relied on agents to go in her stead or went in the company of family members. The choice to return to Girona—rather than remaining in Barcelona to administer her husband's estate—could reflect her preference to avoid venturing alone into male, Christian space. She also might have succumbed to family pressures—her surviving relatives might have encouraged her to return to a city where she could rely on a variety of support networks to navigate Christian notarial culture, whereas she might have had to do so fully independently in Barcelona.[60]

Other women in Barcelona's Jewish community either made different choices or had fewer alternatives available to them. In the wake of the Black Death, several Jewish widows in Barcelona appealed to Christian legal institutions to maintain control over their late husbands' assets. Astruga would have been in a particularly strong position to claim management rights over her late husband's estate as the mother of a minor child.[61] However, by relocating to Girona, Astruga could more easily rely on the assistance of her family and friends to avoid or negotiate the office of the Christian notary. While Astruga was sufficiently well-off to have the luxury of making this choice, her decision, either independently or under pressure, to relinquish direct control of her late husband's estate probably resulted in some financial loss.

Jewish women of lower socioeconomic strata—like the woman Astruga hired as a wet nurse—went to the notary's office even less often than wealthy Jewish women. Some may have possessed so few assets that they did not require the involvement of notaries to manage the meager resources at their disposal. In other cases, however, social rank, religion, and gender may have combined to discourage them from turning to the notaries even when doing so might have helped protect their assets. Overall, Jewish women found themselves less able than either Christian women or Jewish men to protect and increase their wealth by employing the services of notaries.

Jewish women may have played a more active role in economic sectors not subject to notarial intervention, including the buying and selling of goods, waged labor in textiles or other industries, and pawnbroking, as well as intra-Jewish commerce or behind-the-scenes assistance with the work of their husbands or fathers. However, exclusion from notarial culture relegated them to less secure and less profitable forms of business. For example, even if Jewish women played an active role in pawnbroking—a speculation without any direct corroborating evidence—they would have been subject to certain dangers from which colleagues who made registered notarial loans would have been immune. Thanks to royal privileges designed to protect Christian debtors from the supposed predations of Jewish creditors, Jews could lose articles in pawn if a Christian claimed them as "stolen." With the loss of the pawn, the lender would lose all formal evidence of the loan.[62] Even if Jewish women were more heavily involved in intra-Jewish business—again, a speculation not directly justified by surviving evidence—the expectation that they pursue economic endeavors only within the confines of their relatively small minority community would have severely diminished the scope of any potential business ventures.

Conclusions

The rise of notarial culture in the thirteenth-century western Mediterranean required that when Jews did business with Christians, they would often do so within Christian space. This dynamic differed substantially from that prevalent in northern Europe. William Chester Jordan has argued that the experience of entering Jewish homes and handing over household valuables as pledges instilled feelings of hostility toward Jews in Christian debtors and their children.[63] As I have argued elsewhere, the restriction of most Jewish credit transactions to a public space may have allowed for more neutral, perhaps even cordial, relationships of credit and debt.[64] However, the requirement that Jews enter a Christian space and engage with Christian legal culture when lending also worked to remind Jews of their subordinate status. Jewish moneylending, which created a debtor-creditor relationship that positioned Jews in power over Christians, threatened to subvert religious hierarchies. Situating these activities within Christian space reinscribed the proper order of things, from a Christian perspective. These efforts to maintain interfaith boundaries and hierarchies during fraught moments of Jewish moneylending may have contributed to the relative stability Jews enjoyed in the Crown of Aragon for much of their history.[65]

However, the reinforcement of boundaries and hierarchies that took place in the office of the notary affected Jewish men and women differently. Regardless of gender, even those Jews most familiar with notarial culture may have experienced moments in the office of the notary that highlighted their status as members of a marginal minority. Jewish women, however, experienced additional forms of marginalization. Much like Christian women, they experienced the particular challenges of negotiating within a male space. They also faced unique challenges, unlike those experienced by either Christian women or Jewish men, as a result of prevalent Jewish legal norms that made them unlikely to need notarial contracts and hence even more unfamiliar with notarial culture if they were forced to navigate it later in life.

Many Jewish women rarely participated in work that necessitated regular engagement with notarial culture. Even Jewish women with access to financial resources often relied on agents or simply did less business instead of navigating the male, Christian spaces associated with notarial culture. Undoubtedly, Jewish women engaged in profitable forms of labor not visible in the notarial documentation. However, Jewish women's difficulties in negotiating notarial culture, combined with their limited access to financial resources, left them less economically self-sufficient and less able to work in profitable sectors than Christian women.

III

WOMEN'S WORK

5

WORKING WOMEN IN MEDIEVAL CATALAN CITIES

On May 31, 1330, twelve women went before the notary Guillem Borrell of Barcelona to invest in a commercial partnership (*societas*) formed earlier that day between Bernat de Vila, a merchant of Barcelona, and Berenguer Vinot, a merchant of Mallorca, for commerce within and between their two cities as well as across the Mediterranean.[1] Together, these twelve women made nearly half of the investments in Bernat and Berenguer's partnership and contributed slightly over one-third of the capital that the two men received for their budding joint business venture.[2]

All twelve of these women investors not only came from wealthy families but also controlled financial resources independently. As members of the same urban elite as the male merchants who brought ships across the Mediterranean, they would have tapped into family networks to obtain specialized knowledge about the profitability of commercial destinations and the reputation of merchants—a shared practice across the Mediterranean.[3] Valença, widow of Guillem Ferrer d'Odena of Barcelona, made the largest contribution to the *societas*—680 pounds.[4] Even while married, Valença independently owned and controlled vast stores of wealth, which allowed her to purchase property without her husband's involvement.[5] Despite having brothers, both Valença and her sister Sibil·la, wife of Jaume Carbó, had received substantial inheritances, parts of which they held jointly.[6] Like her sister, Sibil·la controlled inherited wealth even as a married woman. She and Jaume made separate investments in Bernat and Berenguer's partnership, and in 1319 they had individually purchased neighboring houses.[7] Upon her husband's death, Valença came into even greater wealth—a recovered dowry worth at least 9,000 sous.[8] She even found herself in a position to make generous gifts of cash and property to her nephews, the sons of her brother Pere Corretger.[9]

References to working women, both Jewish and Christian, are scattered throughout the pages of the notarial registers of Barcelona, Girona, and Vic. Historians have typically understood women's work in the medieval and early modern world as low-paid and low-status.[10] Studies focused on women's access to wealth have treated the management of financial resources as divorced from labor, while the scholarship that addresses women's involvement in high-status, high-skilled trades rarely includes the women who administered household assets.[11] I employ an expanded definition of women's work that encompasses not only artisanal production and waged labor but also the management of household financial and human resources. By placing the women who plied trades and worked for wages in conversation with their counterparts who invested in commerce, borrowed and loaned money, and managed real estate holdings, I emphasize the interconnections between urban economies and household economies and center the crucial contributions that women made to both. Women like Valença and Sibil·la, for example, not only augmented the wealth of their households as managers of family assets but also contributed to the vibrant urban real estate market and to cross-Mediterranean trade—cornerstones of Barcelona's thriving economy.

Women's work was often essential to the solvency of their households, integrated into the economic life of their cities, and in some cases treated as equal in status to similar work performed by men. Yet the reevaluation of the broader social and economic significance of women's work should not obscure the fact that most Catalan men saw the labor of their wives, mothers, and daughters as subsidiary to their own. Family economic strategies might rely on women to play a crucial supporting role in augmenting household resources, or even to temporarily replace their husbands or sons as breadwinners and the primary managers of household wealth. However, despite the tacit recognition that women could profitably manage assets, ensure the solvency of their households, and transmit wealth to the next generation, women's *potential* to contribute through their labor did not always translate into women being given labor opportunities comparable to those of the men of their family. The notarial registers demonstrate conclusively that women worked as weavers and wet nurses, as investors and lessors, although a quantitative overview of the contracts that notaries recorded demonstrates incontrovertibly that women's work accounted for only a fraction of the business recorded by urban notaries. Throughout this chapter, I acknowledge the work women performed and its value while still placing that work in the wider context of a fundamentally patriarchal society.

This chapter offers an overview of women's work in different economic sectors: domestic labor, artisanal production and trade, commercial investment, and credit (reserving the particularly intriguing case of the real estate market for chapter 6). I emphasize how gender, socioeconomic status, and religious identity combined to shape the labor options afforded to women. Jewish women, I argue, nearly always had fewer work opportunities available to them, across economic sectors, than either Christian women or Jewish men. This chapter's intersectional approach throws into sharp relief the ways in which gender combined with other factors to expand or contract working women's options.

Notarial Registers as Sources for Women's Work

Notarial registers offer many advantages for scholars interested in social history—particularly for those who seek to make visible the lives of women and of non-elites. Some scholars have described notarial culuture as "egalitarian," in that the contracts recorded by notaries offer insight into the lives of women as well as men of a wide array of social strata.[12] However, it is equally important to address the limits of notarial contracts as sources, especially for women's work.

Both Jewish and Christian women almost certainly engaged in forms of labor that did not require notarial documentation. The immediate sale of goods in exchange for cash did not require a contract; small loans might have been secured with a pledge and not registered; sellers of goods may have kept their own records of store credit. Urban regulations from Barcelona hinted at such work performed by Christian women when they referred to both men and women who practiced a particular trade: bakers, resellers of goods, fishmongers, grain sellers, and tavernkeepers.[13] However, notaries almost always described women with reference to a husband or father, not a profession, unless the profession was directly relevant to the contract. As a result, even if a Christian woman fishmonger appeared on the pages of a notarial register—perhaps extending a loan using the profits of her trade—notarial practices obscure the work she performed in the marketplace.

Responsa literature offers indirect evidence that some Jewish women practiced trades and earned an income, but offers little detail as to the nature of their work. On the one hand, work of this kind would only create a legal problem requiring rabbinic intervention if a working woman refused to give her husband her earnings, which legally came under his control, or refused to stop working outside the home at his request.[14] On the other hand, the silence of both rabbis and notaries on the subject makes it impossible to determine how common it was for Jewish women to work independently at a trade. Hebrew and Latin evidence taken together prove that Jewish women in the Iberian Peninsula worked as cobblers, food sellers, fur traders, silversmiths, coral cutters, seamstresses, weavers, midwives, and physicians.[15] But it is difficult to determine whether Jewish women's work in these sectors was exceptional, unremarkable, or somewhere in between.

Even though notarial evidence does not represent the totality of women's work, women's access to the economic sectors best represented in notarial documentation still matters to a wider understanding of women's work in medieval Catalan cities. Women may have worked in economic sectors not visible in notarial registers, but such labor was often less profitable or less secure than business that generated notarial documentation. Moreover, the volume of notarial evidence allows us to make quantitative comparisons not possible for other types of women's work. Women fish sellers were common enough that Barcelona's governing council felt the need to refer to them, but the regulation does not tell us if women constituted a quarter of the fishmongers, half of them, or more.

Jewish women probably also worked within their own community and documented their business with Hebrew contracts. Very few such contracts have survived; we can only speculate as to whether Jewish women may have played a more substantive role in business within the Jewish community than in business that required interaction with Christians. However, even if Jewish women worked more regularly in intracommunal business, social norms that pressured Jewish women to do business only with other Jews represented a significant check on Jewish women's ability to support themselves through their work. Jews formed only a tiny minority of the population and therefore generated less internal business than the Christian majority. If Jewish women, unlike Jewish men, were discouraged from transacting with Christians, the economic options available to them would narrow dramatically and undercut their ability to earn a living through their labor.

Domestic Labor: Mistresses, Servants, and Slaves

Women of all social strata were expected to play some role in the basics of household management. However, the nature of women's domestic labor depended on their family's wealth: a woman who belonged to the mercantile elite, an artisan woman, and a laboring-status woman would have had different expectations about what was included in their domestic work. Some women performed tasks like childcare, cooking, and cleaning for their own homes and families. Other women did the same work but in the households of others, as waged servants or even as slaves. Women of wealthy families instead worked to oversee the enslaved and waged laborers brought into their households.[16]

Affluent households in Catalonia and elsewhere in Europe relied on extrafamilial female labor, with the result that domestic service became a particularly common occupation for women.[17] In fifteenth-century Valencia, young women worked as domestic servants to raise funds for their dowries.[18] Waged domestic servants could bring income home, or at least alleviate the financial burden they placed on their families.[19] The most prosperous families also purchased slaves, mostly women of Muslim or Eastern European background, to perform similar labor tasks.[20] Servile and enslaved women performed a range of household tasks, including drawing water, cooking, cleaning, laundry, spinning, caring for children, and purchasing household goods at the market.[21]

Most domestic servants were young women, many of whom left home to seek work in Catalonia's urban centers.[22] While most contracts did not specify servants' ages, the notaries overwhelmingly identified these women as unmarried.[23] Barcelona was a particularly popular destination, able to attract servant girls from both rural villages and smaller cities and towns, whereas most domestic servants in Girona and Vic came from either the city itself or its surrounding rural hinterlands.[24] Similar patterns held throughout the medieval and early modern Mediterranean; large urban centers, including Valencia in the fifteenth century and Venice in the sixteenth, similarly drew women from throughout the region to work in the homes of wealthy urban citizens.[25]

Although lower-status women like these domestic servants could more easily travel to pursue work opportunities than affluent women, many may have relocated for work out of necessity rather than preference. Both their subordinate status and their lack of nearby family support left them vulnerable. Women servants risked physical and sexual abuse, allegations of theft, and withholding of salaries.[26] A 1340 contract involving a servant and her mistress from Barcelona illustrates the precarious nature of maidservants' positions. Margarida, wife of Guillem Constanç of Barcelona, committed to make no claims against her former servant Romeua. Margarida stated, "You served me well and legally and completely for the two years which you promised to remain with me and serve me, with a [notarial] instrument. . . .

I absolve and release you and yours from any question, petition, or demand which I might make or claim against you and your goods, on account of the aforementioned [service]." She further explained that she provided this contract as proof that Romeua committed no wrongdoing as her servant.[27] The need for this contract highlights the potential vulnerability of domestic servants, most of whom lacked a document like this one.

The same wealthy families that could afford to hire girls or purchase slaves as domestic servants also sought out wet nurses to nurse their infant children. Hired wet nurses were usually married and slightly older, but they remained socially and economically vulnerable and, moreover, subject to particularly demanding restrictions on their sexuality.[28] Husbands who allowed their wives to work as wet nurses consented to deprive themselves of their wives' sexual favors: wet nurses were expected to remain celibate, as sexual intercourse or pregnancy could spoil the milk, according to then-current scientific theories.[29] However, in contrast to their counterparts in Italy, Catalan Christian wet nurses normally contracted their own laboring bodies: only one husband in Girona and one in Barcelona contracted out their wives' services without their overt involvement and consent in the notarial contract.[30]

The most vulnerable women in Catalan urban households were enslaved women, who could be transferred between households without their consent and raped or otherwise abused without consequence.[31] The notarial documentation tells us little about these women; most slave sale and manumission contracts specified little beyond the gender, ethnicity, and skin tone of slaves.[32] Ahirona, sold in Barcelona on March 4, 1300, was described as a twenty-five-year-old "white Saracen" (*sarracena alba*).[33] A notary described Erina, sold on December 30, 1311, in Girona, as olive-skinned (*laura*) and of either Greek or Romanian background (*de genere grecorum vel romanicorum*).[34] Families particularly prized women slaves, who could serve as domestic servants or wet nurses, and these women often fetched high prices.[35]

The case of Axona, a Black Muslim ("Saracen") woman sold twice as a slave in 1318, emphasizes enslaved women's vulnerability and lack of control over their circumstances. Her original master, Jaume Andreu of Barcelona, sold Axona to his son-in-law, Ferrer de Riera, for 23 pounds. Jaume then purchased a white Greek slave woman named Cali, for 18 pounds, on the same day.[36] This transfer might seem to suggest that Jaume sought to place Axona in the household of his married daughter, who remained uninvolved in these arrangements. However, Ferrer resold Axona less than two weeks later, at a slight profit—for 25 pounds—to Guillem de Mata of Tortosa.[37] Enslaved men and women in Valencia attempted to subvert sales, either seeking new masters to their liking or behaving poorly to sabotage sales.[38] We have no way to tell if Axona, preferring to remain in a familiar city, attempted to sabotage her sale and failed, if she preferred to leave and hence behaved badly in Ferrer's household, or if she did not care either way.

Affluent Christian women took a leading role in hiring or purchasing the exploited female labor of their households; in Barcelona, women hired almost two-thirds of all female servants in the city.[39] Women's involvement in obtaining and managing other women's labor demonstrates their own importance as household managers. They could make and enforce decisions about the other women who worked in their households precisely because they enjoyed managerial authority over household functions and finances. Florence provides an interesting counterpoint: mothers rarely hired the wet nurses for their own children, a practice that Christiane Klapisch-Zuber linked to mothers' broader exclusion from the family lineage.[40] In Catalan cities, in contrast, women or married couples acting together hired wet nurses in about half of the contracts.[41]

The role played by elite Christian women in exploiting the labor of more vulnerable lower-status women, including those of marginalized ethnic or religious backgrounds, exposes the participation of high-status women in a "patriarchal bargain."[42] Women from wealthy, Christian families collaborated with patriarchal structures in order to preserve their own superiority over others, especially women, of lower socioeconomic status as well as those belonging to marginalized ethnic and religious groups.[43] Those women responsible for managing financial resources treated enslaved women like any other type of asset. They sold slaves more often than they purchased them, perhaps because they needed immediate liquidity more than they needed the women's labor.[44] In 1340, Francesca, wife of Bernat Esteve of Barcelona, sold the Greek slave Anna and her infant daughter Guillema, whom she had inherited from her late brother, Pere Nadal.[45] For Francesca, the price she received for Anna and Guillema—22 pounds—probably outweighed the value of her work, especially if she did not require a wet nurse at the time. Economic considerations of this kind would have shaped most relationships between slave-owning women and enslaved women.

The notarial registers include few examples of domestic service contracts from within the Jewish community. Wealthy Jewish families probably hired servants either informally or with Hebrew contracts. In all extant contracts, Jews hired their coreligionists, rather than Christians, as servants and wet nurses.[46] Both rabbinic and Christian authorities expressed anxiety about the practice of Jews hiring Christian maidservants, owing in part to the presumption of masters' sexual access to women servants.[47] Illicit hires of Christian wet nurses aroused particular concern.[48] As a result, Jews who hired Christian servants may have made these arrangements under the table, without notarial contracts. Other Jewish families hired Jewish girls as servants, in part as a means of supporting impoverished and orphaned Jewish girls.[49] Rabbis tended to be far more concerned about the sexual exploitation of Jewish servant women than non-Jewish ones.[50] Christian families did not typically hire Jewish servants or wet nurses; when hiring non-enslaved labor, they may have preferred to have other Christians rather than Jews in their domestic space.

The sparse contractual evidence suggests that Jewish women might have played a similar role to that of Christian women in working to secure female labor for their households, but they presumably did so without notarial contracts. I found only two examples of Jewish women who hired women servants, both of whom were widowed: Bonadona, widow of Astrug Caravida of Girona, hired Astruga Belida to work as her household servant in 1336, and Astruga, widow of Jucef de Beziers, hired Clara, wife of Salomó Carnisser, as a wet nurse for her infant daughter Druda in 1349.[51] However, Jewish women seeking work as domestic servants were even less likely to sign a contract with a male Jewish householder. The only Jewish man who contracted a female servant—Cresques Jucef of Girona—acted under unusual circumstances. He hired Gentil, wife of Mosse Avempesat of Barcelona, to work as a wet nurse for his infant son Jucef in 1336.[52] Cresques never identified the child's mother, and he did not marry his wife Bonafilla until 1339.[53] Jucef's mother may have died, given birth out of wedlock, or both. These three contracts together suggest that Jewish women servants negotiated with Jewish mistresses of households directly, but the paucity of documents does not allow for firm conclusions. Regardless, most servants working in Jewish households, whether Jewish or Christian, must have worked outside the bounds of notarial culture. If Jewish families hired servants informally, the women working in their households may have had fewer protections afforded to them than in Christian homes.

Jewish women also bought and sold slaves. Muslim slaves could replace the Christian servants and wet nurses that Jews could not licitly hire.[54] Astrug de Mallorca and his wife Astruga, Jews of Vic, obtained labor cheaply by purchasing a Muslim slave woman named Axia for 40 sous in 1268.[55] A Christian servant girl hired in Vic the following year received 6 sous per year as wages; Axia could pay for herself in less than seven years.[56] In other cases, enslaved men and women only passed briefly through the homes of

Jewish men and women, as some Christians used slaves to pay debts.[57] Jewish women moneylenders' sales of enslaved people demonstrate that even women from a marginalized minority community participated in the same patriarchal bargains as wealthy Christian women. Goig, wife of David Canviador, a successful Jewish woman moneylender of Vic, in 1276 sold a white Muslim slave woman for 100 sous in a contract that fails to even mention the enslaved woman's name.[58]

Women in the Market: Artisanal Production and Trade

Work in artisanal production and trade produced far less notarial documentation than economic sectors like credit, investment, and real estate. Except for elite merchants who specialized in high-value goods, most of the people who made and sold textiles, leather goods, metalwork, and foodstuffs either sold their wares for cash in the marketplace or kept their own records of shoppers who bought on credit.[59] While notaries used profession as an identifying marker for Christian men who used their services, they omitted such descriptors for both women and Jews. Religious identity alone identified people of minority faiths, while women's identity was nearly always expressed exclusively in terms of their relationship to men. Similarly, Sharon Farmer noted that male legal professionals in Paris treated work as an essential aspect of identity for men of the urban poor, but not for women.[60] Notaries included women's professional identities if they were directly relevant, as when tradeswomen obtained commercial credit or contracted to train apprentices.

Both Christian and Jewish women found work opportunities in the textile industry. Women across Europe worked in the production and sale of cloth for urban markets. Girls and women often learned sewing, spinning, and weaving as part of their household responsibilities, but these skills also proved useful for work that could directly bring in wages and business profits. In Catalonia, women worked in a range of textile professions, from spinning and sewing at home for piecework rates, to managing workshops as weavers, to controlling large-scale textile businesses.[61] Most women who took apprentices worked in the textile industry, and most girls who contracted as apprentices planned to enter textile trades (see table 7).

Married couples worked together in textile workshops; the weavers Pere and Maria Franch of Vic received an investment together in 1342.[62] Widows took over these workshops after their husbands had died.[63] The Barcelona cotton-workers guild permitted women members, while the weavers' guild

TABLE 7 Professions in apprenticeship contracts involving women

	Barcelona, 1292–1350	Girona, 1311–1350	Vic, 1250–1350
Textiles	13	37	24
Costurera	8	19	1
Teixidor	3	9	21
Seder	2	2	0
Sastre	0	2	2
Sàvenera	0	2	0
Mercer	0	2	0
Draper	0	1	0
Leather	0	9	6
Bosser	0	7	5
Corretger	0	1	1
Albadiner	0	1	0
Unknown	4	3	1
Total	17	49	31

allowed widows to continue their husbands' trades.[64] Work in textiles allowed unmarried or widowed women to support themselves independently. The weaver Elisenda de Mans, who had relocated to Vic from the village of Sant Andreu de la Vola, concluded her marriage contract without her parents' involvement and granted her husband Bernat Pasqual a dowry comprising houses she had purchased with her earnings.[65]

A few women gained wealth and status as cloth merchants and luxury textile producers.[66] The only woman in all three cities who entered a formal, notarized commercial partnership worked as a draper, a merchant specializing in the sale of high-quality textiles.[67] Sobirana, widow of the draper Guillem d'Abadia of Girona, took over her husband's business after his death.[68] However, Sobirana proved much more successful in her late husband's industry than most drapers' widows. While the widows of tailors and weavers often maintained their late husbands' workshops, few drapers' widows continued to work in their late husbands' trade, which occupied the pinnacle of the professional hierarchy in Girona.[69] Sobirana began to sell textiles on credit, mostly for fairly low sums, after her husband's death in 1337.[70] The low prices she charged (ranging from 12 sous 9 pence to 18 sous) could suggest that she felt obliged to sell her products at a discount, or that she began by selling off lower-value textiles. She only attained real success in the textile industry after she formed a business partnership with another Girona draper, Bernat Massot, in April 1338.[71] Her alliance with Bernat allowed her to make a larger number of more profitable sales and establish her professional identity as a draper.[72] Even in the textile industry, the economic sector most open to women, women had difficulty breaking into the most profitable trades, and they benefited from working closely with men.

Laboring-status women worked low-status, non-guild jobs in the textile market, such as spinning, weaving, sewing, and preparing yarn, often as employees of male guild members.[73] Women, especially those of lower socioeconomic status, faced gendered challenges if they sought to operate businesses independently. Guilds in early modern Germany worked to limit women's profits from work like spinning.[74] In Catalonia, investors hesitated to extend commercial credit to women: women acting alone received investments less often than they made them and less often than they received consumption loans (loans of small sums used to meet immediate personal needs).[75] The struggle to obtain commercial credit may have kept many women out of trades that required substantial capital investments. Women textile workers faced uniquely gendered difficulties when obtaining even small commercial loans. In 1338, Agnès, wife of Guillem de Tortosa of Barcelona, needed to provide a guarantor—her husband—when she purchased 20 sous of raw silk on credit for her work weaving silk headdresses.[76] Nevertheless, a few married women sustained independent businesses.[77] Elisenda, wife of Bernat de Vall of Barcelona, worked professionally as a weaver, while her husband was a sailor.[78] As Bernat's work would have frequently taken him out of town, Elisenda might have pursued her own business in order to ensure financial stability during her husband's absences.

While both Christian and Jewish married couples worked together in shared textile workshops, Jewish women textile workers faced additional challenges in establishing and funding independent enterprises. Christian women obtained commercial credit both independently (albeit rarely) and alongside their husbands, whereas Jewish women only received commercial loans in tandem with their husbands. Jewish women might not have maintained independent workshops, even after widowhood. Alternatively, Jewish women may have failed to secure commercial credit, with the result that only the wealthiest women could establish independent workshops. Some Jewish women may have obtained commercial loans within the confines of the Jewish community, using Hebrew contracts, but the expectation that they seek credit primarily from their coreligionists would have severely limited their pool of potential investors.

Several Jewish couples practiced complementary or shared trades and comanaged workshops.[79] The Jews of Barcelona played a particularly prominent role in the silk industry, and the few Jewish women identified as practicing a trade worked alongside their husbands as silk weavers or dyers.[80] Samuel Xaham of Barcelona and his wife Miriam both worked as cloth dyers, while Samuel also worked as a silk weaver; in 1314 they jointly purchased 95 sous' worth of raw silk from a Christian couple "for the work of our aforementioned trades of silk weaving [*sederia*] and dyeing."[81] Samuel wove the raw silk into finished cloth, which the couple then worked together to dye. Bellaire, wife of Mosse Cohen of Barcelona, took full responsibility for production as a silk weaver, while her husband worked as a silk merchant; they also acted together to purchase raw silk on credit, in 1318.[82] They purchased the raw silk from another Jewish woman—Jueva, wife of Fabib Maimó—who had received the silk as *paraphernalia*, suggesting that she may have come from a family of Jewish silk weavers. However, there is no direct evidence that Jueva worked in the silk industry.

These brief references to economic partnerships between Jewish couples working in the textile industry demonstrate the potential importance of Jewish women's labor to their households. However, the apparent inability of Jewish women to obtain commercial credit independently highlights the practical restrictions on Jewish women's labor options. Few women could hope to establish and maintain workshops without relying on either investor credit or the support of male relatives.

While the extant documentation provides no evidence for Jewish women's labor in artisanal production outside the textile market, Catalan Christian women found occasional work in other sectors, particularly in the victualing industry. Only men could work as butchers and meat sellers, but women sold other food products and dominated the baking trade.[83] Women bakers even received commercial investments; in 1305, Pola, widow of Guillem Verdaguer of Vic, received 50 sous "to be invested in my trade of baking and other commercial ventures."[84] Successful bakers also sold their wares to wealthy households on credit; the household of the bishop of Vic purchased 120 sous' worth of bread on credit from local baker Margarida in 1265.[85]

Apprenticeships allowed Christian girls to learn the skills necessary to practice trades, while Christian women artisans could count on the cheap labor provided by apprentices.[86] However, gendered apprenticeship patterns limited both the pool of apprentices available to women artisans and the options available to girls seeking specialized training. Women almost always took on girls rather than boys as apprentices, while girls nearly always apprenticed with either women or married couples rather than adult men.[87]

Apprenticeship contracts often enmeshed husbands in their wives' trades even when the couple otherwise maintained separate businesses. In a 1339 contract, Maria des Bruguer of Sant Martí del Brull commended her daughter Ermessenda to Bernat des Vilar of Vic, so that Ermessenda could learn to weave from Bernat's wife Brunissenda. Although Brunissenda alone practiced the trade of weaving and bore exclusive responsibility for teaching Ermessenda, Bernat legally committed himself as Ermessenda's master in the notarial contract.[88] Apprenticeship involved integration into an artisan household, socially as well as economically. Families therefore had to think carefully about masters' and mistresses' ability to provide a home for their children as well as training.[89]

Apprentice girls were young and vulnerable: although precise ages rarely appear in apprenticeship contracts, one of the two young women who specified their ages stated that she was 14, while another identified herself as between 12 and 15 years old.[90] The tendency for parents or guardians to act on behalf of apprentice daughters corroborates the assumption that most were in their early teens or younger.[91] In Montpellier, girls normally entered apprenticeships between the ages of 12 and 14.[92] The small number of widowed mistresses suggests that families considered independent woman householders less able to care for and protect their vulnerable young daughters than married couples.[93] Nevertheless, a clearly defined apprenticeship system provided certain advantages for both established women artisans, who received nearly free labor, and girl apprentices, who received training that prepared them to establish their own workshops or work alongside their future husbands.

In contrast, Jewish girls did not formally enter apprenticeships in the extant documentation, nor did Jewish women take on apprentices. Several Jewish boys and men signed notarial apprenticeship contracts, which demonstrates that even if most Jews made such arrangements without contracts or with Hebrew writs, at least some turned to the notaries.[94] The absence of Jewish women and girls therefore indicates a limitation not experienced by men and boys of their faith. Those Jewish girls and women who worked trades probably learned skills informally, at home, from their parents or their husbands. Jewish girls and young women therefore had fewer opportunities than their Christian counterparts to learn to practice trades independent of their husbands or fathers, while Jewish women artisans had more difficulty obtaining apprentice labor than Christian women who managed workshops.

Christian Women in Credit: Consumption Loans, Profit, and Social Capital

In addition to the more traditional forms of work like domestic service and artisanal production, women's work also encompassed the management of household assets. Work in the credit market formed an essential part of women's managerial labor, thanks to the deep-rooted importance of credit in the economy of the medieval western Mediterranean. Credit was crucial to trade as well as everyday life; many people lived in a state of constant indebtedness.[95] Small-scale, short-term consumption loans of the *mutuum* type accounted for between one-quarter and one-third of notarial business (see table 5). Work within the credit market, including both extending and obtaining loans, proved crucial to the solvency of urban households and therefore formed part of the managerial work sometimes expected of women.

The work of lending involved keeping accurate records, renegotiating unpaid loans, and, if necessary, turning to the courts to force repayment.[96] Creditors had to evaluate and potentially sell objects given in pledge (*pignus*), which could include clothing, fine metalwork objects, precious stones and pearls, household linens, and a range of church liturgical objects (books, holy vestments, liturgical crosses, chalices, censer bearers, statues, and icons).[97] Those creditors who received real estate holdings as collateral worked to manage the properties under their control.[98]

Christian women played a minor but visible role as creditors, extending just over 10 percent of Christian loans in Girona, around 6 percent in Barcelona, and approximately 3 percent in Vic.[99] Although very few women worked professionally in this economic sector, Christian women could and did turn to credit to augment their assets and to maintain or strengthen social networks. Of course, the business of credit only generated direct income if the creditor charged interest. While Jewish creditors often specified that they extended *mutuum* loans at the legal interest rate of 20 percent per annum, most Christian creditors either provided no information about interest or explicitly described the loan as interest free (*bono amore*).[100] However, anti-usury proceedings indicate that some Christians circumvented restrictions on charging interest with hidden fees.[101] Enterprising women creditors may have used late fees as a *de facto* form of interest. In 1340, for example, Guillema Payana, wife of Pere Payà of Girona, demanded that her debtors pay her an extra 2 sous if they repaid the loan later than the Feast of Sants Pere i Feliu.[102] Catalan creditors also profited off grain loans by taking advantage of fluctuating market prices.[103] Elisenda, wife of Pere Ripoll of Vic, extended four grain loans between August and November of 1268; the notary did not specify whether the debtors would repay Elisenda with goods or in cash, leaving her with some flexibility to demand a profitable cash payment.[104]

Other Christian women did not profit directly off the loans they extended but used credit to build and reinforce social ties that could prove essential to future economic endeavors. Loans in the medieval Mediterranean often signaled amity between creditor and debtor.[105] Although notaries did not normally describe interpersonal relationships outside the bonds of kinship, our limited evidence hints at the existence of social networks that structured women's credit activities. Between one-third and one-half of women's independent loans were either explicitly described as interest free or went to individuals linked to them by kinship, neighborhood, or profession.[106] Women even extended loans to their own husbands, usually drawn from their *paraphernalia*. In 1335, for example, Ramon Vengiu of Girona borrowed 1,000 sous from his wife Caterina, who obtained the cash through her management of inherited real estate holdings.[107] Other women used cash loans to reinforce relationships with their stepchildren, siblings, or neighbors. Margarida, wife of Pere Descortell of Barcelona, loaned money to her stepson in 1336; Berenguera, widow of Francesc Corder of Girona, extended a loan to her brother Berenguer de Carrer of Sant Esteve de Sords in 1331; Bernat de Julià and his wife Elisenda, who lived on Carrer de Manlleu in Vic, received a loan from their neighbor Antonia, widow of Pere de Coniuncta, in 1327.[108]

Unsurprisingly, given their unfettered access to financial resources, widows and economically independent single women extended more loans than married women did.[109] However, married women nonetheless played a visible role as independent creditors—a form of work made possible by the fact that they controlled household assets. Some married women specified that they extended loans out of their *paraphernalia*; in 1300, for example, Guillema, wife of the tanner Pere de Vila of Barcelona, confirmed that the 7.5 pounds she loaned the cobbler Pere Ulric came from the *paraphernalia* she had inherited from her parents.[110] Other married women did not specify the source of their funds and may have drawn on resources from a jointly managed conjugal estate. In 1330, for example, Brunissenda, wife of the jurist Berenguer Renau of Girona, loaned 400 sous to another jurist, Berenguer de Riera, without specifying how she obtained the cash to make such a substantial loan.[111] Although Brunissenda did not publicly comanage household assets during her marriage, her husband demonstrated his faith in her as an administrator of wealth by naming her as one of his testamentary executors, an unusual choice in Catalonia.[112]

Men often trusted their wives to shoulder the responsibility of collecting on loans on their behalf, both during brief absences from the city and after their deaths. Especially in Barcelona, wives of traveling merchants and sailors worked to collect debts owed to their husbands.[113] Men about to embark on travel sometimes signed agency contracts granting their wives generalized authority over their property, including the right to collect debts. Bernat Castelló of Barcelona, helmsman of a small ship (*barquer*), appointed his wife as his agent to handle all his business, administer his estate, and collect on debts in 1328.[114] Christian families also expected that widows would ensure the solvency of their late husbands' estates—often for the benefit of their minor children—by collecting on debts.[115] Caterina, widow of the wealthy merchant Arnau de Conaminis of Barcelona and guardian of her minor son Francesc, collected on three loans owed to her late husband in 1349.[116] In Vic, where women made fewer independent loans than in either Barcelona or Girona, widows collected on debts alongside their adult sons or their husbands' testamentary executors.[117] Pere de Coniuncta and his widowed mother, Antonia, acted together in 1332 to collect on a loan owed to Pere's late father, also named Pere.[118] Although widows in Vic often found their authority over their late husbands' estates mediated by male supervision, women like Antonia may also have successfully asserted a modicum of control over family property by acting alongside their adult sons.

Christian women's domestic labor also included obtaining credit for their own needs and those of their families. Although few women borrowed money independently, married couples and other groups including women received nearly one-quarter of loans in Vic and almost one-third in Girona.[119] When wives participated in their husbands' debts, they lost the right to sequester their dowry funds from creditors. However, their involvement may have given them a greater voice in family finances. Some women borrowed to secure cash for business ventures. In 1340, Joan Morell of Barcelona loaned his wife Margarida 40 pounds to complete repairs on houses she had inherited from her mother.[120] While Margarida had not inherited cash beyond her dowry, she may have planned to profitably lease out the houses to recoup her investment.

Wives of absent husbands and widows also sought credit to support themselves and their families. Sança, wife of Jaume de Forn of Barcelona, borrowed 275 pounds from Berenguer de Riera, whom Jaume had named as his agent while he was traveling on business.[121] Although the need to borrow money highlights Sança's lack of authority over her husband's estate and her limited access to liquid assets, the debt also demonstrates that borrowing money represented part of women's domestic work. In both Girona and Vic, most independent women debtors were widowed. Widows often needed credit, owing to delays in obtaining their dowries or to a lack of liquidity if their assets were in the form of land or movable goods rather than cash.[122] One lower-income widow in Vic specified that she needed to borrow 30 sous to meet her most basic needs while she suffered from illness.[123] Their newfound independence often left widows in a financially vulnerable position. However, the expectation that they would eventually recover their dowries made wealthier widows, at least, a better credit risk than married women acting without their husbands' consent, who might not independently own sufficient collateral to secure their debts.

Jews, Gender, and the Credit Market

Although Jews participated in a range of commercial activities and Christians also loaned money at interest, extending credit was increasingly perceived as a stereotypically Jewish profession in the Crown of Aragon and elsewhere in medieval Europe.[124] Jews could legally lend at interest, subject to royal regulations: Jaume I required all Jewish loans to be registered and stabilized the legal interest rate Jewish creditors could charge at 20 percent per annum.[125] Julie Mell has recently argued that a potent combination of medieval stereotypes and modern ones has led scholars to vastly overemphasize the importance of credit in Jewish economic life. Based on evidence drawn from England and Marseille, Mell claims that only a small fraction of the Jewish population worked as moneylenders.[126]

Although Mell does not directly discuss the Iberian Peninsula, aspects of her argument are supported by decades of scholarship on the Jewish communities of both Castile and Aragon. Most scholars of the Jews of the Iberian Peninsula have treated moneylending as only one of many professions practiced by Jews.[127] Although the credit market remains the best-studied economic sector in such scholarship, the real culprit is source survival, not stereotype. Owing to royal requirements mandating the registration of Jewish loans, combined with the importance of notaries in credit more broadly, Jewish work in credit is disproportionately represented in the surviving documentation from the Crown of Aragon. The evidence for Jewish involvement in a variety of artisanal trades, in commerce, and in the real estate market is clear but scanty in comparison with the sheer volume of documentation on credit.

The precise proportion of Jews involved in credit—either as their main profession or as a supplement to other economic strategies—is difficult to determine and may have varied not only from region to region but even from city to city. The relatively small number of individual Jews who extended one or more loans in Barcelona suggests that most Jews there did not work in credit. In Vic, however, most Jewish households solvent enough to pay taxes had at least one member who worked in credit, either as a main form of income or as a supplement to other forms of work.[128] The sheer volume of documentation requires us to consider that credit formed an important part, albeit not the only part, of the economic profile of elite Jewish households. Credit also matters because the volume of contracts allows for quantitative assessments of the role played by Jewish women not feasible for many other economic sectors. Jewish women may have participated more intensively in economic activities unrecorded in the extant documentation, although by its very nature this possibility remains in the realm of speculation. However, the small number of women working as creditors indicates that most women were effectively barred from work that many Jewish men found profitable and convenient to practice alongside other trades.

Medieval texts and visual culture imagined the Jewish creditor as male, as seen in images ranging from the Castilian *Cantigas de Santa Maria* to the cover of a *liber iudeorum* from Vic.[129] In northern Europe, the masculinity of Jewish creditors in visual art elided the important role Jewish women played in the credit market.[130] In the Mediterranean, in contrast, the visual emphasis on male Jewish moneylenders largely reflected reality. With few exceptions, Jewish women in the western Mediterranean rarely worked in the credit market. In both Barcelona and Girona, Jewish women extended less than 3 percent of new Jewish loans, and women or groups including women collected on about 7 percent of debts Christians owed to Jews in contracts referred to as quitclaims (see table 8).[131] Scholarship on other cities and towns in Catalonia and southern France has yielded similar results.[132]

Despite popular associations between Jews and credit, Jewish women played a far less active role as moneylenders than Christian women did.[133] Jewish women also were less likely than Christian women to extend loans while married. While Christian wives acted as creditors less often than widows, they still extended at least 20 percent of women's loans in all three cities. In contrast, widows extended all of Jewish women's loans in Barcelona and over 80 percent in Girona.[134] The restrictions on Jewish wives' control over both their own property and the conjugal estate left even the wealthiest

TABLE 8 Jewish women's loans in Barcelona and Girona before the Black Death

	Barcelona, 1292–1348	Girona, 1311–1348
New Jewish loans		
Total no. of loans	108	3,339
Women's loans	3 (2.8%)	72 (2.2%)
Mixed-gender loans	0	7 (0.2%)
Jewish quitclaims		
Total no. of quitclaims	177	1,599
Women's quitclaims	10 (5.6%)	65 (4.1%)
Mixed-gender quitclaims	2 (1.1%)	43 (2.7%)

Jewish wives unable to work effectively in a capital-heavy field such as the credit market.

Moreover, while Christian husbands often expected their wives to manage their affairs while they traveled for work, Jewish husbands relied on their wives less frequently. Only two Jewish wives in Barcelona, and none in Girona, collected on loans on behalf of their husbands.[135] One of the Barcelona wives—Dolça, wife of Perfet Issach—enjoyed formal authority as Perfet's agent (*procuratrix*).[136] The other—Bonafilla, wife of Vidal Gracià—lacked such formal authorization. The contract in which she accepted repayment for a loan made by her husband illustrates the tenuous nature of Jewish women's authority over the conjugal estate.

Bonafilla appears only once in the documentary record. On April 8, 1277, she acknowledged that she had received 96 sous in repayment from the cleric Jaume de Santa Eugènia.[137] However, neither Bonafilla nor Jaume had participated in the original loan. Bonafilla claimed to act "in my name and that of my husband," who had extended the loan without her involvement.[138] Jaume agreed to pay the debt because he had purchased property from the original debtor, Berenguer de Sanahuja, and owed him for the sale price.[139] Bonafilla released both Jaume and Berenguer from any further claims and promised that her husband would formally approve the repayment upon his return to Barcelona.[140]

In many ways, this contract looks like a standard debt quitclaim. Yet one odd detail raises questions about Bonafilla's right to collect on this debt. Bonafilla named a guarantor (*fideiussor*): Salomó Gracià, probably a relative of her husband's. Debtors, not creditors, normally named guarantors, who accepted the responsibility to repay loans out of their own assets if the original debtors proved unable to pay.[141] I have found no other example of a notarial contract in which a creditor or a creditor's agent named a guarantor. The intended function of a creditor's guarantor is unclear; presumably, Salomó committed to pay Vidal himself if he refused to acknowledge the repayment and pursued the debt. Intriguingly, Salomó did not sign the document, perhaps because the notary considered his involvement inessential.[142]

Bonafilla may have provided a guarantor because she had no formal right to collect on the loan—and because her husband's Christian debtors did not expect Jewish wives to act on behalf of their husbands. Unlike Dolça, wife of Perfet Issach, Bonafilla apparently could not produce an agency contract. In collecting on this loan, Bonafilla may have acted against the wishes of her husband, or she might have responded quickly to a change in circumstances—for example, if Vidal went away unexpectedly on business or was kept from home longer than anticipated. Yet the infrequent appearances of Jewish wives as substitutes for their husbands may have inspired concern on the part of Bonafilla's Christian debtors. While they and Bonafilla came to what must have been a mutually acceptable solution, the need to provide a male guarantor further circumscribed Bonafilla's authority over the conjugal estate.

Only in widowhood, after they had collected their dowries, could Jewish women take on more economically active roles. Even Jewish widows, however, remained fairly peripheral figures in Catalan urban credit markets, extending less than 2 percent of all Jewish loans. Jewish women's lack of familiarity with notarial culture and experiences of marginalization in the male, Christian space of the notary's office, combined with discomfort on the part of male family and community members about the unaccompanied presence of Jewish women in such a space, discouraged even the most economically self-sufficient widows from regularly working as creditors. The interconnection between credit and notarial culture in Catalonia might even have contributed to the disparity between the Jewish women of Mediterranean Europe and those of northern Europe.[143]

Women in Commerce: Investments in Regional and International Trade

The financial innovation of the *commenda* contract fueled Mediterranean trade. Investors who contributed capital through the *commenda* contract hoped to both recover their initial investment and earn three-quarters of the profits, if the commercial venture proved successful. The merchants and tradespeople who received investments could keep the remaining one-quarter of profits.[144] *Commenda* investments facilitated cross-Mediterranean trading voyages by providing much-needed capital to obtain goods, ships,

TABLE 9 Christian women's *commenda* contracts by type of investment

	Barcelona, 1292–1350	Girona, 1311–1350	Vic, 1250–1350
Deposit			
Wives	23	14	2
Widows	46	66	4
Unknown	12	30	1
Subtotal	81	110	7
Animal			
Wives	0	4	1
Widows	0	4	5
Unknown	1	0	1
Subtotal	1	8	7
Local/regional commerce			
Wives	4	4	1
Widows	9	22	7
Unknown	0	6	3
Subtotal	13	32	11
Extraregional commerce			
Wives	26	0	0
Widows	62	2	0
Unknown	11	1	0
Subtotal	99	3	0
Total	194	153	25

and crew. The flexibility of *commenda* contracts allowed investors to contribute sums of varying sizes as well as to invest in a broad range of economic sectors. Although scholars have mostly focused on the importance of *commenda* investments in international trade, small businesses specializing in local or regional trade also sought investments.

The *commenda* became an important tool for women seeking to profitably manage financial resources, as it allowed women of different social strata to invest what cash they had in a variety of business ventures. While many women invested directly in specific trading voyages or local businesses, others used the *commenda* contract to deposit funds with trusted individuals, who would manage money on their behalf and pay interest to the depositor.[145] Among Catalan Christian women, *commenda* investments formed an essential part of women's financial management strategies. In Barcelona and Girona, women invested using *commenda* contracts more often than they extended loans.[146] Women in the more provincial town of Vic made a larger proportion of investments than loans, but far more total loans than investments.[147] Commercial investment also played an important role in women's economic strategies in other Mediterranean urban centers; women made

TABLE 10 Women investors in Mediterranean commercial voyages in Barcelona

Destination/ type	Date	Total no. of investments	Avg. investment (in pounds)	Women's investments	Avg. women's investment (in pounds)
Calabria & Sicily[1]	November 1319	23	43.5	4	51.6
Cyprus[2]	August–September 1328	80	81.38	19	29.33
Valencia & North Africa[3]	August 1328	16	23.63	1	30
Calabria & Sicily[4]	August 1328	14	50.86	4	54.25
Societas (unspecified destination)[5]	May 1330	28	165	13	127
Syria[6]	April–May 1334	80	41.98	3	16.3
Romania[7]	February–March 1340	20	51.4	6	17.78
		261	67.46[8]	50	56.35[9]

[1]ACB, notaris, vol. 53, fols. 27v–31v.

[2]ACB, notaris, vol. 92, fols. 90v–91r, 154v–155r, 156v, 169v–170r, 184r–v, 186r, 188v–189v, 191v, 192v, 193v.

[3]ACB, notaris, vol. 92, fol. 130r.

[4]ACB, notaris, vol. 92, fols. 139v–140r.

[5]ACB, notaris, vol. 68, fols. 24v–26r.

[6]ACB, notaris, vol. 93, fols. 29r–v, 32v–34r, 43v, 45v–48r, 50r– 51v, 52v, 53v–55r.

[7]ACB, notaris, vol. 94, fols. 122r, 127v, 146r, 152v.

[8]Weighted to take into account the number of investments.

[9]Weighted to take into account the number of investments.

nearly half of all investments in local businesses in Perpignan and about one-quarter in Montpellier, as well as around one-quarter of investments in maritime commerce in Genoa.[148] Widows made the bulk of women's investments—around two-thirds of the total in all three cities—but married women also made investments using their *paraphernalia* (table 8).

The success of Mediterranean trading voyages depended on merchants' ability to secure multiple investments, and merchants turned to women as well as men. In Barcelona, about half of women's investments funded long-distance trade, and nearly one-fifth of investments in cross-Mediterranean voyages came from women (tables 9 and 10). Sea voyages, especially those bound for profitable destinations in the eastern Mediterranean, required substantial funding and brought high risks as well as high rewards.[149] Such voyages could take the better part of a year and required security measures to protect goods, yet they could incur significant losses through shipwreck, piracy, and confiscation of goods by foreign rulers.[150] The trading voyages that embarked across the Mediterranean from Barcelona brought women's money to destinations ranging from nearby Valencia and Mallorca to Venice, Calabria, Sicily, Sardinia, and Corsica, to the Byzantine Empire, Cyprus, Armenia, and Alexandria.[151]

Most women who invested in international trade came from wealthy families and committed large sums; women's average investment in Mediterranean voyages was 56 pounds 7 sous, only slightly lower than the overall average investment (67 pounds 9 sous; see table 10). Some women prioritized investing in a single promising business venture: Valença, widow of Pere Guitart, invested 30 pounds in a *societas* in her own name and another 175 pounds in her capacity as the guardian of her daughter Francesca.[152] Others attempted to diversify their investments; in the summer of 1328, Elisenda, widow of Bernat Pere, invested 10 pounds in a voyage to Cyprus and 30 pounds in a voyage to Sardinia and Corsica.[153] Merchants, aware of women's potential as investors, often turned to their female relatives. When collecting investments for a voyage to Calabria and Sicily, the brothers Guillem and Bonanat de Terré received their largest investments, of 100 pounds each, from their mother, Alamanda, and their sister Francesca.[154]

Regional trade, either spanning Catalonia or limited to a single city and its hinterlands, provided economic opportunities for women looking to make smaller, lower-risk investments. Most investors specified to some degree how the recipients should use their capital; in 1347, for example, Francesca, wife of Jaume de Vall of Vic, invested 100 sous for the recipients to utilize in their work making wine sacks and scabbards "in the county of Osona and not beyond."[155] Small contributions to regional trade also allowed even women of middling status to diversify their investments; Margarida, widow of the tanner Salvator Carbonell of Girona and guardian of her minor children Francesc and Caterina, made ten investments via *commenda* contracts between 1333 and 1337, all for sums of less than 100 sous and all for local trade.[156] Such small, diverse investments may have seemed safer than relying on profits from a single voyage or business venture. Many of the women who invested in local businesses came from families of more moderate means than those who invested in international trade.

The extant notarial documentation includes only a few examples of Jewish women's investments using *commenda* contracts, nearly all of which took the form of deposits rather than direct investments in either regional or international trade. Some Jewish women may have invested using a Hebrew contract similar to the *commenda*.[157] Catalan Jewish men worked as merchants and were especially involved in commerce with Alexandria, Crete, Cyprus, and the Byzantine Empire. They relied on both Christians and their own coreligionists to invest in maritime voyages.[158] However, if Jewish women found themselves limited to investing with the relatively small number of Jewish merchants and tradespeople, they would have had access to a far smaller pool of investment opportunities than Christian women, and they would have experienced greater difficulty if they sought to diversify their investments.

Women's Labor and Women's Networks

In 2008, Monica Green opened a special issue of the *Journal of Medieval History* with a call for more research on interactions between women, particularly those that brought together women of different faiths.[159] This issue, entitled "Conversing with the Minority: Relations Among Jewish, Christian, and Muslim Women in the High Middle Ages," includes excellent work on relationships between women of different faiths as seen through credit, healthcare, and wet-nursing. However, as Green acknowledges, economic spheres like the credit market are not necessarily the most promising place for scholars to look for women's interfaith interactions.[160] Male-dominated notarial culture, I argue, required women to prioritize social and economic ties with men, rather than women, when engaging in business that brought them before the notaries.

Women's networks undoubtedly existed and affected women's lives. In Picardy, credit markets were divided and stratified by gender, with women creditors specializing in consumption loans extended to other women.[161] Credit transactions between Jewish and Christian women in medieval England reveal neighborhood-based interfaith networks between women.[162] Impoverished women in medieval Paris relied on close female friends for survival.[163] In fourteenth-century Montpellier, a detailed web of women's networks shaped social and economic life.[164] Women in Mallorca worked together to sell and purchase enslaved labor.[165] The documentary evidence from Barcelona, Girona, and Vic hints at such connections; girls seeking apprenticeships often contracted with women artisans, pointing to urban-rural women's networks like those Kathryn Reyerson found in Montpellier.[166] Nevertheless, a quantitative assessment of notarial evidence from Barcelona,

Girona, and Vic indicates that women who sought to navigate notarial culture while managing household financial resources found ties with men more useful than ties with other women.

Overwhelmingly, notarial evidence portrays women as enmeshed in business with men, whether within their own community or in transactions that crossed religious lines. In all three cities, around 90 percent of Christian women's loans went either to male debtors or to groups that included both men and women, such as married couples.[167] In Barcelona, Christian women were even less likely than men to extend loans to women; it is possible that far from being motivated by gendered fellowship, cautious women creditors may have seen other women as riskier debtors.[168] Christian women creditors in Vic and Girona loaned money to women debtors slightly more often than male creditors did, but given that most of women's loans still went to men, this disparity hardly provides compelling evidence for the importance of women's networks in the credit market.[169] Moreover, many of the woman-to-woman loans recorded were between close relatives—for example, Francesca de Pausa of Vic borrowed 59 sous from her daughter Blanca in 1334.[170] Kinship ties may have had more power to create a sense of economic obligation than other kinds of connections between women.

Interfaith transactions, especially in the credit market, tell the same story: Jewish women creditors mostly did business with Christian men, and Christian women in need of credit overwhelmingly turned to male Jewish creditors. Christian women acting alone received less than 3 percent of Jewish women's loans in both Vic and Girona.[171] The unusually prominent role Jewish women played in Vic's credit market (see chapter 7) apparently did not dispose them to offer credit to women acting alone: Jewish women creditors in Vic were even less prone than their male counterparts to lend to Christian women.[172] As within the Christian community, Jewish women creditors in Girona extended loans to Christian women at slightly higher rates than male Jewish creditors did.[173] Nevertheless, the grand total of two loans between Jewish and Christian women in Girona hardly provides a rich portrait of interfaith women's networks, especially when placed in a broader quantitative context. Jewish women creditors working in Girona extended 97.5 percent of their loans to Christian men, and Christian women borrowing from Jews in the same city received 96.4 percent of their loans from Jewish men. Evidence from other cities and towns in Catalonia and southern France similarly indicates that Jewish women creditors did not disproportionately lend to other women.[174]

Post-plague Barcelona offers something of a counterpoint: between 1348 and 1350, Jewish women creditors were more than twice as likely as Jewish men to lend to Christian women.[175] A quantitative assessment indicates that Jewish women working as creditors still did most of their business with either Christian men or mixed-gender groups, who received well over three-quarters of Jewish women's loans. However, Christian women may have appreciated the sudden entry of Jewish women into the credit market: Jewish women made around 20 percent of all Jewish loans, but 30 percent of Christian women borrowing from Jews turned to Jewish women creditors. Together, these numbers hint at interfaith networks between women, foregrounded when Jewish women suddenly played an expanded role in the local credit market (see chapter 7). It is unclear, however, whether loans between women stemmed from preference or constraint. Male Jewish creditors may have sought to relegate the women of their community, who entered the market suddenly after the deaths of their husbands, to a gendered niche of the credit market. Among Christians in medieval and early modern Europe, guilds adopted a variety of strategies to stifle competition from women nonmembers; only the lack of such formal cooperative structures would have made it difficult for Jewish men to do the same.[176] However, whether women in post-plague Barcelona preferred or felt constrained to work with other women, the male-dominated notarial credit market still required most women to do business with men.

Two case studies—one Christian and one Jewish—further highlight women's tendency to rely on ties with men, rather than with other women, when negotiating notarial culture. When Valença, widow of Guillem Ferrer d'Odena of Barcelona—with whom this chapter began—invested in the *societas* formed by Bernat de Vila and Berenguer Vinot, she revealed her involvement in a kinship network that wove together the men and women of her extended family. Three individuals related to Valença by blood or marriage also invested in the *societas*: her sister Sibil·la, Sibil·la's husband Jaume Carbó, and Jaume's sister Agnès, widow of the jurist Bernat Ermengaud.[177] Although these contracts reveal the links that connected Valença to women as well as men, the other contracts in which Valença participated suggest that at least when she needed to navigate the norms of notarial culture, she particularly prized her relationship with her brother-in-law Jaume.

Jaume Carbó was undoubtedly a useful man to know. As a merchant, he may have been the one who discovered and assessed the profitability of the *societas*.[178] He had also served as one of Barcelona's five leading city councilors in 1327, and his brother Galceran would serve in the same position in 1332.[179] By the time Valença invested in the *societas* in 1330, she had a long history of working closely with Jaume, who had acted as her agent and as the testamentary executor of her late husband.[180] In contrast, the notarial documentation reveals very little overt economic cooperation between Valença and her sister Sibil·la. Valença's economic ties with Jaume may have stemmed from her close relationship with her sister, but it was Jaume who worked publicly alongside Valença to help her manage and increase household assets. Strikingly, Valença's generous *donatio inter vivos* grants went to young men of her family—her nephews, the sons of her brother Pere Corretger.[181] While this choice might simply indicate personal affective ties, it could also reflect an effort to reinforce a relationship with male kin, who would prove more useful than women relatives as future business partners or agents.[182]

Jewish women similarly cultivated social and economic relationships primarily with their male relatives. Much like Valença, Bonadona, widow of Astrug Caravida of Girona, found her closest business associate in a man related to her by marriage through a close female relative. Throughout the 1330s and 1340s, she regularly worked with her son-in-law Bellshom Scapat, who acted as both her agent and a cocreditor.[183] Bonadona's close connection with Bellshom could indicate the strength of her relationship with her daughter Bonafilla, but the notarial evidence yields no direct insight into the mother-daughter relationship. Even though Bonadona's command over her late husband's wealth had virtually disinherited both her daughters, Bonadona did not publicly attempt to involve Bonafilla in her business.[184] Bonafilla appeared independently in the documentary record only after her husband's death.[185] We can speculate about the training in financial management Bonafilla might have received from her mother, or her role in facilitating a profitable business connection between her mother and husband. Yet when business took Bonadona to the notary, her relationship with her son-in-law, not her daughter directly, benfited her most.

The reality of patriarchal inequalities meant that for most women, social and economic ties with men were nearly always more useful than those with other women, especially in the male-dominated economic sectors most closely interconnected with notarial culture. Nor were women in Catalan cities unique in this regard. Women in fourteenth-century Ghent were far more likely to make loans to men than to other women.[186] Jewish women in medieval Egypt depended primarily on male kin to access a social order rooted in patronage networks that excluded them.[187] Women presumably established social networks with the women in their families and communities—networks that might even be indirectly reflected in some of women's business relationships with men. But in their working lives, they depended first and foremost on their connections with the men in their families and communities.

The idea of women-to-women networks is compelling. It often posits solidarity between women as a subtle challenge to a fundamentally patriarchal gender system. Studies of vertical ties between women, moreover, at times portray such connections as free of the hostility and tension that could characterize relationships rooted in power inequalities: between Jews and Christians, between rich and poor, between masters (or mistresses) and their servants or slaves. However, despite the importance of such networks for scholars' efforts to reconstruct the gendered structures of the medieval past, we cannot assume that solidarities between women played a central role in women's efforts to manage financial resources, nor that gender solidarities provided a counterweight to power disparities. Connections with the men who would help them navigate male-dominated economic systems remained paramount.

Conclusions

The expansion of our concept of women's work allows us to see that both Jewish and Christian families relied on women to perform profitable labor tasks, including the management of household financial resources for women of various social strata, as well as artisanal work and domestic service for middling and lower-status women. Overall, however, Christian women consistently appear as more active than Jewish women in the notarial economy. The expanded labor options available to Christian women could have a real impact on their financial security, including their ability to support themselves during moments of family crisis.

The set of options available to women of both faiths differed across economic sectors. Jewish women found most of their labor opportunities in the credit industry but proved less successful there than Christian women. The artisanal trades, particularly the textile industry, allowed women to work in a range of occupations, although Jewish women both found fewer opportunities overall and experienced greater challenges to pursuing independent work. As the next chapter will demonstrate, the real estate industry represents a particularly intriguing case: both Jewish and Christian women played a more prominent role in real estate than in most economic sectors, but they nevertheless found the available options circumscribed.

6

CHRISTIAN AND JEWISH WOMEN IN THE INTERRELIGIOUS REAL ESTATE MARKET

In August 1285, Dura, widow of Samuel Cap, a Jew of Barcelona, went to the Christian notary Jaume Carnisser to sell a vineyard located just outside the city walls.[1] Although Dura's family origins remain obscure, she had married into an elite Jewish family of Barcelona. Her late husband, a prominent moneylender, had served as an elected official of the city's Jewish community.[2] Her father-in-law, Bonjuda Cap, had been dubbed a *nasi*, a member of Barcelona's Jewish communal elite, with close ties to royal power.[3] Dura had borne her husband three sons, Issach, Abraham, and Sento, and a daughter, Ester, who had married into the de Tolosa family, which was on the rise socially and economically.[4] Dura resembled the few other Jewish women active in business that required notarial documentation: wealthy and widowed.

Dura's vineyard was located just beyond one of the city gates, near the Hospital d'en Pere Vilar, which provided care for the poor, sick, and elderly.[5] She owned the property allodially, meaning that it was not subject to any higher overlord.[6] Rather than working the land directly or renting it out through a sharecropping agreement, Dura exploited the land economically by collecting cash rents. A Christian tenant held the land from her through an emphyteusis tenure agreement, a perpetual lease in which he committed to work and improve the property.[7] After his death, his heirs continued to hold the land, for which they paid Dura three morabatins per year.[8] The notary specified that the property bordered another rural holding to the east, a public road to the south, and a stream to the west.

On August 29, Dura sold the property for the sum of 39 pounds to two Christians, Ramon d'Abellan and Arnau Aleman, and committed to fully transfer all ownership rights to the two men. Like many other women, Christian as well as Jewish, she renounced the benefit of the Velleian senatus consult, an institution derived from Roman law that imposed both legal protections and restrictions on women's ability to transact freely.[9] Dura also specified that she would not take advantage of either "Hebrew" (Jewish) or "Latin" (including both Roman law and Catalan customary law) legal loopholes. One of her sons, Sento Cap, approved the sale and promised Ramon and Arnau that he would not contest it on account of his inheritance rights. Dura appended her signature in Latin and authorized another Jew to sign on her behalf in Hebrew—a choice that might indicate that she did not know how to write in Hebrew.[10]

On the one hand, this sale contract demonstrates the possibilities open to women as property owners and as participants in Catalonia's vibrant urban real estate markets. Dura, a Jewish widow, owned land and had for some amount of time effectively administered the property by leasing it to Christian laborers. She then independently sold the land to Christian buyers, a task that involved communication and negotiation with both the buyers themselves and the notary who recorded the contract. However, the sale contract was only the first step in a complex process of transferring the vineyard from Dura's ownership to that of Ramon and Arnau; the three additional contracts related to this sale highlight the obstacles a Jewish woman like Dura faced when managing real estate.

Dura then appointed an agent to transfer corporeal possession of the property—a legal ritual that required both buyer and seller, or their appointed agents, to appear in person on the grounds of the property.[11] Her agent, Llobell Gracià, belonged to another elite Jewish family of Barcelona.[12] In a subsequent document, signed the following day, Llobell approved the sale and agreed not to contest it on the grounds of any rights he might have.[13] As agency conferred no legal property rights, Llobell's action is puzzling; it could indicate that he had ownership claims via a family relationship with Dura. The text does not explicitly identify them as kin, but we do not know Dura's family background, and a marriage tying together these two elite families certainly seems plausible. The same day, Llobell transferred corporeal possession of the property to Ramon and Arnau, finalizing the sale.[14]

Taken together, these four contracts reveal the gendered legal and social structures that impeded women as owners and managers of real estate—yet still left open possibilities for women to buy, sell, and lease property. Dura had to obtain the approval of both her son Sento and of Llobell, who was certainly her agent and perhaps also a relative. She negotiated the sale contract and signed it in person but balked at traveling outside the city walls to accomplish the final property transfer. Although some men also appointed agents to accomplish this potentially time-consuming and onerous task, women almost never left the city to finalize property transfers, and they sometimes even abstained from trips to properties within the city walls.[15]

This chapter will consider how both Jewish and Christian women worked to manage real estate holdings in medieval Catalan cities as well as the legal systems and social expectations that sometimes enabled, and at other times restricted, their control over real property. I consider real estate separately from other economic sectors for two major reasons. First, both Christian and Jewish women participated in a higher proportion of their own faith group's real estate contracts than any other type of transaction. Second, Jewish families came closer in the real estate market than in any other economic sector to adopting Christian expectations about women's claims over family assets, although Jewish women still faced restrictions not experienced by their Christian counterparts.

For Christian women, inheritance law and the legal norms that distinguished real property from cash gave more people, including women, meaningful claims over real estate holdings. I begin the chapter with a discussion of how Catalan Christian legal culture shaped understandings of family property in ways that required women to participate in property management. A case study of three wealthy Christian women active in the Barcelona and Girona real estate markets of the 1320s and 1330s highlights the possibilities open to women in the upper echelons of urban society. I then place those women in context with a quantitative assessment of Christian women's real estate transactions, which indicate that the women real estate tycoons who leap from the pages of notarial registers were unusual but not unique.

The chapter then turns to Jewish women, who participated in a substantial proportion of their community's real estate transactions but remained less active in urban property markets than their Christian counterparts. In the thirteenth and early fourteenth centuries, property flowed freely back and forth between Jews and Christians. Jews in real estate contracts acted as both buyers and sellers, both lessors and lessees. As a result, Jews buying and selling property felt more pressure than in other economic sectors to negotiate between Jewish customs and the legal expectations of their Christian buyers. Concessions to Christian expectations integrated Jewish women into the work of managing family property, but halakhic norms still left Jewish women with less authority over real property than Christian women. After a discussion of Jewish legal norms surrounding gender and property, I employ a documentary case study to explore how Jewish families might handle the tensions between Jewish and Christian legal culture that arose when they sold property to Christians. Finally, I contextualize Jewish women's property transactions in a study of Jewish real estate contracts to demonstrate that Jewish women retained only tenuous authority over real property.

Property and Gender in Medieval Catalan Legal Culture

Christian women in the western Mediterranean inherited, owned, and managed real estate. Although Diane Owen Hughes argued that the rise of the dowry system in Mediterranean Europe excluded women from control over real property by the end of the thirteenth century, extensive documentary evidence from the Iberian Peninsula and southern France suggests that Hughes's thesis requires some revision.[16] Women in Montpellier were especially well represented as sellers of property, but they also appear in the city's notarial registers as purchasers of land and as lessors.[17] About one-quarter of the brides in the southern French town of Manosque, and about half of the brides in Perpignan, brought dowries including real estate to their husbands.[18] Castilian women maintained property rights after marriage, and spouses typically acted jointly when selling land owned by either party.[19] Case studies of individual women and families in both Catalonia and southern France have revealed that women effectively administered real property and transmitted it to succeeding generations.[20]

Scholars have typically envisioned women of Mediterranean and southern Europe as economically disempowered relative to their northern European counterparts.[21] However, the evidence of women's activities in Mediterranean urban real estate markets complicates this dichotomy. Christian women in Barcelona, Girona, and Vic worked in the real estate market in much the same way as the women of northern European cities. In late medieval London, women sold property more often than they purchased it, and most women who participated in the real estate market acted jointly with their husbands.[22] Rural English widows may have enjoyed a somewhat greater degree of economic independence but also faced the very real threat of poverty.[23] Women in Ghent routinely sold property alongside their husbands, but they less often managed property independently.[24]

The model of Mediterranean Europe as a more economically restrictive place for women stems largely from Italian evidence. Italian women enjoyed both property rights and economic power in the eleventh century, but they experienced a decline in their right to own and manage financial resources, including real property, in the thirteenth century.[25] In Florence, the economic position of women worsened in the fifteenth and sixteenth centuries.[26] Elite women in Venice and Milan maintained greater control over financial resources but still lost some formal property rights.[27] In Catalonia, in contrast, women maintained property rights not only after the rise of the dowry system in the thirteenth century but even into the early modern period.[28] Women in other regions of the Iberian Peninsula similarly owned and managed property through the sixteenth century.[29] Although women in Catalonia undoubtedly experienced meaningful economic limitations, their example nevertheless undermines the supposed contrast between northern and southern Europe.

The notarial documentation from Barcelona, Girona, and Vic contributes to the growing picture of Christian Mediterranean women as active managers of real estate. Catalan customary law and local notarial practice constructed a legal culture that enabled women to own and manage real estate and upheld the claims wives, daughters, and sisters made over family property. Daughters and sisters enjoyed full inheritance rights under a system of partible inheritance that took seriously their potential claims to patrimonial property.[30] As Marie Kelleher has argued, women became implicated in the real estate market not only because they owned property directly but also because their dowries gave them claims over their husbands' assets.[31] Husbands accepted the obligation to repay the full value of their wives' dowries in exchange for the right to manage and profit from dotal assets for the duration of the marriage. However, wives maintained ownership over their dotal wealth, and on the basis of their dowry claims, they could invalidate their husbands' transactions or even sue for the return of their dowries.[32]

Real estate sales raised distinct legal concerns over the potential claims of family members, including daughters, wives, mothers, and sisters. According to Catalan customary law, jointly owned property could only be permanently alienated (irrevocably transferred to another's ownership) with the full permission and consent of all parties with ownership claims. If one person sold jointly owned real estate without the knowledge or consent of a co-owner, the aggrieved party could recover the property without compensating the buyer.[33] The immutability of real property endowed it with a legal status very different from fungible cash resources. Thomas Aquinas made this distinction in his *Summa Theologica*. Cash disappeared through its usage; if you allowed someone the use of your money—through a loan, for example—you would expect to be repaid, but you could not expect the same coins to return to your hands. In contrast, if you granted someone else the use of your house or field, you expected the same property to eventually return to your possession.[34]

The treatment in Catalan law of cash dowries in comparison with real estate further illuminates this fundamental difference between money and property. Husbands undertook the obligation to repay the entire value of a cash dowry, but the money quickly became incorporated into the estate at large.[35] Wives approved their husbands' debts because it was impossible to distinguish between the sum designated as a dowry and other household monetary resources. In contrast, husbands could not licitly alienate real property that their wives had brought as dowry unless the woman or her family chose to estimate its value formally, thus conceptually transforming it into cash.[36]

Real estate was also treated differently from cash as a heritable resource. Heirs had no right to contest debts; a son named as universal heir, for example, could not refuse to repay a debt incurred by his late father on the grounds that he had not consented to it. He could only avoid repayment by repudiating the inheritance entirely—a reasonable financial choice if the value of the estate was insufficient to pay its debts, but not necessarily feasible in less extreme cases.[37] However, children could, and did, contest the alienation of patrimonial real property.[38] While family members had no inherent right to cash or movable goods dissipated by a wastrel relative, the unilateral alienation of property considered essential to the family estate raised questions about whether the seller had the right to alienate the property at all.

Given the status of real property in Catalan customary law, buyers took care to obtain documentary confirmation that potential claimants—including women—had renounced their property rights. Some sellers even accepted the obligation to repay the buyer if they failed to obtain the consent of their minor children once they reached adulthood. In 1327, for example, Miquel de Tressera, a notary of Barcelona, obligated himself and a guarantor to repay the 27 pounds he had received as purchase price for houses in the city of Barcelona if he failed to obtain the consent of his minor son and daughter.[39] The traditions of Catalan customary law, combined with a notarial legal culture that emphasized the value of formal documentation, required women to publicly participate in the alienation—if not necessarily the management—of real property owned by their husbands and fathers.

Christian Women Property Managers in Barcelona and Girona: Agnès, Valença, and Blanca

On May 5, 1319, Agnès, daughter of the Barcelona draper Arnau de Busquets, signed a contract with her husband Ramon Calvet, a jurist of Girona, in which they agreed to an unusual arrangement. Agnès and Ramon confirmed an agreement made at the time of their marriage, according to which the 12,500 sous Agnès had brought as dowry "would be converted into the purchase of honors and possessions, for my work (*ad opus mei et meorum*), and that I would give the same honors and possessions to you as a non-estimated dowry."[40] With these words, recorded by the notary Bernat de Vilarrubía in her home city of Barcelona, Agnès not only transformed her cash dowry into real property but also identified the management of these properties as her work or trade, using the same language as a cobbler or weaver would. Agnès apparently understood the business of real estate as income-generating labor—and acted decisively to ensure that she could support herself with her work.

Like most Catalan brides, Agnès received a cash dowry; unlike most, she not only preferred to transform her assets into landed wealth but even came to a formal agreement with her husband that enabled her to do so.[41] Although the contract does not directly specify who instigated this arrangement, it clearly benefited Agnès more than Ramon. The choice to convert a cash dowry into real property kept considerable cash resources out of Ramon's hands while transforming Agnès's assets into secure forms of property, which would potentially increase in value over the ensuing years. Ramon would enjoy any income generated by this property during the marriage, but he lost the flexibility that came with cash: he could not alienate these real estate holdings without his wife's permission. The contract specified that the properties would become a non-estimated dowry—a savvy decision on Agnès's part, as dotal real estate with an estimated value could be sold and replaced with cash.[42]

By 1319, Agnès had transformed her cash dowry into an impressive array of landed wealth: houses near the smithy (*ferreria*) of Girona; a *hospicium* where she lived with her husband; a mill, located in the marketplace (*mercadal*) of Girona, half of which she had inherited from her grandfather and half of which she had purchased; and houses and a field outside the city.[43] The mill, in particular, proved to be a good investment. As a widow, she leased the rights over the mill to a married couple for 16 pounds per year in July 1330.[44] In June 1331, she renewed the couple's lease for two years, raising their annual rent to 17 pounds.[45] However, if Agnès worked to manage her property during her marriage, she only did so behind the scenes: after she signed this contract, she disappeared from the notarial documentation of both Barcelona and Girona until her widowhood in 1329.

After her husband's death, the notarial registers offer glimpses of Agnès as a powerful family matriarch who negotiated with her son Jaume over the division of family property in 1329, secured her daughter Francesca's marriage to the wealthy moneychanger Guillem de Sant Martí in 1331, and then facilitated Francesca's entry into the convent of Santa Clara in 1333, perhaps after she too had been widowed.[46] Agnès's business had apparently made her quite wealthy; in 1333 she loaned 3,420 sous to the draper Pere Gironès.[47] Strikingly, however, she relied on an agent to act on her behalf when she leased out her mill.

The agreement Agnès made with her husband is unparalleled, but she was hardly unique as a Christian woman who worked in the management of real property. The same week that Agnès signed her contract with Ramon, another Barcelona notary, Guillem Borrell, was occupied with the business of Valença, wife of Guillem Ferrer d'Odena, who purchased two substantial urban properties in May 1319. On May 3, she bought two urban *hospicia* with attached workshops, becoming the new landlady to the current noble tenant, the knight Bernat de Serrià.[48] On May 12, she purchased several houses in the city, then rented out to various tenants, from a canon of Barcelona.[49]

Valença cuts a powerful figure as a property owner: she purchased properties worth a total of 1,500 sous in the span of ten days, paid in cash shortly after the purchase, and placed herself in a position of authority over high-status male tenants. Both in marriage and widowhood, she appears as a confident player in Barcelona's bustling urban economy. In 1324 she took possession of urban property owned by her late husband as payment for her 9,000-sou dowry.[50] In 1330, as discussed at the beginning of chapter 5, she made the largest single investment in the *societas* established by the merchants Bernat de Vila of Barcelona and Berenguer Vinot of Mallorca: 680 pounds.[51]

Like Agnès, however, Valença relied on male agents for part of the work of managing property. Valença designated her brother-in-law Jaume Carbó (husband of her sister Sibil·la) as her agent to take corporeal possession of the properties. She may have hesitated to appear in person for business that required her to trek to unfamiliar spaces across the city.[52] Properties scattered across and outside the city, owned as investments rather than personal dwellings, may have felt less familiar and secure, and more likely to pose a potential threat to a woman's security and honor, than a notary's office or a public square. Borrell might even have accommodated Valença by drawing up the sale contract in her home. When men bought property within city walls, they were less likely than women to rely on agents; even a powerful figure like Valença had to maneuver within social expectations different from those faced by men.

Valença was not alone among women real estate tycoons in Barcelona. Blanca, widow of Berenguer Albanell of Barcelona, owned properties across the city and in its rural hinterlands.[53] Although the available documentation provides no information about Blanca's family background, she had married into the city's commercial elite. At his death in 1323, Blanca's husband Berenguer was owed sizable sums of money by both King Alfons IV of Catalonia-Aragon and the Hafsid king of Tunisia, Abu Bakr II. Both debts were related to Berenguer's involvement in international commerce. Blanca controlled the late Berenguer's estate—and collected on these debts—in her capacity as guardian of her minor children.[54] She also orchestrated the marriage of her eldest daughter, Blanqueta, to the merchant and vice-admiral Galceran Marquet, who was one of the most important men of the city.[55] Unlike the widows of men in the textile industry, Blanca did not have the option to adopt her late husband's profession: Catalan women did not work as merchants in international Mediterranean commerce. Although she could collect on his mercantile debts and settle his affairs, there is no evidence that her work in international commerce extended beyond these obligations. Instead, Blanca worked in the real estate market.

She appeared on the scene in the 1320s as a wealthy and propertied widow who earned money by renting urban and rural properties to tenants, most of whom were men of middling status. In some cases, Blanca did not even directly participate in the transaction recorded; the notary mentioned her name as leaseholder when describing and identifying a piece of rental property.[56] Blanca purchased some real estate holdings during widowhood.[57] However, she may also have inherited property as dowry or *paraphernalia*; as guardian of her minor children, she may have managed her late husband's real estate holdings as well as those she owned outright. Blanca's powerful position as an owner and manager of property is undeniable—but if she engaged in such work during her marriage, it remained behind the scenes. She only became a prominent player in the real estate market during widowhood.

Gender, Family, and Power: Christian Women in Real Estate Contracts

The case studies of Agnès, Valença, and Blanca offer a glimpse into what the wealthiest Christian women of Catalan cities could accomplish as owners and managers of property. Their work in the real estate market was made possible by a constellation of social and economic structures that granted women authority over landed wealth. These three women were not unique: the pages of notarial registers from Barcelona, Girona, and Vic are populated with women who sold, bought, and leased property. Nevertheless, women property owners faced very different challenges from men, and work in real estate brought very few women the level of success enjoyed by Agnès, Valença, and Blanca.

Most of the women who worked in the real estate market belonged to the upper echelons of urban society. Landed wealth, including both rural and urban holdings, formed a central part of the patrimony of elite urban families in Mediterranean Europe. The management of those properties helped ensure the solvency of urban households.[58] The real estate market was also critical to urban economies. Vibrant and ever-growing land markets had contributed to Barcelona's economic takeoff and early urban growth.[59] Over the course of the thirteenth and fourteenth centuries, contracts dealing with the sale and rental of real property represented a substantial share of notarial business in Barcelona, Girona, and Vic. In Vic, real estate generated almost one-quarter of notarial contracts, second only to credit.[60] In both Barcelona and Girona, the real estate market was the third-largest sector of the notarial economy.[61]

Women participated both in sales, which permanently transferred property to new owners, and in rentals, which gave the lessee usage rights in exchange for either fixed annual rents or a portion of the land's produce. Although some families directly sold or leased out properties over which they held full ownership rights, Catalan urban real estate markets also relied on the regular circulation of rental properties. Holders of long-term leases, especially perpetual leases of the emphyteusis type, could freely sell or sublet their rights for substantial profits.[62] In 1297, for example, Alamanda, widow of Bernat Andreu of Barcelona, made 18,000 sous off the sale of houses in Barcelona that she held from the moneychanger Guillem Pere d'Usay, who in turn held the property from the nobleman Bernat de Centelles.[63]

The sale of a property, whether owned allodially or rented, could bring instant liquidity to those in need of cash, while rentals provided a steady but small yearly income. Long-term emphyteusis rentals, in which lessees received usage rights in perpetuity in exchange for a fixed annual rent (*census*) and the obligation to cultivate and improve the property, kept valuable agricultural land and urban workshops occupied and productive.[64] New tenants paid an entry fee (*entrada*) as well as an annual rent. The regular circulation

TABLE 11 Real estate contracts with Christian women participants

	Barcelona, 1290–1350	Girona, 1311–1350	Vic, 1250–1350
Sellers			
All sellers	164	154	451
Christian women sellers	49 (49%)	71 (46.1%)	268 (59.4%)
Buyers			
All buyers	164	154	451
Christian women buyers	17 (10.4%)	44 (28.6%)	85 (18.8%)
Lessors			
All lessors	116	142	453
Christian women lessors	20 (17.2%)	23 (16.2%)	117 (25.8%)
Lessees			
All lessees	116	142	453
Christian women lessees	23 (19.8%)	30 (21.1%)	89 (19.6%)

of emphyteusis tenures allowed landlords to treat these entry fees as a semi-regular source of income, less frequent but more substantial than yearly rental payments.[65]

A landlord could also lease out property for a specific sum over a shorter period of time. This strategy left landlords more open to the risk of properties remaining unoccupied but allowed them to rake in larger annual rents and to adjust rental fees as the market dictated.[66] Alamanda, widow of Nicolau Ros of Barcelona, may have sought to compensate for the risks inherent in short-term rentals by charging an astronomically high yearly rent. She owned a *hospicium*—a large urban dwelling that could include workshops and storefronts as well as living space—near the old shipyard in Barcelona, and in 1332 she rented it to Barcelona's city council. She promised that she would neither expel her tenants to get a better rate nor sell the property out from under them. In exchange, the councilors would pay her 30 pounds for the first year and another 35 pounds for the second.[67] It seems unlikely that she could have gotten a better rate from another lessee. Few tenants would pay upward of 30 pounds per year in rent; in the same year, the sum of 35 pounds could buy a set of contiguous houses just outside the city walls.[68]

Women participated in a larger proportion of real estate contracts than in any other type of notarial transaction—yet still confronted limitations distinct from those experienced by men. Even women who possessed wealth in real property and the economic know-how to manage it effectively worked in real estate only with the support of men. As women were discouraged from traveling, they nearly always acted through agents for the final part of most real estate sales and rentals: the transfer of corporeal possession.

Especially when property was located outside city walls, women were reluctant to travel in person to transfer or receive possession of land. Male relatives could thereby gain some modicum of authority over property to which they had no legitimate ownership claim. In 1333, for example, Bartomeua, wife of Berenguer de Vic of Barcelona, sold two plots of land, both located in the territory of Barcelona outside the city walls.[69] She had inherited the property from her late father, Guillem Ermengaud, and presumably held it as *paraphernalia*. Her husband did not provide consent, but he still participated in the transaction as her agent and accomplished the transfer of corporeal possession. Even in sales of urban property, women more often than men remained physically at a remove when the sale was finalized.

In all three cities, Christian women property sellers acted independently less than half the time.[70] Although men engaged in joint action when selling property more frequently than in other types of transactions, men still sold property independently far more often than women.[71] The independent sale of real estate was more common in Barcelona than elsewhere, and women of Barcelona were more likely to sell property without male intervention than their counterparts in Girona and Vic. However, independence was a double-edged sword: compared to women living in smaller cities, women in Barcelona may have sold a larger proportion of properties independently, but they were less represented overall as property sellers. Moreover, relatively few women owned and managed property independently, even in Barcelona; in all three cities, most of women's opportunities to participate in the real estate market stemmed from their shared management of family-owned property.

In Barcelona, Girona, and Vic, Christian women primarily appeared as property sellers rather than as purchasers, lessors, or lessees (see table 11). In other words, women most often entered the real estate market to permanently alienate valuable financial resources rather than to invest in those resources through accumulation or to manage them by collecting rents. Women were not legally barred from purchasing property. However, the tendency for women to sell rather than buy or lease out property could indicate that women faced more obstacles than men if they sought to manage property beyond a home in which they lived. Alternatively, women may have sold off real estate holdings to remedy a lack of liquidity—perhaps because they faced more difficulties than men in either earning an income or independently obtaining credit.

It is no coincidence that women were both least active and most independent in Barcelona, where elites treated real property as a short-term investment rather than long-term family patrimony.[72] Barcelona was the only one of the three cities in which most property sellers acted independently.[73] Properties purchased for quick resale were less subject to family inheritance claims and less likely to function as collateral for dowry debts. As a result, fewer property sales required the involvement of women, whose claims usually stemmed from either inheritance or from the lien they held on their husbands' estates due to their dowries. The language of individual sale contracts suggests that women often participated not as joint owners and managers of property but as potential claimants, with the ability to invalidate sales made by their husbands or male relatives.

Catalan partible inheritance traditions gave both sons and daughters equal claim to family property, and as a result, families expected older children to accompany them to notaries' offices and younger children to provide consent once they came of age. Property owners obtained consent from daughters as well as sons, and sisters as well as brothers, when they sold family property. Especially in Vic, families often called upon multiple children and other relatives to participate in or consent to sales. In 1303, for example, Ramona, her husband Ramon Jordi of Vic, their sons Nicolau and Lleonet, and their daughter Simona jointly sold rented houses in Vic for 1,750 sous—a sizeable sum, suggesting that the sale of this property could seriously impact the family estate. They also promised to obtain the consent of Ramon's sisters, Maria and Berenguera.[74] Daughters' involvement in these sales almost certainly did not indicate that they actively participated in the management of family-owned property. However, the need to seek out their participation or consent indicates that their potential claims to these family real estate holdings were taken seriously. Women as well as men could even challenge their relatives' charitable donations of land to local monasteries, on the grounds that their kin could not alienate the property without obtaining their consent.[75]

Husbands obligated all their goods for the repayment of their wives' dowries, with the result that wives could contest transactions that jeopardized the security of their dotal assets. Some wives regularly participated in real estate sales made by their husbands that could affect the security of their dowries. Cilia, wife of Andreu Ripoll of Vic, twice sold property alongside her husband, once in 1313 and again in 1324.[76] Married couples also owned property jointly; in some cases, women's dowries may have helped fund real estate purchases. The cobbler Francesc de Strata of Vic and his wife Maria jointly sold three properties over the course of almost twenty-five years, and all three contracts explicitly state that Maria and Francesc owned or held the property jointly.[77]

A comparison of property sellers and lessors suggests that women's ownership claims over property did not necessarily translate into rights of management. In all three cities, family groups including women were more than twice as likely to sell property as to lease it to a tenant.[78] Although women's domestic responsibilities included their formal involvement in the alienation of family property, they more rarely shared in the everyday public management of properties that remained under family ownership.

Some women may have found that restrictions on their mobility and their control over financial resources made them less able to effectively manage real property than their husbands or fathers. The challenges posed by collecting rents may have encouraged some women to alienate inherited property, rather than temporarily lease it, and to avoid buying property as an investment. Widows, often without ready access to cash and in need of liquidity to support minor children or divide their husbands' estates, may have felt forced to sell family property for an immediate cash infusion.[79]

Gender, Money, and Property in Rabbinic Legal Culture

Catalan rabbis worked to strike a balance between the peculiar status of real property, on the one hand, and halakhic norms that restricted wives' and widows' authority over the conjugal estate, on the other. Solomon ibn Adret denied wives the right to contest their husbands' cash debts or to collect on their dowries if their husbands became bankrupt.[80] Widows could collect on their dowries before other creditors sought repayment from their husbands' estates. But if a man repaid his debts and then died in a state of insolvency, his widow had no legal recourse against her late husband's former creditors. A widow could, however, overturn her late husband's real estate sales. Husbands obligated their real property for the debt of the dowry, comparable to a pledge. If the sale of that property left the estate too depleted to muster the capital to repay a widow's dowry, she could void the sale. Ibn Adret therefore provided a set of guidelines that undermined widows' ability to overturn their husbands' real estate sales. Wives should not only consent to sales but also act formally as joint sellers. The wife's name should even appear before that of her husband to emphasize her free consent and participation.[81]

Most ordinary Jews would not have read rabbinic responsa directly, but local leaders would have shared the guidance they received from rabbinic luminiaries. Ibn Adret was an immensely influential figure in Catalan rabbinic culture and, during his lifetime, an important source of advice for communal leaders throughout and beyond Catalonia.[82] The influence of rabbis like ibn Adret, spread to ordinary Jews via local communal leaders, could explain why Jewish married couples sold real estate together more often than they jointly incurred debts, made investments, or purchased property. Both Latin notarial contracts and Hebrew writs demonstrate that Jews regularly followed ibn Adret's recommendation to name the wife before her husband, a practice seen much less frequently among Christians. For example, when Cresques Alfaquim and Sobredona jointly sold property in 1281 with a Latin contract, the notary listed the parties as "I, Sobredona, wife of Cresques Alfaquim, and I, the aforementioned Cresques Alfaquim."[83] In both the extant Hebrew contracts in which married couples sold property, the wife's name preceded that of her husband.[84]

However, ibn Adret also maintained distinctively Jewish restrictions that hampered widows' ability to exert ownership claims to jointly owned real estate after they had collected their dowries. He even challenged whether married couples could jointly own property at all. His response to a property dispute between a widow and her husband's heirs insisted on a complete separation between the property of husband and wife.[85] Christian legal culture took for granted joint ownership over real property, which they saw as subject to a broad range of overlapping claims from the purchasers and their kin.[86] In contrast, ibn Adret refused to acknowledge the possibility of overlapping claims or of commingling and confusion of goods. The houses under dispute, ibn Adret dictated, had belonged either to the husband or the wife, and therefore now belonged either to the heirs of the deceased or to his widow. Property had a clearly defined owner or owners, and neither vague claims over an estate nor participation in transactions involving those claims constituted ownership.

Elka Klein has argued that thirteenth-century Catalan Jewish families developed ideas of family property drawn from a "complex interpenetration of Jewish law and local custom."[87] Yet despite the moments of voluntary partnership cited by Klein, widows' rights and heirs' claims to a deceased man's property remained legally distinct. Some families undoubtedly saw themselves as participating in a joint enterprise and acted to meet the needs of the entire family. Nevertheless, Jewish families and communities maintained a clear understanding of the differences between Jewish law and local custom, and when they relied on the latter, they did so carefully and deliberately. Individuals or families might occasionally embrace local Christian ideas of shared family property for the good of the household, but Jewish men also remained ready to appeal to halakhic justifications to limit women's claims over family property.

Although ibn Adret provides justification for the practice of Jewish married couples jointly selling property, other Jewish family strategies adopted in the real estate industry remained outside the realm of halakhah. The real estate market, I argue, encouraged Jews to adapt to Christian practices in ways other economic sectors did not. Widows and heirs, according to ibn Adret, should not jointly own property, yet they jointly sell property in several contracts.[88] Husbands and wives could not jointly own property, but Jewish couples acted together to buy real estate.[89] Some of the Jewish couples who sold property together even treated the wife as co-owner of the property, not merely a problematic claimant. When Cresques Alfaquim appointed an agent to transfer corporeal possession of a vineyard he and his wife Sobredona had sold, he referred to Sobredona as a co-owner of the property and specified that they had jointly received yearly rent on it before the sale.[90] Finally, although ibn Adret took seriously the claims of widows unable to collect on their dowries as a result of their husbands' irresponsible alienation of real property, he provided no recourse for heirs, whether male or female. Under Jewish law, fathers would have no need to involve their sons, much less their daughters, in sales of real property. However, Jewish property sales sometimes brought together a wider web of kin, many of whom could make claims in Christian courts, but not Jewish ones.[91]

In the following sections, I argue that Jewish families selling property adhered to Christian legal norms to meet the expectations of their Christian buyers. However, these adaptations did not necessarily give Jewish women a meaningful role as comanagers of family property. While a few Jewish families chose to assert the property claims of their wives and daughters, most of the Jewish families selling real estate employed Christian contractual practices without granting women real authority over family-owned property.

Selective Acculturation in the Real Estate Market: The de Tolosas of Barcelona

In November 1277, the brothers Issach and Abraham de Tolosa, Jews of Barcelona, sold to a group of Christian buyers a plot of land that they had inherited from their late brother Saltell, who in turn had inherited it from their late father, Astrug de Tolosa. As proof of their ownership over the property, they appended a copy of Astrug's Hebrew will, which had divided his estate among his three sons.[92] However, Issach and Abraham were not

Astrug's only surviving children; they also had two sisters, Astrugona and Dolça. Under Jewish law, Astrug's heirs were expected to provide his daughters with appropriate dowries, but the two girls could make no formal inheritance claims over the estate of either their father or their brother. Only if Issach and Abraham also died childless would the estate pass to Astrugona and Dolça. Nor had Astrug treated his daughters with special consideration in his will, which mentioned the girls only to place them, along with their brothers, under the guardianship of their grandfather Samuel Cap. Astrug made no inheritance provisions for them whatsoever, not even specifying appropriate dowries.

Issach and Abraham nevertheless took their responsibility to appropriately dower their sisters seriously. In the sale contract, they stated that they had chosen to sell this plot of land partly in order to liquidate assets to secure a dowry for their sister Astrugona.[93] The notary did not use the term "dowry," however, but instead referred to the "inheritance" (*hereditas*) owed to Astrugona now that she had reached marriageable age—even though Astrug de Tolosa's will granted her no such inheritance. Moreover, although they had no valid halakhic claim to the sold property, Astrugona and the siblings' widowed mother, Ester, consented to the sale. In a separate contract, Issach promised that he would also obtain the consent of his younger sister Dolça once she came of age.[94]

In her analysis of this case, Elka Klein argued that it provided evidence for shared inheritance practices among Catalan Jews and Christians. The choice to represent Astrugona's dowry as her inheritance reveals that Catalan Jews, like their Christian neighbors, conceptually linked the two.[95] Klein saw the difference between Astrug's will, which assumed standard halakhic protections for his daughters, and the Latin documentation, which overtly described the girls as having rights over the family patrimony, as negligible; ultimately, she suggests, "the end result was essentially the same."[96]

In contrast, I read this disjunction between Astrug's 1268 Hebrew will and the 1277 Latin notarial sale contracts as evidence for tensions between Jewish and Christian legal norms. Rabbinic texts from medieval Catalonia challenged the equivalency of dowry and inheritance by distinguishing clearly between the nature of rights enjoyed by sons and those held by daughters. While sons had grounds to contest legacies that left them with less than their share of the patrimony, both Rabbi Asher ben Yehiel and Rabbi Solomon ibn Adret emphasized that fathers had the right to unilaterally determine what their daughters received as dowry, and young women had no legal grounds to challenge these decisions.[97] At least some Catalan Jews—including Astrug de Tolosa—upheld these distinctions between dowry and inheritance. Jewish fathers granted their daughters appropriate dowries but often stopped short of treating them as heirs.

Interaction with Christian notaries and buyers required some Jewish families, who might otherwise have upheld the standard halakhic position, to entertain an alternative vision of daughters' inheritance claims, at least temporarily. Issach and Abraham in this sale contract treated their sisters and widowed mother as if they exercised meaningful claims over the family patrimony. However, it seems plausible that they made this choice to alleviate the concerns of their Christian buyers, who probably had little understanding of the nuanced distinctions between Jewish and Christian inheritance practices and therefore assumed that Astrugona, Dolça, and Ester had valid claims. Their buyers easily might have balked at making a purchase that, according to their own legal assumptions, left them in danger of losing their newly acquired property to future inheritance claims. The alternative explanation—that despite the silence of their father's will, the brothers chose to actively treat their sisters as coheirs—ascribes an immense amount of generosity to the two young men. Outside this contract, there is certainly no evidence that they considered their sisters as heirs with rights comparable to their own.

Nor can we assume the word "inheritance" in this contract accurately represents the way Issach and Abraham understood the funds they would transfer to Astrugona, as opposed to the way the notary and the Christian buyers understood Astrugona's claims. When notaries worked with Jewish clients, they sometimes had to translate Jewish legal concepts into Latin terminology and concepts—and at times did so imperfectly.[98] The notary might not even have realized that the distinction between dowry and inheritance was sharper for Catalan Jews than for the Catalan Christians who probably accounted for most of his clientele.

This case study offers a clear example of a moment in which Jewish understandings of daughters' inheritance, as represented in Astrug's will, conflicted with Christian ones, as represented in the notarial sale contracts. Such moments of tension and accomodation were far more frequent in the real estate market than in other economic sectors. The following section will place this case in the wider context of a real estate market that brought Jews and Christians into constant contact and forced members of the Jewish minority community to reckon with how their Christian neighbors understood women's claims over landed wealth.

Jewish Women in the Interreligious Real Estate Market

Although Jewish law defined women's property rights very differently from Catalan customary law, Jewish women nevertheless played a more visible role in their community's real estate transactions than in any other economic sector. Credit contracts provide a particularly good point of comparison. Jews turned to the notaries to record their loans to Christians more than for any other type of transaction: in each city, the surviving notarial registers include hundreds or even thousands of Jewish credit contracts. In contrast, a mere 128 Jewish real estate contracts have survived from Barcelona, Girona, and Vic combined. Jewish women selling property appeared in fewer total contracts than Jewish women lending money to Christians, but they accounted for a much more substantial proportion of the Jewish community's real estate business. Jewish women (or groups including women) sold one-third of all properties alienated by Jewish owners in Barcelona, half of such properties in Girona, and all properties sold by Jews in Vic (see table 12). The thirteenth-century parchment contracts from Barcelona yield additional examples of Jewish women selling property: Jewish women, or groups including women, made another four real estate sales between 1250 and 1292, while Jewish wives or women relatives consented to two sales.[99]

The apparent prominence of Jewish women in the real estate market comes with a few caveats. In this economic sphere, like others, they played a less active role than their Christian counterparts. In both Barcelona and

TABLE 12 Jewish real estate contracts

	Men	Women	Married couples	Group (men)	Group (mixed)	Total
Barcelona, 1292–1350						
Tenants	3	0	0	0	0	3
Landlords	1	1	0	0	0	2
Sellers	11	2	2	1	2	18
Buyers	7	2	0	0	0	9
Girona, 1311–1350						
Tenants	7	2	0	6	1	16
Landlords	13	0	0	4	1	18
Sellers	6	2	2	2	4	16
Buyers	18	0	1	0	0	19
Vic, 1250–1350						
Tenants	22	1	4	4	0	31
Landlords	2	0	0	0	0	2
Sellers	0	2	0	0	2	4
Buyers	8	1	0	1	0	10

Girona, Jewish women sold property independently less often than Christian women: women acted independently in only three of the ten real estate contracts involving Jewish women sellers from Barcelona (30 percent), and two of eight from Girona (25 percent).[100] Jewish women only enjoyed greater independence than Christian women as property sellers in Vic—which was also where Jewish women played an unusually prominent role in the credit market, as I will discuss in the next chapter.[101] Women sellers acted alone in half of Jewish women's four sale contracts (50 percent), whereas Christian women of Vic acted independently in only 14.3 percent of women's sale contracts.

However, comparisons between Jewish and Christian women are made difficult by the fact that we have far fewer examples of Jewish real estate contracts. In comparison with the 128 Jewish real estate contracts found in all three cities combined, the registers of each city record hundreds of real estate contracts between Christians. Jews consistently enjoyed the right to own land in the Crown of Aragon, and real estate management formed a crucial element of the economic portfolios of elite Jews, who often worked in multiple economic sectors.[102] However, the precise financial significance of real estate in the economic strategies of Jewish families is hard to pinpoint. Although Jews participated in fewer real estate contracts than credit contracts, real property assets were of higher value than most Jewish loans. Christians as well as Jews also generated more credit contracts than real estate contracts, although the disparity was less pronounced. Moreover, the notarial documentation probably underrepresents Jews' participation in the real estate market; Jews selling, leasing, or transferring property to other Jews often would have done so with Hebrew contracts, few of which survive.[103]

The evidence we do have portrays Catalan urban real estate markets as bringing together Christians and Jews in a variety of configurations. Jews participated in the purchase, sale, and exploitation of urban and rural real estate holdings, and property flowed freely between Jewish and Christian hands.[104] As members of a relatively small minority community, Jewish property owners expected to sell or rent to Christians, and Jews seeking to purchase or lease property looked toward Christian sellers and landlords. Nor, apparently, were Christians unwilling to do business with Jews, especially not during the period between 1250 and 1348, when Jewish-Christian relations were relatively stable. In both Barcelona and Girona, about two-thirds of Jewish real estate contracts involved Christian transacting partners.[105] Even more dramatically, Jews interacted with Christians in forty-five of the forty-six Jewish real estate contracts from Vic (97.8 percent). The real proportion of intra-Jewish transactions was almost certainly higher; nevertheless, the substantial number of interreligious real estate contracts remains striking evidence of the regular transfer of property between Jews and Christians.

Most Catalan cities with Jewish communities had a Jewish quarter, known in Catalan as a *call*. Although Jews could legally live outside the *call*, many preferred to take advantage of the easy access it provided to synagogues, kosher butchers, and other communal institutions.[106] Jewish quarters could also provide a modicum of protection; the walls of Girona's Jewish quarter protected its inhabitants from Christian harassment and attacks during Holy Week, an annual issue in the early fourteenth century.[107] However, Jewish quarters never remained entirely closed, and Jews were never completely segregated. Some urban Catalan Jews lived in predominantly Christian neighborhoods, while Christians sometimes chose to live within the principally Jewish *call*.[108] In 1307, Reina, wife of Asser Toros of Barcelona, sold houses in the *call* of Barcelona to Bernat des Cases, a Christian.[109] Despite the intermingling of Jewish and Christian homes, the *call* remained a Jewish space, and some Christians who owned property in the *call* may have preferred to sell or rent it to Jews. Bonanat de Puig, a Christian who owned a house in the *call* of Girona, sold it to a Jewish couple in 1311.[110]

The particularly high rate of interreligious real estate contracts in Vic probably stems from the fact that the city lacked a defined Jewish quarter until the mid-fourteenth century.[111] As a result, no neighborhood became sufficiently Jewish in character to either disproportionately attract Jewish buyers or discourage Christian inhabitants. Moreover, as the Jews of Vic were relatively recent arrivals to the city, fewer Jews owned local property there than in longer-standing communities like Barcelona and Girona. Jews bought or leased property from Christian owners in forty of forty-five interreligious real estate contracts (88.9 percent).

Christian buyers of Jewish-owned property expected the wives, daughters, and sisters of male property sellers to formally relinquish their rights, and they expected them to do so in terminology comprehensible in Christian courts. As discussed in the case study above, Astrugona, sister of Issach and Abraham de Tolosa, swore that she would not seek to invalidate the sale made by her brothers "on account of my inheritance, paternal or maternal, or as successor of my late brother Saltell, or for any other reason."[112] Her renunciation of inheritance claims was identical to those of Christian potential heiresses, whose example provided the model by which the Christian buyers understood her inheritance claims.

Jewish wives, who had different types of property claims under Jewish and Roman law, renounced their rights in hybrid formularies that referred to both legal systems. When Preciosa, wife of Salves Astrug of Girona, sold half of a *hospicium* alongside her husband and son in 1324, she renounced the benefit of the Velleian senatus consult, her rights of lien on account of her dowry and dower, and rights held under Jewish law.[113] Other women did not refer to specific categories of rights but broadly agreed not to contest the sale on the basis of claims derived from either legal system. In both cases, Jewish property sellers acted in accordance with concepts of women's property rights derived from Christian legal culture.

Occasionally, Jews who purchased property from one another acted in accordance with Christian practices that affirmed the theoretical claims of women. When Jewish buyers drew up Latin contracts to record a purchase, they expected Jewish sellers to adhere to Roman legal formularies for nullifying the claims of wives. Cruxia, wife of Bonjueu Vidal, a Jew of Barcelona, renounced the Velleian senatus consult when her husband sold property to Jewish buyers.[114] Even when buying and selling property amongst themselves, the Jews of Barcelona would have remained very aware of the interreligious nature of the real estate market. If Bonjueu's Jewish buyers wanted to resell the property to Christians, they would want to be able to present Latin contracts that raised no questions about their ownership of the property.

Jewish women experienced no direct legal obstacle, under either Catalan or Jewish law, to owning and managing property. However, the ways in which Jewish law circumscribed daughters' inheritance rights left very few Jewish women heiresses in control of real estate holdings. Jewish brides received cash dowries in all extant Catalan dowry contracts, both Hebrew and Latin.[115] Responsa indicate that some Jewish brides did bring dowries including real estate. Elka Klein found only a few examples of Jewish brothers and sisters who co-owned property, and her studies of Hebrew and Latinate Jewish wills suggest that daughters with brothers rarely inherited real estate holdings.[116] My own research has yielded only two cases, one from Girona and one from Barcelona, in which Jewish brothers and sisters jointly inherited real estate.[117]

Even when Jewish women did own property, they may have faced more legal and social obstacles in managing it than Christian women. A responsum of Yom Tov ben Avraham Ishbili suggests that husbands, at least in theory, remained in firm control of their wives' dotal property; a husband could use, improve, or damage these holdings with no meaningful intervention from the ostensible owner.[118] Jewish women relied more heavily than their Christian counterparts on male agents, not only to transfer corporeal possession, but even to negotiate sale and rental agreements in the notary's office. Notarial culture, the province of Christian men, doubly marginalized Jewish women, both as women and as Jews.[119] Many Jewish women may have sought to avoid public activity in the notary's office when possible. As a result, while most Christian women sellers and lessors of property dealt with financial arrangements in person and concluded contracts in the office of the notary, Jewish women more often remained at a physical remove when negotiating sales and collecting rents or purchase prices.

The need to travel in order to manage distant inherited properties raised additional challenges for Jewish women, who did not ordinarily travel on business.[120] Bonosa, wife of Bonsenyor des Cortal, lived in the town of Vilafranca del Penedès but had inherited houses in the Jewish quarter of Barcelona—about sixty kilometers away—from her late father and brothers.[121] When she collected rents owed on the property in 1349, she was represented by Samuel ça Porta, a Jew of Barcelona, who went before a public notary of Barcelona and received payment from Bonosa's tenant on her behalf. Given the timing, her father and brothers may have died unexpectedly in the Black Death, which reached Barcelona in May 1348, or in the subsequent massacres of many members of Barcelona's Jewish community.[122] Bonosa may have felt unprepared to engage in regular travel to manage properties that she (as a daughter with two brothers) had never expected to inherit.

Distance also posed challenges for Bonadona, daughter of Bramon de Torroella of Girona, who inherited both outstanding loans and real property from her late father. Bonadona had married a Jew of Mallorca, Vidal Bonet, and after collecting on a single loan in 1326, she relied on Vidal to manage her inherited resources.[123] Although she arrived in Girona around the time of her father's death, her continued absence after 1327 suggests that she may have returned permanently to Mallorca, leaving her inheritance entirely in her husband's hands. His final act as her agent in the extant notarial registers was to sell, in 1336, the *hospicium* she had inherited from her father in Girona's Jewish quarter.[124]

However, even Jewish women managing local properties sometimes acted through agents rather than appearing in person in the offices of Christian notaries. When Reina, widow of Abraham Cap of Barcelona, sold a *hospicium* in the Jewish quarter of Barcelona in 1328, she acted through agents to sell the property and collect the sale price as well as to transfer corporeal possession.[125] As the transaction required no significant travel, Reina simply may have preferred to avoid public economic activity in a Christian setting.

Jewish women property sellers also demonstrated more caution than Jewish men in obtaining consent from a wide range of family members with potential inheritance claims. Dura, the widow of Samuel Cap with whom this chapter began, sold her vineyard independently but obtained consent not only from her son but also from her agent, Llobell Gracià, who may have been a relative. The 1307 real estate sale made by Reina, wife of Asser Toros, provides an even more extreme example. When Reina sold houses in the Jewish quarter of Barcelona to a Christian buyer in 1307, she obtained consent from her husband, father, brother, sister, and daughters.[126] The consenting parties represent an extensive grouping of Reina's potential heirs.[127] Their involvement in the sale neutralized any future claims they might have over the property, thus securing the purchase claim of Reina's Christian buyer.

In contrast, Jewish men rarely gathered quite such a wide network of kinfolk and claimants when they sold property. In both Barcelona and Girona, Jewish men sold property alone more often than Jewish women. Some men even sold property without obtaining the consent of individuals with seemingly obvious inheritance claims. In 1347, for example, Bonsenyor Malet, a Jew of Barcelona, sold a Christian merchant his share of a vineyard that he co-owned with his brothers.[128] Under prevailing patterns of partible inheritance, his brothers would have expected to incorporate Bonsenyor's share into their own holdings if he died childless.[129] Yet Bonsenyor made no apparent effort to obtain their consent.

Intriguingly, however, Bonsenyor did obtain the consent of his wife, who agreed not to contest the sale on the grounds of her dowry claims. Jewish married couples rarely adopted the Christian practice of obtaining a wife's consent for her husband's cash debt. However, Jewish husbands selling property often involved their wives in real estate sales. In some cases, the couple owned the property jointly, perhaps because they had combined funds drawn from the husband's estate and the wife's assets to purchase it. When Sobredona and her husband Cresques Alfaquim, Jews of Barcelona, sold a vineyard to a Christian buyer in 1281, they acted together when collecting the purchase price. Sobredona alone appended her signature in Latin, although they both signed in Hebrew.[130] Although Cresques acted alone when he appointed an agent to transfer corporeal possession of the property, he once again affirmed in the agency contract that the property belonged to both him and his wife, and that they had sold it jointly.[131]

Other Jewish wives, however, co-sold properties over which they had no apparent ownership claims. Although widows could potentially lay claim to their husbands' real estate holdings in order to collect their dowries, Jewish law did not permit wives to inherit from their husbands.[132] Jewish men seeking to circumvent this prohibition characterized legacies to their wives as "donations" or gifts or even recorded their wishes in Latin, rather than Hebrew, wills.[133] Despite their lack of formal claims, however, some Jewish couples jointly sold properties that probably belonged to husbands' inherited patrimonies. In 1332, Salvat Mosse of Girona and his wife Bonadona jointly sold a rented vineyard to another Jew with the explicit consent of Salvat's parents and other relatives.[134] The involvement of not only Salvat's parents but also more distant kin (probably an aunt and uncle) suggests that the property came from his family. Bonadona's sole claim would have stemmed from her dowry rights.

Similarly, a 1342 contract from Barcelona does not specify the origins of the sold property but implies that it belonged to the Jewish seller as inheritance. Abraham Astrug de Torre of Barcelona and his wife Ferrera sold a *hospicium* located in the Jewish neighborhood of the town of Montalbà.[135] The notary referred to Abraham Astrug as the "son and universal heir" of the late Astrug de Torre of Montalbà. The emphasized inheritance relationship, combined with the location of the property in Abraham's father's hometown, suggests he had inherited the *hospicium* from his father, perhaps quite recently. However, Ferrera not only participated fully in the sale but also renounced any claims over the property on account of her dowry, *sponsalicium*, the "help" (*auxilium*) of the Velleian senatus consult, and any other rights of lien "in the goods or over the goods of my aforementioned husband." By renouncing these claims, all standard in Christian notarial culture, Ferrera implies that she had them in the first place—even though under Jewish law, she would have had difficulty laying any claim to property her husband had inherited from his father unless he had specifically obligated it for her dowry.

Several Jewish property sellers adopted the Christian practice of obtaining the formalized written consent of their daughters and sisters, who under Jewish law had no right to challenge the sale of family property. In 1253, Reina, wife of Bonastrug Bonissach of Vic, her sons Bonmacip and Bonissach, and her daughter Dolça consented to a real estate sale made by her husband. The children attested that they had reached the age of majority and renounced all claims over their father's property.[136] Dolça behaved differently from her brothers only in that she, like her mother, renounced the Velleian senatus consult. The contract implies that she and her brothers enjoyed equal inheritance claims. In a 1305 sale contract from Barcelona, the Jewish property seller, Bondia Zarch, obtained the consent of his married daughter Preciosa as well as his son Zarch Bondia, despite the fact that Preciosa had already received her dowry and could make no further claims under Jewish law while her brother lived.[137]

Some Jews specified that they sought Latin notarial contracts for intra-Jewish property transactions precisely for the sake of clarity if they needed to prove their ownership to Christians. In 1329, Fabib Maimó, a Jew of Barcelona, granted his son Maimó Fabib a *hospicium* in Barcelona with a Latin notarial contract. He explained that although he had already accomplished the grant with a Hebrew writ (*ebraicum instrumentum*), "because at some point you might need to transact or deal with Christians and they would wish to see the title by which you hold the land, and it is difficult for you to show them the title which you have in the form of a Hebrew contract, you asked me, in order to avoid such difficulty regarding this donation, to make for you a Latin public instrument."[138] If Maimó ever needed to sell the property to a Christian, he did not want to risk the particular challenges of proving his ownership with only a Hebrew contract. Similarly, Jews who had purchased property from other Jews would want to avoid trying to prove their ownership with a contract that had failed to legally nullify other claims on the property. Potential concerns about future transactions with Christians thus led some Jews to adhere to Christian practices even when selling property within the Jewish community. As a result, the real estate market created a space for Jewish women that looked much like the role carved out for their Christian counterparts.

Conclusions

The real estate market provided opportunities for both Jewish and Christian women. Women enjoyed some property rights under both legal systems, although Jewish law limited women's inheritance rights, and fewer Jewish women may have owned property independently. Christian custom allowed women to exercise their theoretical claims to real property owned by their husbands, fathers, and brothers; they regularly participated in real estate sales on the grounds of their dowry and inheritance claims. Undoubtedly some women only consented in a purely formulaic sense, providing uncritical assent to men's transactions; we cannot assume that girls (or boys) in their early teens made reasoned determinations about whether to consent to their fathers' real estate sales. However, evidence from court cases suggests that many women were deeply aware of and invested in the financial solvency of their households and would have taken seriously the question of whether to alienate family-owned real property.

Although Jewish law permitted women to own property, rabbinic authorities remained unwilling to grant women joint ownership with their husbands, fathers, and brothers, cutting off an avenue that granted Christian women authority over family-owned real estate. Jewish daughters could not lay claim to specific pieces of property nor contest their sale on the grounds of their limited inheritance rights. Widows could recover alienated property if their husbands' estates proved insufficient to repay their dowries, but even when they purchased property jointly with their husbands, rabbis like ibn Adret and his student Ishbili did not necessarily respect their shared ownership claims. However, the interreligious real estate markets of Catalan cities allowed Jewish women to become more involved in the real estate transactions of their husbands and male relatives. Although Jews might willingly purchase property without the consent of the owner's wife or children, Christian buyers proved more reluctant to do so. Unfamiliar with the content of Jewish law, they certainly would not have trusted Jewish families' attempts to deny women's theoretical property rights.

Catalan Jewish communities used the sphere of family law, including women's property rights, to resist acculturation. Jewish families maintained distinctive marriage and inheritance customs, which restricted wives' and daughters' access to financial resources more strictly than contemporary Catalan Christian practice. However, this posture of principled resistance proved more difficult to maintain in the face of pragmatic economic challenges. Local Christians were unconcerned with the question of whether Jewish daughters inherited equally with their brothers or whether Jewish wives could recover dowries from still-living husbands. But if they were investing in real estate, they wanted assurance that Jewish sellers could not overturn the sale. In practice, if not in theory, Jewish women gained somewhat greater rights over family-owned real property, albeit only as part of an effort to reassure Christian buyers. Overall, however, they remained at a disadvantage relative to their Christian counterparts.

7

CREDIT, CHANGE, AND CRISIS IN CATALAN JEWISH COMMUNITIES

On November 11, 1293, Reina, daughter of Bonmacip of Vic, loaned 60 sous to Agnès, widow of Pere de Puig Carbó of Sant Quirze de Muntanyola and her son Bernat, due to be repaid at the end of August.[1] With this loan, Reina began a successful seventeen-year career as a moneylender, which continued through her marriage to her second husband. What circumstances allowed Reina to embark on a successful career in the credit industry as a married woman, while most Catalan Jewish women worked as creditors only in widowhood or not at all?

Reina belonged to a family and a local Jewish community that encouraged women to contribute economically to their households by working as moneylenders. Her mother, also named Reina, worked occasionally as an independent creditor while still married.[2] Although the elder Reina was never as successful as her husband, who was one of Vic's leading creditors, her public work in the credit market would nevertheless have been unusual in most other Catalan cities. Both mother and daughter followed the example set by the previous generation. Bonmacip's parents, Bonastrug Bonissach and Reina Cabrida, both worked in credit, while his maternal aunt Goig, wife of David Canviador, dominated Vic's Jewish credit market in the mid-thirteenth century.[3] The choices made by Reina Cabrida's and Goig's generation—the founders of Vic's fledgling *aljama*—continued to shape their community for decades.[4] Until the 1330s, the Jewish women of Vic played a far more prominent role in their local credit market than Jewish women of any other city or town.

This chapter seeks to explain two anomalies in the pattern of Jewish women's work in the credit markets of medieval Catalan cities. Jewish women in Girona and Barcelona extended only about 2 percent of Jewish loans before 1348; Jewish women in Vic extended 3.5 percent of Jewish loans between 1330 and 1350. These findings conform to our expectations for Jewish women's moneylending in Catalonia and southern France. However, the notarial evidence from Barcelona, Girona, and Vic reveals two glaring exceptions to the norm. Between 1250 and 1330, the Jewish women of Vic played a more substantial role in credit than in any other city in the region; women extended 15 percent of Jewish loans over the course of these eighty years, including a staggering 38 percent of loans in the 1260s. What made this small Jewish community, populated with settlers from cities across Catalonia, develop such a distinct approach to women's work—and what made them abandon this approach around 1330?

Nearly two decades later, when the last of Vic's Jewish women moneylenders had ended their careers in the credit market, Jewish women in both Barcelona and Girona suddenly (and briefly) became more visibly active as creditors than ever before. Between 1348 and 1350, Jewish women's share of the credit market in Barcelona and Girona leapt from around 2 percent to 20 and 10 percent, respectively, of all Jewish loans. Why did the labor expectations for Jewish women change so dramatically in the wake of the Black Death—and why did those women so quickly exit the credit market in the 1350s?

These two cases differed in many ways. The unusual pattern in Vic was sustained over decades, while in Barcelona and Girona, women's new prominence in credit lasted only a few years. Moreover, the change in Barcelona and Girona coincides with a major moment of communal crisis—the Black Death—whereas the Vic anomaly appears in the context of the slow but steady growth of a small yet flourishing community. I argue that both, however, represented local, intracommunal responses to change and crisis. In Vic, the challenges of establishing a new community led families to adapt by embracing alternative models of women's work; women's role in credit declined as the community became a stable fixture of the city. In Barcelona and Girona, the demographic and social crisis wrought by the Black Death briefly required Jewish women, mostly widows, to work in credit to support their families; as their children grew older or they remarried, many of these widows ceased working as moneylenders.

Although both cases clearly represent anomalies in the general pattern, the reasons behind these exceptions enrich our understanding of the cultural and legal norms that governed most Jewish communities most of the time. At the same time, careful consideration of the Jewish women who did work in credit adds nuance to our wider portrait of Jewish women's work. The challenges of living as a minority community often encouraged Jewish families to adhere closely to local halakhic restrictions on women's control of assets but could also, on occasion, require flexibility.

The Jewish Women Creditors of Vic: A Golden Age

Reina, daughter of Bonmacip of Vic, built a career unimaginable for most Catalan Jewish women. Individual circumstances, as well as the preferences of her family and community, made it possible for Reina to enjoy such success as a creditor. Around 1282, Reina married Jucef Darahi and moved to his home city of Barcelona.[5] By 1288, the marriage was failing. In June of that year, Reina and Bonmacip appointed agents to prosecute a lawsuit against Reina's father-in-law, Issach Darahi.[6] Two months later, Bonmacip appointed agents to evict tenants, installed by Reina and Jucef, from houses he owned in the *call* of Barcelona.[7] These two contracts hint at prolonged efforts to untangle the social and financial relationship marriage had created between Reina and Jucef. The notary who recorded the two agency contracts remained silent on the reasons why Reina and her father had soured on the marriage. They may have been concerned about the security of Reina's assets; Jucef had a serious enough gambling habit that in 1285, Issach petitioned the king for permission to control his son's estate.[8]

After her divorce, Reina returned home to Vic and began to support herself through work in moneylending. She made her first loan five years after her marital troubles began in 1288; the delay could indicate that she and her father had trouble securing her divorce, recovering her dowry, or both—relatively common problems.[9] Once she recovered her dowry from her ex-husband, Reina maintained control over financial resources both as a single divorcée and after her remarriage in 1294. As her parents' only child and expected universal heiress, Reina certainly would have brought her husband a substantial dowry and might have held extradotal assets as well.[10] However, wealth alone did not enable Jewish women—especially married Jewish women—to manage their assets independently.

Reina must have enjoyed the support of her father, who had no apparent qualms about either his wife's or his daughter's work as a creditor. It is tempting to wonder whether her remarriage was contingent on receiving such encouragement from her husband; Astrug Caravida certainly did

TABLE 13 Jewish women's independent loans by decade in Vic, 1250–1350

Decade	Jewish loans to Christians	Loans extended by Jewish women	% loans extended by Jewish women
1250–1260	107	29	27%
1261–1270	129	49	38.0%
1271–1280	152	35	23.0%
1281–1290	230	25	10.9%
1291–1300	336	30	8.9%
1301–1310	113	12	10.6%
1311–1320	715	96	13.4%
1321–1330	337	45	13.4%
1331–1340	282	14	5.0%
1341–1350	262	5	1.9%
	2,663	340	12.8%

not prevent his wife from continuing her work. The marriage made sense for both families: Bonmacip was among the leading members of the Jewish community of Vic, while Astrug belonged to to a wealthy and politically connected family from the larger city of Girona.[11] Marriage allowed Astrug to build connections in an expanding market and linked Bonmacip back to the wealthier Jewish community from which his parents had emigrated.[12] There is no reason to think Reina's status as a divorcée carried any significant stigma.[13]

Personal factors remain in the realm of speculation, but it is possible that Astrug valued his new wife's financial acumen and expertise. Reina might have appreciated Astrug's willingness to move to Vic; she would not have to relocate to another community with a much less encouraging attitude toward married women working outside the home. For his part, Astrug appears to have adjusted quickly to life in Vic. He had moved from Girona either for his marriage or shortly beforehand; only a few months later, in January 1295, he had begun to describe himself as a "Jew of Vic," a phrase that emphasizes his integration into his new city of residence.[14]

Reina and her parents might also have appreciated that Astrug showed no inclination to discourage his wife from working in credit. The couple maintained distinct lending businesses through the first decade of the 1300s, with Reina contributing nearly 40 percent of their household's income from

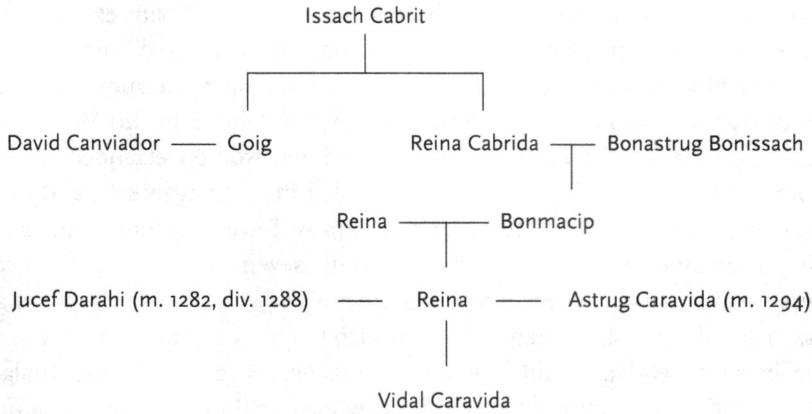

FIG. 5. Family tree of Reina, daughter of Bonmacip of Vic.

moneylending.[15] For over a year after her marriage, Reina styled herself as "Reina, daughter of Bonmacip," perhaps to associate herself with her father's prolific and well-established lending business rather than her husband's much newer enterprise.[16] She, or the notaries, transitioned into using her husband's name only after he had established his own business.

Individual circumstances must have been crucial to Reina's success: support from her father and husband; perhaps also personal ambitions or qualities omitted from the sparse lines of Reina's loan contracts. Community, however, appears as the defining factor: there is no woman like Reina in either Barcelona or Girona, where the few Jewish women creditors entered the market only in widowhood. In Vic, Reina shared her experience of working as a creditor with many other women in the city's Jewish community, including both married women and widows, within her family and beyond it.

The numbers from the *libri iudeorum* of Vic almost speak for themselves. As table 13 demonstrates, in the 1260s, when Vic's Jewish community was still in its infancy, women extended a staggering 38 percent of Jewish loans.[17] Over the course of the ensuing decades, Jewish women's level of activity in Vic declined but remained high for the region: Jewish women extended nearly a quarter of Jewish loans in the 1270s, and about 12 percent of loans made between 1281 and 1330. Only in the 1330s did the Jewish women of Vic start to look more like their counterparts in neighboring Jewish communities; between 1330 and 1350, women extended an average of only 3.5 percent of Jewish loans. Even this low rate, however, remained higher than the rate of women's lending in Barcelona or Girona for most of the period under study, although it is comparable to the proportion of loans extended by Jewish women in thirteenth-century Perpignan and Castelló d'Empúries.[18]

Individual women creditors in Vic aspired to longer and more successful careers than those open to Jewish women elsewhere in the Mediterranean. Between 1250 and 1350, twenty individual women extended ten or more loans; thirteen of these women extended more than twenty, and four extended eighty or more. Moreover, while most Jewish women lenders in Girona remained active for less than a decade, seven women in Vic had careers lasting over twenty years, while another eight worked as creditors for at least a decade. Jewish women in Vic had such lengthy careers in part because they began to work as creditors while still married, whereas in most Catalan cities Jewish women almost never publicly worked in the credit market before widowhood.[19] Married women thrived in Vic's credit market, where they extended over two-thirds of Jewish women's loans (see table 14).

The unusual story of the Jewish women creditors of Vic begins with the community's foundation in the mid-thirteenth century. Jews began to settle in Vic at a moment of economic growth, probably at least in part to take advantage of increasing local demand for Jewish credit.[20] The men who belonged to the community's founding families did not necessarily intend to work as full-time lenders; Jews in the Iberian Peninsula and beyond worked in a wide range of sectors besides credit, and many Jews either never extended loans at all or did so only occasionally to supplement their incomes.[21] The local demand for Jewish credit—and the lack of interest in moneylending among some of the men who shaped this new community—may have led Vic's founding families to pioneer an unusual division of labor for Catalan Jewish families.

Goig, wife of David Canviador, played a crucial role in setting the tone for the Jewish women of her new home for years to come. Around 1250, Goig and David had relocated to Vic from Girona along with Goig's sister, Reina Cabrida, and Reina's husband Bonastrug Bonissach.[22] David, who (based on his last name) probably worked as a moneychanger, rarely extended consumption loans to the Christians of Vic.[23] Goig, meanwhile, dominated the credit market through much of the latter half of the thirteenth century. In the 1250s, she extended more loans than any other Jewish creditor, and she remained a major player in the credit industry through the early 1280s.[24]

The example set by Goig and David remained influential in her immediate family, and the collective memory of these founding members may have inspired the Jewish community of Vic to preserve the distinct culture surrounding Jewish women's work that began with them. Goig's daughters never played a major role in the credit industry, but the wives of her sons and

TABLE 14 Jewish women's independent loans by marital status in Vic, 1250–1350

Decade	Widows	Wives	Unknown	Total
1250–1260	1	26	2	29
1261–1270	70	54	6	130
1271–1280	36	59	6	101
1281–1290	19	58	10	87
1291–1300	3	64	11	78
1301–1310	32	49	13	94
1311–1320	43	136	11	190
1321–1330	21	68	2	91
1331–1340	5	110	3	118
1341–1350	4	2	0	6
Total	234	626	64	924

grandsons worked as creditors, albeit less successful ones than the family matriarch.[25] The choices made by two generations of her family over a period of nearly seventy years to foster women's work as creditors suggests Goig's influence ran deep in her immediate family. In a small community, the model provided by these leading families may have helped shape men's and women's expectations about how women could contribute to their households through their labor.

The Jewish women creditors of Vic needed capital to make loans; their authority over financial resources probably stemmed not from vast stores of extradotal wealth but from an alternative understanding of wives' control over a shared conjugal estate. Although women rarely extended loans alongside their husbands, married couples would act together to collect on loans.[26] In most cases where married couples jointly released debtors from further obligations, both husband and wife worked independently as moneylenders. For example, both Astrug Jucef and his wife Tolsana were major players in Vic's credit market from about 1310 to 1333. Tolsana only once extended a loan alongside her husband, in 1309, prior to establishing her own impressive career.[27] However, on four separate occasions, Astrug and Tolsana together released Christian borrowers from all debts owed to the couple.[28] These joint repayment contracts hint at a commercial partnership between husbands and wives, in which both extended loans out of a shared conjugal fund.[29] Although several extant contracts demonstrate that Tolsana and her family worked diligently to ensure the security of her dowry, *ketubah*, and *tosefet ketubah*, none refers to extradotal assets.[30] At least some of the Jewish women lenders of Vic may have drawn on a shared conjugal estate when making independent loans.

Scholars of medieval Iberia have suggested that communities in frontier zones developed creative legal solutions in response to the unique challenges of attracting settlers—including generous terms for women.[31] Heath Dillard argued that women in Castile benefited from efforts to bring women as well as men into new settlements. Castilian *fueros* granted women extensive property rights by treating marriage as an egalitarian "society of acquisitions," one in which the wife was a "full partner in supporting the couple and brightening their economic future."[32] Vic in the 1260s had long since ceased to be part of a Christian frontier zone, and legal and ecclesiastical culture had stabilized as a result.[33] For Vic's new Jewish community, however, this Catalan town represented a new frontier for Jewish settlement. The Jews of Vic worked to establish an economically stable community amid battles over jurisdictional authority, as the bishop and the Montcada viscount clashed over control of the Jewish community of Vic and the *collectas* of Barcelona and Girona both fought to absorb the new *aljama* of Vic.[34] Such challenges undoubtedly required a flexible approach; the particular choices made by the Jewish community of Vic may have been facilitated by the fact that the city never became a center of rabbinic culture. Although Jews in Vic must have sought rabbinic guidance on thorny problems, they might have been less influenced by unsolicited rabbinic advice than their counterparts in Girona and Barcelona.

However, the unique opportunities enjoyed by the Jewish women creditors of Vic proved short-lived. Women's share of the credit market began to decline by the end of the thirteenth century. As the fourteenth century wore on, the Jewish women of Vic came to look much like their counterparts in neighboring Barcelona and Girona: between 1340 and 1350, they extended less than 2 percent of Jewish loans, and for the first time, widows outnumbered wives in the credit market. Although two of Vic's most successful women lenders—Tolsana, wife of Astrug Jucef, and Goig, wife of Salomó Vidal—continued working into the 1330s, no new Jewish women creditors rose to prominence after 1320. Demographic growth and increased stability, as well as the arrival of more and more Jews from communities with less flexible attitudes toward women's control over financial resources and public work as creditors, contributed to the narrowing of opportunities for Jewish women creditors.[35] While communal change and transformation created space for Jewish women to play an expanded role in the management of conjugal property, communal stability reinstilled gendered norms.

Barcelona and Girona After the Black Death: Communities in Crisis

While the Jewish women of Vic came to look more like their counterparts elsewhere in Catalonia, the Jewish women of Barcelona and Girona experienced a sudden yet brief transformation in their social and economic lives. Prior to 1348, only a few sparse references briefly illuminate the work performed by the Jewish women of Barcelona, few of whom appear more than once in the surviving documentation. Yet in the wake of the Black Death, Jewish women suddenly populate the pages of the few registers specializing in Jewish transactions. Although the Barcelona notariate did not formally relegate Jewish transactions to designated registers, certain notaries, such as Bonanat Rimentol, evidently cultivated a largely Jewish clientele.[36] Rimentol's registers, combined with scattered Jewish loan contracts found in other notarial documentation dating from 1348 to 1350, demonstrate that Jewish women's involvement in Barcelona's credit market suddenly skyrocketed as the city and its Jewish community confronted plague and violence. Whereas before 1348, women had extended only 2 percent of Jewish loans, women extended 20 percent of Jewish loans between 1348 and 1350 (see table 15). Girona saw an almost equally dramatic transformation: women extended 10 percent of Jewish loans between 1348 and 1350, compared to about 2 percent before the arrival of the Black Death. Jewish women also collected on old loans in quitclaim contracts at unprecedented rates.

The crisis of the Black Death transformed the lives of both Christians and Jews across Catalonia. The plague reached Barcelona by March 1348, traveling on ships from either Rosselló or Mallorca, and by the beginning of May it had taken enough of a toll to inspire a response in the form of religious processions. Girona saw the arrival of plague in early May, probably also from Rosselló.[37] Within a year, approximately 60 percent of the population of Barcelona and 40 percent of the population of Girona had succumbed to plague.[38]

TABLE 15 Jewish women's loans in Barcelona and Girona, May 1348–December 1350

	Barcelona	Girona
Jewish new loans to Christians		
Total no. of loans	154	86
Women's loans	31 (20.1%)	9 (10.5%)
Mixed loans	0 (0%)	1 (1.2%)
Jewish quitclaims to Christians		
Total no. of quitclaims	54	111
Women's quitclaims	16 (29.6%)	20 (18%)
Mixed quitclaims	0 (0%)	5 (4.5%)

Continued social conflicts and crises wrought demographic and economic challenges in Catalonia in general, and Barcelona in particular, through the rest of the fourteenth and the fifteenth centuries.[39] Several Catalan Jewish communities—including that of Barcelona—experienced the most serious threat thus far to their physical safety and security. Christians, fearing that the plague was either a divine punishment for Jewish sin or the deliberate result of Jewish malice, attacked and murdered Jews.[40] While the Jews of Barcelona confronted a serious threat to their survival, the Jews of Girona faced ritual attacks on the *call* and isolated murders, albeit not a large-scale massacre.[41]

The Black Death and the subsequent persecutions must have taken a serious demographic toll on the Jewish communities of Barcelona and Girona. Such drastic losses concentrated property in fewer hands, leaving individual survivors in control of far more wealth than previous generations. The sudden proliferation of Jewish women creditors in Barcelona and Girona suggests that the Black Death and the subsequent massacres of Jews may have left an unusual number of young widows, many of whom were either childless or mothers to very young children.[42] In Vic, intriguingly, the decline of Jewish women's moneylending continued unabated during and after the Black Death. There is no direct evidence that the Jews of Vic faced attacks during the plague; the combination of pandemic and massacre may have been crucial in creating the circumstances that required Jewish widows to take greater control over finances.

Under normal circumstances, Jewish widows were rarely tasked with the responsibility of publicly managing household wealth. Many Jewish widows, especially those with adult sons, probably refrained from collecting their dowries in exchange for maintenance from their husbands' heirs.[43] After the Black Death, however, high mortality rates left widows with few options other than to manage their late husbands' estates—and Jewish families and communities with little alternative but to promote Jewish widows' economic self-sufficiency, at least temporarily.

Whereas the Jewish women creditors of Vic carved out an economic niche for themselves rooted in a distinct understanding of women's role in managing the conjugal estate, those in Barcelona and Girona maneuvered within a more typical set of labor expectations for Jewish women. Widows still extended most of women's loans; in many cases, women probably took on a more prominent role in credit only because their families had no other adult members.[44] However, Jewish widows in this period selectively appealed to Christian law in new ways to justify their authority over their late husbands' estates. Christian widows could claim the right of *tenuta*, which allowed them to administer their late husbands' property on account of the debt of their dowries and *sponsalicia*.[45] Prior to 1348, Jewish widows did not claim this customary right in notarial documentation. In post-plague Barcelona, however, several women explicitly identified themselves as holding their late husbands' property in accordance with Barcelona's customary law.[46] Local rabbis seemingly refrained from critiquing this practice in responsa; their silence could indicate either ignorance of the practice or a pragmatic recognition of the immediate and unusual need for widows to control their late husbands' property for the good of their families and the Jewish community.

Although an unusual number of Jewish widows shouldered new labor responsibilities as creditors in the wake of the Black Death, these women never achieved the levels of success open to the male lenders who still lived and worked alongside them. Jewish men and women extended loans of similar size, probably in response to general demand from Christians seeking credit.[47] However, individual women lenders extended far fewer loans than men of comparable stature, and as a result, they had less valuable lending practices. Between 1348 and 1350, nine Jewish women in Barcelona made two or more loans. The most active of these women—Dura, widow of Bonjueu Issach de Bellcaire—extended only five. Even among the subset of women who made two or more loans, the average woman lender extended only three. During the same two-year period, fifteen Jewish men extended two or more loans, and the most successful—Issach Bonjueu de Bellcaire, probably Dura's stepson—extended twenty-three.[48] If we eliminate lenders who only extended a single loan, Jewish male creditors on average made seven loans during this period—more than twice the number of loans extended by an average woman lender. In Girona, only one Jewish woman—Bonafilla, widow of Cresques Jucef—extended more than one new loan between 1348 and 1350, whereas twelve Jewish men extended multiple loans in the same period.[49] Bonafilla extended only five loans during this period, whereas the most successful male lender—Bonjueu Cresques—made thirteen new loans.

Because they extended fewer total loans, Jewish women's businesses remained far less profitable than those built by Jewish men. Whereas Issach Bonjueu de Bellcaire loaned out a total of 3,361 sous between 1348 and 1350, his stepmother Dura lent 1,094 sous, less than a third as much. In Girona, Bonafilla, widow of Cresques Jucef, loaned 923 sous between 1348 and 1350; her competitor Bonjueu Cresques loaned 5,700 sous. Although the surviving documentation illuminates only a small fraction of the total business generated by these Jewish lenders, there is no reason to suspect that additional documentation would dramatically alter the overall picture. In the wake of the Black Death, Jewish women played a more prominent role in the credit markets of Barcelona and Girona than ever before but still could not maintain lending businesses comparable to those of successful men of their own faith and socioeconomic status.

Communal crisis left the Jewish widows of Barcelona and Girona in control of significant assets and with the responsibility to profitably manage them. However, sudden need could not erase decades of cultural pressures that dissuaded Jewish women from independently managing financial resources and, in particular, from relying on the services of Christian notaries. Anna Rich Abad presents the women creditors working in fourteenth-century Barcelona as having entered the credit market with enthusiasm and economic savvy.[50] However, some Jewish widows may have hesitated to work in areas that would require regular interaction with Christian notaries.[51] Elka Klein, similarly, has argued that Jewish women in thirteenth-century Catalonia selectively relied on husbands and male relatives to avoid public appearances in both Jewish and Christian courts.[52]

The patterns of women's lending in post-plague Barcelona and Girona suggest that Jewish women either hesitated to embrace their new economic role, working in credit only out of necessity, or that family pressures soon reasserted themselves to limit women's engagement in public economic life. The small number of loans extended by individual women meant that despite playing a more prominent role as creditors than ever before, Jewish women still refrained from regular work that required them to interact with Christian men, including both their clients and the notaries. When women collected on loans extended by their late husbands or family members, they often acted through appointed agents rather than going in person to the notary.[53] Some women never collected on a loan independently, despite going to the notaries with some regularity.[54]

Other women made choices, either of their own volition or under pressure, that ended their work in credit shortly after it began. Bonadona, widow of Samuel de Piera, collected on several old loans and extended new ones in the first two weeks of April 1349.[55] Her late husband had worked as a lender, and his death—probably from plague or in the subsequent massacres—left Bonadona in charge of the family business.[56] Overall, she demonstrated herself capable of both pursuing debts and of justifying her rights; although she served as guardian of her minor son Bondia, when collecting loans she emphasized her claims on the basis of her uncollected dowry, in accordance with Christian custom.[57] The Christian notary, her late husband's Christian debtor, and the Christian witness to the contract might not even have realized that her actions lacked justification under Jewish law. Intriguingly, the second witness was not only one of Bonadona's coreligionists but also a member of her family: her brother-in-law, Issach de Piera. Issach presumably would have been aware of the halakhic norms surrounding widows' authority (or lack thereof) over their late husbands' estates. However, he apparently recognized that desperate times called for desperate measures, and that supporting Bonadona's control over his late brother's assets was the best way to preserve the estate during this moment of crisis.

Christian women in similar positions spent years working as the financial caretakers of their late husbands' estates. Bonadona's contemporary Francesca, widow of the jurist Francesc d'Alda of Vic, began to manage Francesc's assets after he died in early 1346, and she remained active through late 1349.[58] Bonadona, in contrast, disappeared from the record soon after her brief flurry of activity in April. When she resurfaced on June 30, it was to remarry; she transferred 5,000 sous' worth of debts to her new husband, Astrug Vidal Biona, in payment for her dowry.[59] Bonadona's marriage marked the end of her credit activities as well as the end of her guardianship over her son, which went to her brother-in-law Issach.[60] She remained absent from the registers until October 1351, when, as her husband's agent, she collected on a loan ceded to her husband by Issach. Bonadona's involvement might indicate that the ceded debt was linked to her dowry.[61] Her second marriage would end tragically, leaving Bonadona twice widowed; Astrug Vidal Biona was executed for an alleged host desecration in 1367.[62] Once again, Bonadona briefly acted on behalf of her late husband to recover his confiscated goods, perhaps after a postmortem pardon.[63] She did not, however, return to work as a creditor.

Within a few years after the Black Death, the Jewish credit markets of Barcelona and Girona gradually returned to normalcy. Even during the moment of crisis of the late 1340s and early 1350s, many women limited or mediated their work in the notarial credit market, whether by remarrying or relying on agents. Others may have engaged in pawnbroking—away from the male, Christian, public space of the notary's office. After decades, perhaps centuries, of discouraging Jewish women from involvement in credit, few Jewish families saw change as desirable. Some families may have pressured widows to remarry or hand the reins of businesses to sons when they reached their teens. Some widows may have perceived work in the credit market as a hardship, not an opportunity.

Conclusions

Although Jewish women typically played a much more minor public economic role than their Christian counterparts, the smaller size and greater vulnerability of this minority community meant that in moments of change and crisis, Jewish women could take on vastly expanded roles in the credit market. The ability to offer credit was a crucial element of Jewish communities' value to Christian rulers; even new communities and communities in crisis may have felt pressured to meet local demands for loans. During these moments, Jewish women briefly played a role unequalled by Christian women. The changes experienced by Christian women, even in the wake of the crisis of the Black Death, tended to be less drastic. Shona Kelly Wray argued for the overall stability of urban communities during and after the plague; this stability may have placed a lower ceiling on the changes wrought for women who belonged to the Christian majority.[64]

However, Jewish women's prominence in local credit markets proved short-lived. While Vic may be unique among Catalan cities for the opportunities it afforded Jewish women creditors over a period of eighty years, even this community eventually began to resemble those elsewhere in Catalonia. The Jewish community proved particularly responsive to crisis and willing to carve out space for a different kind of women's public economic activity during moments of crisis and change, yet Jewish women would eventually return to levels of economic participation lower than those of their Christian counterparts.

CONCLUSION

Over a year of research in the archives of Barcelona, Girona, and Vic yielded thousands of contracts that together wove a rich tapestry of women's work in medieval Catalan cities. The thrilling volume of contracts provided incontrovertible evidence that women worked within and outside the home—as servants and wet nurses, as silkweavers and leatherworkers. Women worked as managers of household assets; as creditors and debtors; as investors in small businesses and international commercial ventures; as lessors, lessees, buyers, and sellers of real property both within and beyond city walls. Christian women played a visible role in all these sectors of urban economic life; Jewish women worked in most of them, although credit contracts vastly outnumbered other records of their work. However, the extensive evidence of women's work should not obscure the fact that women participated in well under half the contracts that notaries recorded. Women's work mattered, but women never had the same opportunities as those available to men.

The volume of contracts involving Jewish women allows us to recover something of their working lives, but they represent only a tiny fraction of the business recorded by the Jewish community. Outside of Vic and the immediate post-plague years in Barcelona and Girona—all exceptional cases, as shown in my own research and that of other scholars—Jewish women played a minor role in public economic life not only when compared with the men of their own faith community but also when compared with the women of the Christian majority among whom they lived.

The evidence from the notarial registers of Barcelona, Girona, and Vic challenges three common narratives that have shaped scholars' understanding of both Jewish history and women's history in the Iberian Peninsula: the "Golden Age" of the Jewish communities of the Crown of Aragon, the cultural openness of the Jews of Sepharad in comparison with the Jews of Ashkenaz, and the economic disempowerment of women in medieval southern Europe compared to their counterparts further north. The final pages of this book will address how the Jewish and Christian women of Barcelona, Girona, and Vic undermine all three of these assumptions.

Centering the experiences of Jewish women complicates the idea of the late thirteenth and early fourteenth centuries as a Golden Age for Jews in the Crown of Aragon. Yom Tov Assis characterized the period between 1213 and 1327 as a near-idyllic moment in which the social and economic stability and vibrancy of the Crown of Aragon brought similar benefits to the kingdom's Jewish community.[1] During this era, Jews confronted little serious persecution and enjoyed "the most exciting and fruitful cultural and religious experiences in their history."[2] Assis highlights the security brought by royal privileges, the benefits of Jewish self-governance, and the rich rabbinic culture of the region. In a separate volume, he described the same period as an economic Golden Age, in which relatively low rates of taxation and support for Jewish moneylending allowed individual Jews and Jewish communities to flourish financially.[3]

Scholars have since complicated and nuanced the narrative of an Iberian Golden Age followed by decline. Jonathan Ray and Mark Meyerson have both emphasized that economic opportunity and social integration in this period coexisted alongside active efforts to reinforce boundaries between Jewish and Christian communities, including sporadically enforced laws regulating Jewish dress.[4] Meyerson questioned the historiographical utility of a Golden Age that in some regions proved extremely brief, and he challenged the decline narrative through his analysis of the social and economic resurgence of the Jewish community of Morvedre between 1391 and 1492.[5] However, scholars have not addressed how a gender-based analysis undermines our positive assessment of Jewish life overall in the late thirteenth- and early fourteenth-century Crown of Aragon.

In her work on Jewish self-government in the early modern ghetto of Florence, Stefanie Siegmund argues that the same institutions of self-governance that empowered Jewish communities also entailed "a loss of autonomy to individuals and to some groups of Jews"—particularly Jewish women.[6] Similarly, the primary beneficiaries of the Golden Age in the Crown of Aragon were elite Jewish men. Did the supposed economic Golden Age visibly affect the everyday lives of impoverished Jewish men and women forced to rely on communal charity? Would uneducated Jews—a group that includes most women but also some men—have found meaning in the vitality of rabbinic elite culture? Would Jewish women, who confronted an array of restrictions under Jewish law, have enjoyed this Golden Age of Jewish self-governance as much as the men who empowered themselves as communal officials? Gender and socioeconomic status prevented many members of the Jewish community from experiencing the benefits wrought by this Golden Age. Jewish self-governance in family law—which Assis described as a "source of spiritual strength and comfort"—even left Jewish women less able to support themselves financially, if needed, than their Christian counterparts were, owing to the differences between Jewish and Christian legal constructions of women's access to financial resources.[7]

Jewish efforts to resist acculturation might have increased communal strength and cohesion. Yet such efforts also helped close off avenues through which marginalized and disempowered Jews—particularly women—could pursue their social and economic goals. Elsewhere in the medieval and early modern Mediterranean, Jewish women selectively used non-Jewish courts to achieve more favorable outcomes than they might have found within the community.[8] In the Crown of Aragon, however, court-shopping of this kind was more effectively stifled by the combined efforts of rabbinic authorities and their royal allies, who benefited from semi-autonomous Jewish communities.[9] Communal autonomy, cohesion, and boundary policing maintained not only separation between faith communities but also a gender system designed to keep property in the hands of men.

In the Jewish communities of Catalan cities, rabbinic elites challenged efforts to use Christian legal culture to expand women's control of assets, and most affluent Jewish men and women adhered to halakhic norms that left Jewish daughters, wives, and widows less able to assert authority over financial resources than the Christian women around them. The visible differences between Jewish and Christian working women, and the efforts on the part of rabbis and other members of the Jewish community to maintain those differences, run counter to the traditional narrative that contrasted the acculturated Jews of the Iberian Peninsula with their more insular coreligionists of northern Europe. Yitzhak Baer, a central figure in the construction of this contrast, disparaged Iberian Jews as too concerned with philosophy, Christian politics, wealth, and sex—and therefore willing to embrace Christianity under duress, unlike their northern European counterparts who pursued martyrdom rather than convert.[10] Other scholars have instead praised the Jewish courtiers, poets, philosophers, and physicians of Sepharad for their openness and integration into surrounding Muslim and Christian cultures.[11]

Increasingly, however, scholarship on both Ashkenaz and Sepharad has worked to narrow the supposed gap between these two medieval Jewish communities. Work on the Jews of northern Europe has emphasized interconnections and influences between Jews and Christians, while studies on the Jews of the Iberian Peninsula have underlined efforts to maintain intercommunal boundaries and preserve distinct Jewish identities.[12] Recently, Paola Tartakoff argued for an approach to Jewish conversion that treats the communities of Sepharad and Ashkenaz in tandem, without assuming major differences in their level of acculturation.[13] This book leaves some standard distinctions between Ashkenaz and Sepharad intact—very few Jewish women in Catalonia achieved a level of independent economic success even approaching that enjoyed by some Jewish women in Ashkenaz—but suggests that we continue to revise our assumptions about Jews' integration into Christian culture in the Iberian Peninsula and consider how active efforts to resist acculturation affected ordinary Jewish men and women.

The distinction between the Jewish women of Ashkenaz and Sepharad still stands in this study, but the gap between the Christian women of northern and southern Europe has narrowed considerably. First, it should be noted that this disparity further undermines claims about Jewish acculturation in Sepharad: the Jewish women of Ashkenaz may have resembled their Christian women neighbors more than their counterparts to the south. Second, my research suggests that traditional distinctions that portray Mediterranean women as less economically self-sufficient than women of northern Europe should be revisited. Christian women's work in Barcelona, Girona, and Vic looks much like Christian women's work in London, Paris, and Ghent. Further regional and microregional studies could indicate that local legal and cultural distinctions shaped women's work more than broad macroregional dichotomies.

I conclude this book with a call for future studies that continue to take intersectional approaches to women's history and explore differences among women in the medieval world. As I hope to have demonstrated in these concluding remarks, comparative work on women of different faith communities and socioeconomic strata has the potential to challenge long-held assumptions about not only women's history but also the history of the communities to which they belonged.

Notes

Abbreviations

ACB	Arxiu Capitular de Barcelona
ACF	Arxiu Biblioteca Episcopal de Vic, Arxiu de la Curia Fumada
AHCB	Arxiu Històric de la Ciutat de Barcelona
AHPB	Arxiu Històric de Protocols de Barcelona
AHG	Arxiu Històric de Girona, secció Girona

Introduction

1. Proverbs 31:10–31. "She considers a field . . ." is verse 16.
2. Eiximenis, "Dotzè del Crestià," cap. 563, 81–82; Vinyoles, *Les barcelonines*, 33–35.
3. Christine de Pizan, *Book of the City of Ladies*, 43, 89–90.
4. Bennett, *Ale, Beer, and Brewsters*, 77–97; Farmer, *Surviving Poverty*, 134; Bennett, *History Matters*, 72–79.
5. Howell, *Women, Production, and Patriarchy*, 27–33; Winer, *Women, Wealth, and Community*, 33, 80; Hanawalt, *Wealth of Wives*, 6; Farmer, "Merchant Women"; Comas, Muntaner, and Vinyoles, "Elles no només filaven," 25–31, 36–37; Farmer, *Silk Industries*, 106–36. For an exception to this tendency, see Reyerson, "Women in Business."
6. Stuard, "Burdens of Matrimony," 66–68; Kelleher, *Measure of Woman*, 53–54.
7. Winer, *Women, Wealth, and Community*, 2; Farmer, "Merchant Women," 90.
8. For a useful working definition of women's agency in a medieval context, see Wessell Lightfoot, *Women, Dowries, and Agency*, 6–8.
9. The term "intersectionality" was coined by Kimberlé Crenshaw ("Demarginalizing," 140). For medievalists' use of the term and concept, see Bennett *History Matters*, 142–45; Winer, *Women, Wealth, and Community*, 2–4; Farmer, *Surviving Poverty*, 1, 107; Seal and Sidhu, "Feminist Intersectionality"; Lavezzo, "Antisemitism and Female Power"; Rajabzadeh, "Alisaundre Becket."
10. Klein, "Widow's Portion"; Klein, "Splitting Heirs"; Baumgarten, *Mothers and Children*; Caballero-Navas, "Care

of Women's Health"; Baumgarten, "'A Separate People'?"

11. Castro, *España en su historia*; Cohen, *Under Crescent and Cross.*
12. Nirenberg, *Communities of Violence*; Ray, "Beyond Tolerance and Persecution," 1–18; Meyerson, *Jews in an Iberian Frontier Kingdom*, 57–97; Klein, *Jews, Christian Society, and Royal Power*; Ray, *Sephardic Frontier*, 145–72; Soifer, "Beyond *Convivencia*," 19–35; Safran, *Defining Boundaries*; T. Barton, *Contested Treasure*; Nirenberg, *Neighboring Faiths*; Haskell, *Mystical Resistance*; Soifer Irish, *Jews and Christians.*
13. Shatzmiller, *Shylock Reconsidered*, 104–22.
14. Klein, "Splitting Heirs"; Klein, *Jews, Christian Society, and Royal Power*, 16.
15. Catlos, "Contexto social y 'conveniencia'"; Catlos, *Muslims of Medieval Latin Christendom*, 522–35; Catlos, *Kingdoms of Faith*, 428–30.
16. Nirenberg, *Communities of Violence*, 158–59, 217–21; Ray, "Beyond Tolerance and Persecution," 4–9; Safran, *Defining Boundaries*, 5–9, 18–27.
17. Cuffel, *Gendering Disgust*, 117–55; Haskell, *Mystical Resistance*, 87–97. For a similar phenomenon in Ashkenaz, see Marcus, *Rituals of Childhood*; Baumgarten, *Practicing Piety*, 85–102.
18. Nirenberg, *Communities of Violence*, 141; Furst, "Captivity, Conversion, and Communal Identity,"; S. Barton, *Conquerors, Brides, and Concubines*, 45–75; Safran, *Defining Boundaries*, 128–33, 139–40.
19. Assis, *Golden Age*, 267–68.
20. Jordan, "Jews on Top"; Hoyle, "Bonds That Bind"; Bartlet, *Licoricia of Winchester.*
21. Translated in full with accompanying analysis in both Marcus, "Mothers, Martyrs, and Moneymakers," 40–42, and Baskin, "Dolce of Worms." See also Baskin, "Mobility and Marriage," 233.
22. Schwartzmann, "Gender Concepts of Medieval Thinkers," 195–201; Alfonso, "Medieval Portrayals," 131–48.
23. Lalinde Abadia, *La Corona de Aragón*, 217–18.
24. Baiges i Jardí, "El notariat català," 135–36.
25. Assis, *Golden Age*, 45–46; Bensch, "Baronial Aljama," 24–30; Llop i Jordana, *Vides i veus*, 71–75.
26. Assis, *Golden Age*, 1.
27. Meyerson, *Jews in an Iberian Frontier Kingdom*, 5–45; Meyerson, *Jewish Renaissance*, 65–108.
28. Mell, *Myth of the Medieval Jewish Moneylender*, 1:1–17, 199–208.
29. Gyug, "Effects and Extent of the Black Death"; Guilleré, "La peste noire," 106, 115–22; Benedictow, *Black Death*, 80–81, 279–81; Riera Melis, "Crisis frumentarias y políticas," 144–56; Rodriguez, "Spain," 185–86.
30. Benedictow, *Black Death*, 80–81.
31. Benedictow, *Black Death*, 278–79; Gyug, "Effects and Extent of the Black Death"; Guilleré, "La peste noire," 106, 115–22.
32. Einbinder, *After the Black Death*, 32–56, 88–116.
33. Rodriguez, "Spain," 185–86.
34. Benedictow, *Black Death*, 281; Rodriguez, "Spain," 182; Lopez de Meneses, "Una consecuencia de la peste negra," 97–106; Rich Abad, "Able and Available," 71; Muntané i Santiveri, "Aproximació a les causes de l'avalot"; Einbinder, *After the Black Death*, 117–47.
35. Bennett, *History Matters*, 60–65.
36. Baucells i Reig, *Vivir en la edad media*, 1:69.
37. Bensch, *Barcelona*, 41–44.
38. Ibid., 38.
39. Ibid., 230–32.
40. Ibid., 332–33.
41. Carreras i Candi, "Desenrotllament de la institució notarial," 753–55, 764; Garcia i Sanz, "Precedents, origen, i evolució," 169, 174.
42. Carreras i Candi, "Desenrotllament de la institució notarial," 767; Conde y Delgado de Molina, "Notaries i conflictes entre notaris," 15–17.
43. Klein, *Jews, Christian Society, and Royal Power*, 5.

44. Rich Abad, *La comunitat jueva de Barcelona*, 52–53.
45. Yitzhak Baer estimates the Jewish community at two hundred families: see Baer, *History of the Jews*, 1:194. Kenneth Stow calculated a household coefficient of 3.69 for Jewish families in the Rhineland, and scholars of the Jewish communities of medieval Catalonia have typically adopted this coefficient as well: see Stow, "Jewish Family," 1093; Winer, *Women, Wealth, and Community*, 83; Bensch, "Baronial Aljama," 35, 39n47.
46. Mora, "Un recorregut per la història d'antic call," 90; Rich Abad, *La comunitat jueva de Barcelona*, 53–54.
47. Klein, *Jews, Christian Society, and Royal Power*, 162–67.
48. Guilleré, *Diner, poder, i societat*, 48–49.
49. Ibid., 16–17.
50. Ibid., 19–23, 36.
51. Ibid., 69–70, 153; Ferrer i Juanola and Villar i Torrent, "L'eclosió urbana de Girona," 227–28.
52. Marquès i Planagumà, introduction to *El "Cartoral del Rúbriques Vermelles,"* 75–84.
53. Carreras i Candi, "Desenrotllament de la institució notarial," 754; Baiges i Jardí, "El notariat català," 142; Garcia i Sanz, "Precedents, origen, i evolució," 168.
54. Carreras i Candi, "Desenrotllament de la institució notarial," 760, 767, 769–73; Guilleré, *Diner, poder, i societat*, 221.
55. Baer, *History of the Jews*, 1:194; Planas i Marcé, "Les primeres notícies de jueus a Girona," 203–5; Sagrera and Sureda, "Comunitat jueva i espais urbans," 36–37.
56. Riera i Sans, *Els jueus de Girona*, 32–37, 41.
57. Sagrera and Sureda, "Comunitat jueva i espais urbans," 41–45.
58. Junyent, *La ciutat de Vic*, 69–78, 95–96; Freedman, *Diocese of Vic*, 141–42.
59. Freedman, "Unsuccessful Attempt."
60. Junyent, *La ciutat de Vic*, 81–82.
61. Carreras i Candi, "Desenrotllament de la institució notarial," 754, 761; Baiges i Jardí, "El notariat català," 142; Garcia i Sanz, "Precedents, origen, i evolució," 169; Ginebra i Molins, "Les escrivanies eclesiàstiques," 90, 101.
62. Junyent, *La ciutat de Vic*, 88–89; Llop i Jordana, *Vides i veus*, 78–79.
63. Llop i Jordana and Ollich i Castanyer, "Els espais de la comunitat jueva," 69; Llop i Jordana, *Vides i veus*, 42–43.
64. Assis, *Golden Age*, 168, 184.
65. Llop i Jordana, *Vides i veus*, 58–65.
66. Brundage, *Medieval Origins*, 394–97.
67. Bartoli Langeli, "'Scripsi et publicavi,'" 58, 68; Hardwick, *Practice of Patriarchy*, 20; Nussdorfer, *Brokers of Public Trust*, 11–12.
68. Brundage, *Medieval Origins*, 394–95.
69. Smail, "Notaries, Courts, and the Legal Culture," 23–26; Smail, *Imaginary Cartographies*, 20–30; Meyer, "Hereditary Laws and City Topography," 225–26; Bresc, "Rhétorique et culture notariale," 454–55.
70. Carreras i Candi, "Desenrotllament de la institució notarial," 753; Baiges i Jardí, "El notariat català," 133–35.
71. Baiges i Jardí, "El notariat català," 136; Pagarolas i Sabaté, "Notariat i cultura," 342–43.
72. Ferrer i Mallol, "L'instrument notarial," 41.
73. Denjean, "Crédit et notariat," 188–89.
74. Assis, *Jewish Economy*, 20–21; Winer, "Jews in and out of Latin Notarial Culture," 115–16.
75. For example, Emery, *Jews of Perpignan*; Assis, *Jews of Santa Coloma de Queralt*; Courtemanche, *La richesse des femmes*; Smail, *Imaginary Cartographies*; Denjean, *Juifs et Chrétiens*; Winer, *Women, Wealth, and Community*; Milton, *Market Power*; Reyerson, *Women's Networks*; Llop i Jordana, *Vides i veus*.
76. Cases i Loscos, *Inventari de l'Arxiu Històric*; Cases i Loscos and Ollich i Castanyer, *Catàleg dels arxius notarials de Vic*.
77. Emery, *Jews of Perpignan*, 3–9; Winer, *Women, Wealth, and Community*, 8.
78. Pere de Torroella: ACB, notaris, vol. 97, fols. 1r–44v; Bonanat Rimentol: AHPB 18/1, ACB, notaris, vol. 221, fols.

97r–128r. The latter was not previously linked with Rimentol, but close examination reveals that he referred to himself as the notary in the text: ACB, notaris, vol. 221, fol. 105v.

79. Berner, "On the Western Shores"; Klein, "Protecting the Widow"; Klein, "Widow's Portion"; Klein, "Splitting Heirs"; Klein, "Public Activities"; Klein, *Jews, Christian Society, and Royal Power*; Rich Abad, *La comunitat jueva de Barcelona*; Bensch, "Jewish Merchant in Romania"; Rich Abad, "Able and Available," 71–86.
80. Vinyoles, *Les barcelonines*; Comas i Via, "Una adroguera barcelonina"; Comas, Muntaner, and Vinyoles, "Elles no només filaven"; Vinyoles Vidal and Muntaner i Alsina, "Acreedoras y deudoras."
81. Riera i Sans, *Els poders públics;* Riera i Sans, *Els jueus de Girona*; Donat Pérez, *Jueus del rei i del comte.*
82. Guerson and Wessell Lightfoot, "Crises and Community"; Guerson and Wessell Lightfoot, "Mixed Marriages and Community Identity"; Guerson and Wessell Lightfoot, "Tale of Two Tolranas."
83. Guilleré, *Diner, poder, i societat*, 80–87.
84. Corbella i Llobet, *L'aljama de jueus de Vic*, 31.
85. Llop i Jordana, *Vides i veus.*
86. To Figueras, "Wedding Trousseaus."

Chapter 1

1. "Donamus tibi Bernardo Osona Martinam filiam nostrum et sororem in uxorem": ACF, vol. 3301, fols. 56v–57r.
2. ACF, vol. 3302, fols. 49v–50v. Ermessenda is also absent; she may have married (though the contract is not extant), or entered a convent, or even died.
3. ACF, vol. 3302, fols. 92r–93r. Sometime between 1262 and 1267, as the contract indicates, the young women's mother, Berenguera, had died.
4. ACB, notaris, vol. 44, fols. 161r–164r. For more on the practice of signing the *capítols matrimonials* in medieval Catalonia, see Vinyoles, *Les barcelonines*, 83–88; Ferrer i Mallol, "L'instrument notarial," 49–50; To Figueras, "Las funciones sociales del notariado," 175–86. For parallels elsewhere, see Hardwick, *Practice of Patriarchy*, 60.
5. Donahue, *Law, Marriage, and Society*, 1, 4, 17; McDougall, "Women and Gender," 167–68.
6. Farías Zurita, *El mas i la vila*, 215.
7. ACB, notaris, vol. 44, fols. 174v–175r.
8. ACB, notaris, vol. 44, fol. 189r.
9. Vinyoles, *Les barcelonines*, 69–70; To Figueras, *Família i hereu*, 73–77.
10. Hughes, "From Brideprice to Dowry," 276; Courtemanche, *La richesse des femmes*, 77–79; Bensch, *Barcelona*, 262–64; Stuard, "Dominion of Gender," 138–40; Skinner, *Women in Medieval Italian Society*, 164–67; Winer, *Women, Wealth, and Community*, 25–26. The dowry system also became dominant in some regions outside the Mediterranean, particularly England; see Hanawalt, *Wealth of Wives*, 55–61.
11. Courtemanche, *La richesse des femmes*, 121–27; Mosher Stuard, "Burdens of Matrimony," 65–68; Bensch, *Barcelona*, 270–72; Skinner, *Women in Medieval Italian Society*, 196; Winer, *Women, Wealth, and Community*, 32–33; Hanawalt, *Wealth of Wives*, 95–104; Kelleher, *Measure of Woman*, 51–52; Bermejo, "Law, Women, and Marriage," 330–41.
12. S. Epstein, *Wills and Wealth*, 120–26; Winer, *Women, Wealth, and Community*, 37–39; Reyerson, *Women's Networks*, 148–71.
13. Hughes, "From Brideprice to Dowry," 276–78, 280–82.
14. Klapisch-Zuber, *Women, Family, and Ritual*, 117–31, 213–46; Chabot, "Widowhood and Poverty"; Kuehn, *Law, Family, and Women*, 239, 257; Kuehn, "*Dos Non Teneat Locum Legittime*," 232, 239–42, 246, 248; Kuehn, *Heirs, Kin, and Creditors*, 128–30.
15. S. Epstein, *Wills and Wealth*, 83.

16. Chojnacki, *Women and Men*, 147, 250.
17. Guzzetti, "Women's Inheritance," 82–83.
18. Courtemanche, *La richesse des femmes*, 39–45, 76–79; Reyerson, *Women's Networks*, 55; Reyerson, *Mothers and Sons, Inc.*, 109.
19. Bensch, *Barcelona*, 270–72; Winer, *Women, Wealth, and Community*, 27–28.
20. Hanawalt, *Wealth of Wives*, 51–57; Hardwick, *Practice of Patriarchy*, 69.
21. Davis, *Fiction in the Archives*, 3–4.
22. AHG Gi-5, vol. 1, fol. 55r–v.
23. Brides' inheritance quitclaims were especially common in Girona and Vic, where about half of all *capítols matrimonials* included an inheritance quitclaim (46.5% in Girona; 50.2% in Vic). Although this formulation remained less common in Barcelona, nearly a third of brides either released their parents from inheritance claims or explicitly referred to their dowries as all or part of their inheritance (29%).
24. Font y Rius, "El desarrollo general del derecho," 290–92; Bensch, *Barcelona*, 78–80; Bowman, *Shifting Landmarks*, 39–47; Rucqoi, "Maintien et création du droit," 124–33.
25. Bensch, *Barcelona*, 245–46; To Figueras, *Família i hereu*, 111–12, 117–19.
26. Bensch, *Barcelona*, 253; To Figueras, *Família i hereu*, 122–23.
27. To Figueras, *Família i hereu*, 15–17, 124–26.
28. Font y Rius, "El desarollo general del derecho," 295–98; Bellomo, *Common Legal Past*, 99–101; Kelleher, *Measure of Woman*, 20–24.
29. Bensch, *Barcelona*, 257; S. Epstein, *Wills and Wealth*, 11–12. While Roman law weakened the inheritance rights of women in the Iberian Peninsula, it moderated the exclusion of women from inheritance in the Italian peninsula, as derived from Lombard law. See Kuehn, "*Dos Non Teneat Locum Legittime*," 241.
30. Bensch, *Barcelona*, 257.
31. Ibid.; To Figueras, *Família i hereu*, 17.
32. Font y Rius, "El desarollo general del derecho," 304–6, 314–15; Kelleher, *Measure of Woman*, 23–24; T. Barton, *Victory's Shadow*, 248–50.
33. Pons de Guri, *Les col·leccions de costums de Girona*, 120–21; Massip i Fonollosa, *Costums de Tortosa*, 6.4.2, 13–14, 22–24.
34. Massip i Fonollosa, *Costums de Tortosa*, 6.10.
35. Ibid., 4.7.1; 5.1.2, 19; 5.3.4; Winer, *Women, Wealth, and Community*, 32, 35–36.
36. Bensch, *Barcelona*, 259–60.
37. To Figueras, *Família i hereu*, 124–28.
38. Winer, *Women, Wealth, and Community*, 22–24.
39. Ibid., 26–27.
40. Two or more family members gave brides in marriage in 31 of 145 dowry contracts in Barcelona (21.4%), 64 of 130 in Girona (49.2%), and 332 of 699 in Vic (47.5%). Family groups sold property in 21 of 164 real estate sale contracts in Barcelona (12.8%), 22 of 154 in Girona (14.3%), and 117 of 451 in Vic (25.9%). See Ifft Decker, "Gender, Religious Difference, and the Notarial Economy," 74, 110.
41. Bensch, *Barcelona*, 259–60.
42. To take the example of real estate sales, family groups made 83 of 271 sales in Vic (30.6%) between 1250 and 1300, but only 34 of 180 (18.9%) between 1300 and 1350.
43. "Et nos dicti infantes renunciamus beneficio minoris etatis et cetera": ACF, vol. 24, fol. 64v.
44. Men and women reached full majority at age twenty under Visigothic law: see Winer, *Women, Wealth, and Community*, 26.
45. Her husband had named her as administrator of his property after entering the monastery of Santa Creu: ACB, notaris, vol. 17, fols. 23r–24r.
46. ACB, notaris, vol. 16, fols. 171r–173r.
47. Kuehn, *Heirs, Kin, and Creditors*, 11–13, 91–92.
48. Although the legal meaning of the Roman term *heres* referred to a single individual who assumed all the legal responsibilities and liabilities of the

deceased, testators in thirteenth-century Barcelona referred to multiple heirs (*heredes*), necessitating the use of the term "universal heir" (*heres universalis*) to differentiate a single child from the larger group of heirs: Bensch, *Barcelona*, 257. Elka Klein found that thirteenth-century Jewish wills took this process even further, referring to two or more children as joint universal heirs (*heredes universales*): Klein, "Splitting Heirs," 59–60. My research demonstrates that Christians also employed the term *heredes universales* to refer to a group of coequal heirs.

49. In contrast, customary laws from Occitan cities explicitly excluded married, dowered daughters from making claims in cases of intestacy. See Smith, "Unfamiliar Territory," 30–31.

50. "Heredes universales ab intestato": ACB, vol. 94, fols. 104r–105v. Notably, Constança's husband did not participate in the sale overtly, although he did act as her agent to transfer the property to the buyer.

51. ACF, vol. 3305, fol. 26r–v.

52. ACF, vol. 90, fol. 57r–v. As Berenguera had presumably moved to Barcelona with her new husband, this contract not only provides an example of a married woman who owned property jointly with her mother and brother but also represents a very rare example of a well-off woman traveling on business.

53. In Barcelona, men acting alone made 66 of 125 inheritance payments (52.8%), and family groups 7 (5.6%). In Girona, men acting alone made 43 of 70 inheritance payments (61.4%), and family groups 4 (5.7%). In Vic, men acting alone made 97 of 205 inheritance payments (47.3%), and family groups 27 (13.2%); see table 1.

54. Groups of executors, mostly men, made 15.2% of inheritance payments in Barcelona.

55. S. Epstein, *Wills and Wealth*, 220–27. Executors also had the right to sell property from the estate in order to pay both legacies and debts. See Cohn, *Death and Property*, 68–71.

56. In Barcelona, 71 of 103 (56.8%) inheritance payments went to individual men, 36 (28.8%) to individual women, and 11 (8.8%) to family groups, including groups of male relatives, groups of female relatives, and mixed-gender groups of relatives. Individual men received 43 of 70 (61.4%) inheritance payments in Girona, while individual women received 19 (27.1%), and family groups 4 (5.7%). In Vic, individual men received 111 of 205 (54.1%) inheritance payments, while individual women received 56 (27.3%), and families received 18 (8.8%); see table 1.

57. Family groups acted as landlords in 2 of 116 rental contracts from Barcelona (1.7%), 9 of 142 in Girona (6.3%), and 49 of 453 in Vic (10.8%). See Ifft Decker, "Gender, Religious Difference, and the Notarial Economy," 95.

58. ACF, vol. 8A, fol. 1bisv.

59. ACF, vol. 15, fol. 37v.

60. AHG Gi-5, vol. 22, fol. 82v.

61. AHG Gi-6, vol. 36, fols. 16v–17r; 158r–159r.

62. ACF, vol. 3310, fols. 22r–23r.

63. *Paradiso* XV.103–5. For the phenomenon of dowry inflation in the late medieval and early modern Mediterranean, see Mosher Stuard, "Dowry Increase," 799–803; Klapisch-Zuber, *Women, Family, and Ritual*, 124–25; Chojnacki, *Women and Men*, 58–60, 132–34. On the stability of dowry size in thirteenth- and fourteenth-century Catalonia, see Bensch, *Barcelona*, 357; Winer, *Women, Wealth, and Community*, 25; Kelleher, *Measure of Woman*, 49–50.

64. See table 2. The elevated median dowry in Barcelona presumably reflects the city's economic dominance relative to other Catalan cities; see Baucells i Reig, *Vivir en la edad media*, 1:69.

65. ACF, vol. 3305, fol. 55v.

66. Dana Wessell Lightfoot identified similar cases in fifteenth-century Valencia:

Wessell Lightfoot, *Women, Dowries, and Agency*, 120.

67. ACB, notaris, vol. 28, fols. 58v–59v.

68. To offer just one example of the practice of paying the dowry gradually over the course of years: on July 28, 1330, Francesca, daughter and heiress of Jaume Ros of Girona, married Ramon Ribot of Girona with a dowry of 11,000 sous (AHG, Gi-8, vol. 23, fols. 29v–30v). The alliance between these two families included another marriage: on the same day, Francesca's brother Francesc wed Ermenjarts, Ramon's sister, with a dowry of 5,000 sous (AHG, Gi-8, vol. 23, fol. 31r–v). The double marriage further complicated the exchange of dowry, but it nevertheless took another three months for Francesc to have paid off 7,000 sous of his sister's dowry (AHG, Gi-5, vol. 10, fol. 8r–v), and he would not manage to pay the final 4,000 sous until January 1333, about two and a half years after the marriage (AHG, Gi-6, vol. 3, fol. 34r). Bensch found similar evidence of delayed dowry transfers among Barcelona elites and suggested that the practice strengthened ties with the wife's natal family. See Bensch, *Barcelona*, 272. The practice of paying the dowry in installments was also seen elsewhere in Mediterranean Europe: see Kirshner, *Marriage, Dowry, and Citizenship*, 10.

69. Hughes, "From Brideprice to Dowry," 281.

70. Courtemanche, *La richesse des femmes*, 104; Winer, *Women, Wealth, and Community*, 27. Further afield, Barbara Hanwalt also found dowries including real estate in medieval London; see Hanawalt, *Wealth of Wives*, 56–58.

71. Chojnacki, *Women and Men*, 106–7.

72. Dillard, *Daughters of the Reconquest*, 54–55; Bermejo, "Law, Women, and Marriage," 335; Smail, *Legal Plunder*, 41–42; To Figueras, "Wedding Trousseaus."

73. Smail, Smail, and Duroselle-Melish, "Démanteler le patrimoine," 353.

74. In Barcelona, 9 of 66 women in the sample who leased out property independently and 4 of 49 who sold property independently did so after the onset of the Black Death in May 1348; in Girona, the numbers of women lessors did not noticeably rise, but 3 of 37 women who sold property independently did so after the arrival of the Black Death. Especially in Barcelona, even the larger number of total registers available in the later years of this study does not fully account for the rise in women's sales and rentals per year after the Black Death.

75. Groups including women leased out property in 71 of 249 rental contracts (28.5%) from Vic between 1250 and 1300, versus only 11 of 204 contracts (5.4%) between 1300 and 1350. However, women acting independently leased out property in 13 of 249 rental contracts (5.2%) from Vic between 1250 and 1300, but 22 of 204 contracts (10.8%) between 1300 and 1350. See table 11; Ifft Decker, "Gender, Religious Difference, and the Notarial Economy," 321.

76. Bensch, *Barcelona*, 263–64; Hughes, "From Brideprice to Dowry," 276.

77. Bensch, *Barcelona*, 268.

78. Hughes, "From Brideprice to Dowry," 278; Bensch, *Barcelona*, 268; Winer, *Women, Wealth, and Community*, 27–28. For a *sponsalicium* worth less than half the dowry, see, for example, the 1330 marriage contract between Margarida, daughter of Ramon Sitjar of Girona, and Arnau de Viveres, who had relocated to Girona from Sant Joan les Fonts. Margarida provided a dowry of 11,000 sous; Arnau granted her only 2,000 sous in *sponsalicium*. AHG Gi-5, vol. 10, fols. 16v–18r.

79. Although dowry contracts virtually never included an appraised value for dotal real estate—as estimation made the property subject to alienation without the wife's consent—grooms and their families made their own estimates and offered a *sponsalicium* based on their understanding of the value of the real property they received as dowry. In

December 1334, for example, Francesc de Sitjar of Carrer de Sant Pere of the city of Vic provided a *sponsalicium* of 300 sous for a dowry of 350 sous plus a planted piece of rural land brought by his bride Sibil·la, daughter of the late Pere Garriga, who lived on the same street (ACF, vol. 3311, fol. 157r–v). Two days later, Maria, daughter of Bernat de Coll of Vic, married Jaume d'Ulm, a milliner living in Carrer de Gurb, with a dowry of 400 sous plus houses with a backyard in Carrer de Sant Joan in the city of Vic. Jaume provided a *sponsalicium* of only 200 sous, precisely the value of the cash dowry, without accounting for the extra value generated by the real estate (ACF, vol. 3311, fols. 158v–159r).

80. Bensch, *Barcelona*, 272.
81. Winer, *Women, Wealth, and Community*, 28–29; Wessell Lightfoot, *Women, Dowries, and Agency*, 98–100.
82. Dillard, *Daughters of the Reconquest*, 72–79; Howell, *Marriage Exchange*, 29–34.
83. Lalinde Abadia, "Los pactos matrimoniales catalanes," 177.
84. Winer, *Women, Wealth, and Community*, 28–29; Wessell Lightfoot, *Women, Dowries, and Agency*, 97, 100–106.
85. The single *mig per mig* contract from Girona represented less than 1% of the total 130 contracts. In Vic, 19 of 699 couples (2.7%) married under the *mig per mig* system.
86. See, for example, the one *mig per mig* marriage from Girona, which brought together an agricultural laborer and a woman of unknown background (AHG Gi-8, vol. 23, fols. 70v–71r), and a marriage in Vic between a seamstress who supported herself by her own labor and a man from a nearby rural parish (ACF, vol. 3308, fol. 27r).
87. ACB, notaris, vol. 3, fol. 92r.
88. ACB, notaris, vol. 27, fols. 18v–20r.
89. Mosher Stuard, "Burdens of Matrimony," 66–68; Kelleher, *Measure of Woman*, 53–54.
90. Bensch, *Barcelona*, 268–70.
91. Kelleher, *Measure of Woman*, 54–57; Wessell Lightfoot, *Women, Dowries, and Agency*, 151–88.
92. Kelleher, *Measure of Woman*, 59–60.
93. Kirshner, "Wives' Claims Against Insolvent Husbands"; Winer, *Women, Wealth, and Community*, 32–33; Trivellato, *Familiarity of Strangers*, 261–62; Kelleher, *Measure of Woman*, 56.
94. For background on the origins of the *senatus consultum Velleianum* in Roman law, see Benke, "Why Should the Law Protect Roman Women?," 42–52; Halbwachs, "Women as Legal Actors," 450.
95. Ferrer i Mallol, "L'instrument notarial," 76–77.
96. Winer, *Women, Wealth, and Community*, 35–36; Kelleher, *Measure of Woman*, 57–59; cf. Mummey, who emphasizes the renunciation of the Velleian senatus consult as simultaneously an affirmation of patriarchal expectations and of women's engagement in economic life: Mummey, "Measuring the Margins," 118–19.
97. AHG Gi-4, vol. 8, fol. 75v; Gi-5, vol. 28, fol. 34r–v; Gi-6, vol. 34, fol. 60r–v, 79v, 85v–86r. Bernat controlled the notariate of the city by royal concession; see Carreras i Candi, "Desenrotllament de la institució notarial," 760, 767, 769–73; Guilleré, *Diner, poder, i societat*, 221. Margarida was the daughter and heiress of Jaume de Bordils, another member of the Girona urban elite: AHG Gi-5, vol. 37, fols. 19r–20r. On the Bordils family, see Guilleré, *Diner, poder, i societat*, 81.
98. Bernat also received an additional eight loans from Jewish lenders between 1346 and 1350, but Margarida may have died by then; she last appeared in December 1345, when she and Bernat jointly took out an interest-free loan from Bernat's colleague, the notary Ramon Egidi: AHG Gi-6, vol. 40, fol. 8r–v.
99. Winer, *Women, Wealth, and Community*, 36; Kelleher, *Measure of Woman*, 59–61;

Wessell Lightfoot, *Women, Dowries, and Agency*, 151–88; Carvajal de la Vega, "La mujer castellana," 124–35.

100. Winer, *Women, Wealth, and Community*, 40–44; Kelleher, *Measure of Woman*, 51–52.
101. Chabot, "Widowhood and Poverty"; Hardwick, *Practice of Patriarchy*, 130; Kelleher, *Measure of Woman*, 62–65.
102. De Brocá y Montagut, *Historia del derecho de Cataluña*, 870–72; Kelleher, *Measure of Woman*, 69; Vinyoles Vidal and Muntaner i Alsina, "Acreedoras y deudoras," 279; Mikes, "Legislació històrica de la família catalana," 183–85.
103. "Maria, que censeor tenere et possidere pro dote mea et sponsalicio meo et aliis iuribus meis omnia bona dicti mariti mei quondam ex [scripta] consuetudine Barchinone": ACB 32, fols. 34r–35r, 210r–211v. In the first contract, dated April 8, 1336, Geralda and Maria collected on the first 100 pounds; they collected on the remaining 400 pounds on June 12, 1336. For more on the Marquet family, see Ferrer i Mallol, "Una família de navegants," 137–267.
104. ACF, vol. 94/2, fols. 12v, 13v; ACF, vol. 97/2, fol. 107v; for a similar case in Perpignan, see Winer, *Women, Wealth, and Community*, 56.
105. Kelleher, *Measure of Woman*, 70–71.
106. Winer, *Women, Wealth, and Community*, 47–50.
107. Ibid., 51.
108. ACB, notaris, vol. 68, fol. 25r.
109. Blanca as landowner: ACB 28, fols. 24v–25r; ACB 31, fols. 168v–170r, 176v–178v, 186v–190r; ACB 33, fols. 109r–110v. As guardian of her minor children, collecting on debts owed to her late husband: ACB 20, fol. 130v; ACB 33, fols. 83v–84r; ACB 48, fols. 22r, 41v–42r. Marriage between Blanqueta and Galceran Marquet: ACB 20, fol. 32v; Ferrer i Mallol, "Una família de navegants," 217–18. Their son Galceran's occasional use of his mother's surname Albanell highlights the importance of this match for the Marquet family: Ferrer i Mallol, "Una família de navegants," 219.
110. For establishment of *societas*, see AHG Gi-6, vol. 16, fols. 99v–101v. Kathryn Reyerson has extensively studied the approximately contemporary case of Martha de Cabanis, a businesswoman from Montpellier who began as guardian of her minor children and later formed a partnership with her adult sons: Reyerson, *Business, Banking, and Finance*, 33; Reyerson, *Art of the Deal*, 123–25; Reyerson, *Mothers and Sons, Inc.*, 90–108, 129–47.
111. ACF 316, fol. 91r–v; ACF 317, fol. 133r–v; ACF 378, fols. 4r–5r, 48v–49r.
112. Elisenda, widow of Joan Benet of Vic and guardian of her minor children, in 1311 appointed her brother Pere de Cuspineda as her agent to collect a debt: ACF, vol. 53, fol. 6r.
113. In 1346, Bonanata, widow of Berenguer Cervera of Girona and guardian of her minor children, sold off a plot of rural agricultural land owned by her late husband: AHG Gi-5, vol. 15, fols. 146r–147r.
114. Inventories drawn up by widowed guardians: ACB, notaris, vol. 48, fol. 13r–v; ACB, notaris, vol. 29, fols. 16r–20r; ACB, notaris, vol. 33, fols. 86v–102v; AHG Gi-5, vol. 6, fols. 37v–38r; AHG Gi-5, vol. 14, fol. 1.17r–v; AHG Gi-6, vol. 13, fols. 30v–31v; AHG Gi-6, vol. 23, fol. 46v; AHG Gi-6, vol. 30, fols. 105r–107v.
115. Winer, *Women, Wealth, and Community*, 67–69.
116. ACB, notaris, vol. 17, fols. 134v–135r. Childcare and wet-nursing were standard duties of enslaved women engaged in domestic service: Blumenthal, *Enemies and Familiars*, 82; Winer, "Conscripting the Breast," 168–70.
117. ACB, notaris, vol. 9, fol. 37r–v, 119r–121r.
118. Winer, *Women, Wealth, and Community*, 69.
119. AHPB, vol. 14/1, fols. 151v–152r. The contract refers to Sibil·la as Constança's grandmother but does not specify if

she was Caterina's mother or Guillem's. If the latter, based on the name of her husband, she clearly had also remarried after her first husband's death.

120. ACF, vol. 378, fol. 70r–v.

121. In the larger sample of women's transactions, widows made 62 of 90 women's inheritance payments in Barcelona (68.9%), 33 of 58 in Girona (56.9%), and 54 of 100 (54%) in Vic. See Ifft Decker, "Gender, Religious Difference, and the Notarial Economy," 139.

122. AHG Gi-5, vol. 52, fols. 46v–47r.

123. Two Barcelona widows made payments for their husbands' burial expenses to executors: Benvinguda, widow of the weaver Ferrer Riquer, in 1326, and Romeua, widow of the merchant Guillem de Camos. Benvinguda acted in her capacity as heiress to one-sixth of her husband's estate, with the consent of her children and coheirs—two married daughters and a son (ACB, notaris, vol. 48, fol. 27r–v). Romeua was the guardian (*tutrix*) of her minor children (ACB, notaris, vol. 95, fol. 47r). While Romeua's responsibilities and obligations stemmed from her relationship to her children, Benvinguda formally acted as her husband's heir—an unusual choice for a husband with children, and one that had its own implications, to be discussed later in this section, for Benvinguda's involvement in the estate.

124. During marriage: AHG Gi-4, vol. 2, fols. 59v, 67v–68r; Gi-5, vol. 6, fol. 27r–v; Gi-5, vol. 8, fol. 43v; Gi-5, vol. 9, fol. 16r. As executor: AHG Gi-4, vol. 6, fol. 19r–v.

Chapter 2

1. AHG Gi-5, vol. 5, fols. 7v–9r; Ifft Decker, "Between Two Cities," 490–93.

2. The Latin term used for the grant is *donatio inter vivos*, which literally translates to "grant between the living." The term is employed to describe a wide range of transfers of wealth, often but not exclusively between family members, which effectively represent a form of premortem inheritance. The *donatio inter vivos* allowed parents to help establish their children in new households before their death. Givers also may have used these grants strategically to circumvent inheritance laws or other financial obligations.

3. For rates of morabatins to sous, see Schraer, *Stake in the Ground*, xii, 244–45. The largest cash dowry found among Christians in Girona was valued at 12,000 sous. See table 2.

4. First reference to Bonjueu as secretary: AHG Gi-5, vol. 8, fol. 14v. Bonjueu's first loan: AHG Gi-5, vol. 5, fol. 34v. Between 1322 and 1350, Bonjueu extended 470 extant new loans. For background on the *secretarii*, see Assis, *Golden Age*, 76–78, 86–93; Riera i Sans, *Els jueus de Girona*, 40–42.

5. In 1334, when he still would have been in his early twenties, Saltell extended a loan of 450 sous to a Christian of neighboring Cassà de la Selva, on which he earned about 100 sous in interest: AHG Gi-6, vol. 4, fols. 120v–121r.

6. Bonjueu Cresques last appears in this capacity on April 5, 1346: AHG Gi-6, vol. 43, fol. 15r–v. Saltell Gracià first appears as secretary in September 1346: AHG Gi-6, vol. 43, fol. 16r–v.

7. The loans were for 700 and 400 sous, respectively: AHG Gi-5, vol. 45, fols. 4v, 81r. For more on Bernat Taialà and his family, see Carreras i Candi, "Desenrotllament de la institució notarial," 760, 767, 769–73; Guilleré, *Diner, poder, i societat*, 221.

8. Latin: "ratione partis hereditatis et legitime mee paterne et materne"—the typical Christian formulation. Reina referred to herself as having "passed the age of 12 years" and could therefore have been as young as thirteen. Although most Catalan Jewish girls married in their late teens, age at marriage varied, with girls from the wealthiest families perhaps marrying younger. See Winer, *Women, Wealth, and Community*, 91.

9. In January 1334, Bonjueu and his wife Sobredona jointly repaid a debt to a Jew from Perpignan: AHG Gi-5, vol. 38, fol. 18v.
10. Assis, "Jewish Attitudes," 300–301; Assis, *Golden Age*, 145–60; Klein, *Jews, Christian Society, and Royal Power*, 45–50; Ray, *Sephardic Frontier*, 136; T. Barton, *Contested Treasure*, 77–78, 147–49, 167–68.
11. Marcus, *Rituals of Childhood*, 8–13. For use of this concept elsewhere, see Stow, *Theater of Acculturation*, 67–76, 92–93; Baumgarten, *Mothers and Children*, 8–9; Klein, *Jews, Christian Society, and Royal Power*, 10–16.
12. Marcus, *Rituals of Childhood*, 94–101; Baumgarten, *Mothers and Children*, 27–28, 59–61, 81–83; Baumgarten, *Practicing Piety*, 51–53, 85–94; Haskell, *Mystical Resistance*, 15–23.
13. Siegmund, "Division of the Dowry," 86–89; Stow, "Ethnic Amalgamation," 111–15.
14. Lauer, *Colonial Justice*, 151–54.
15. Grossman, *Pious and Rebellious*, 241–42; Simonsohn, *Common Justice*, 174–204; Marglin, *Across Legal Lines*; Zinger, "'She Aims to Harass Him.'"
16. Winer, *Women, Wealth, and Community*, 120, 125.
17. Klein, "Widow's Portion," 153–58; Klein, "Splitting Heirs," 62–65.
18. Nirenberg, *Communities of Violence*, 158–59, 217–21; Ray, "Beyond Tolerance and Persecution," 4–9; Safran, *Defining Boundaries*, 81; Baumgarten, *Practicing Piety*, 190–94; Ackerman-Lieberman, *Business of Identity*, 181–93; T. Barton, *Contested Treasure*, 91.
19. Nirenberg, *Communities of Violence*, 141; Ray, *Sephardic Frontier*, 165–74; Cuffel, *Gendering Disgust*, 236–38; Furst, "Captivity, Conversion, and Communal Identity," 202–11; S. Barton, *Conquerors, Brides, and Concubines*, 46–62.
20. Septimus, *Hispano-Jewish Culture in Transition*, 55–57; Assis, *Golden Age*, 69.
21. Lorberbaum, *Politics and the Limits of Law*, 94.
22. Roth, "Regional Boundaries and Medieval Halakhah," 76.
23. Lorberbaum, *Politics and the Limits of Law*, 94; Roth, "Regional Boundaries and Medieval Halakhah," 81–84.
24. Maimonides, *Mishneh Torah*, Hilkhot Nakhalot 1:1–2. This summary is derived from the Babylonian Talmud, Ketubot 69a–b.
25. Maimonides, *Mishneh Torah*, Hilkhot Nakhalot 1:2, 8–9; Hilkhot Ishut 12:3.
26. Ibid., Hilkhot Nakhalot 6:2.
27. Burns, *Jews in the Notarial Culture*, 82–84, 91–92, 97–99, 108–9; Klein, "Splitting Heirs," 53–55, 58–59; Winer, *Women, Wealth, and Community*, 90–91; Schraer, *Stake in the Ground*, 137–39.
28. Maimonides, *Mishneh Torah*, Hilkhot Nakhalot 6:2.
29. Ibid., 1:5.
30. Ibid., 1:3–4.
31. For background on Solomon ibn Adret and his views on women and marriage, see in particular I. Epstein, *Studies in the Communal Life*, xiii, 79–88; Grossman, *Ve-hu Yimshol Bakh*, 259–84.
32. Ibn Adret, *She'elot u-Teshuvot*, 1.1165.
33. Ibid., 2.211.
34. Klein, "Splitting Heirs," 59–62.
35. Jacob ben Asher, *Arba'ah Turim, Even ha-Ezer*, 118; ibn Adret, *She'elot u-Teshuvot*, 3.432; Grossman, *Pious and Rebellious*, 151–52.
36. Isaac ben Sheshet Perfet, *She'elot u-Teshuvot*, 179.
37. Maimonides, *Mishneh Torah*, Hilkhot Nashim 12:2.
38. Ibid., Hilkhot Nakhalot 5:2.
39. Ibid., Hilkhot Nakhalot 5:2.
40. Ibid., Hilkhot Ishut 1:2.
41. Ibid., Hilkhot Ishut 11:1.
42. Hebrew *ketubot* from thirteenth- and fourteenth-century Barcelona specified an exchange rate of 8 zuzim per sou; Lacave, *Medieval Ketubot*, 31–36.
43. Ibn Adret, *She'elot u-Teshuvot*, 2.138, 6.5, Klein, "Widow's Portion," 149–50; Winer, *Women, Wealth, and Community*, 94–95.
44. Ibn Adret, *She'elot u-Teshuvot*, 2.2, 3.12, 5.237; Klein, "Widow's Portion," 149;

Winer, *Women, Wealth, and Community*, 94; Lacave, *Medieval Ketubot*, 86–90.

45. Klein, "Widow's Portion," 163.
46. Babylonian Talmud, *Ketubot* 68a–69b.
47. Hezser, "Roman Law and Rabbinic Legal Composition."
48. Goitein, *Mediterranean Society*, 3:118–31; Krakowski, *Coming of Age*, 143–53.
49. Based on four *ketubot* published in Lacave—Barcelona 1, Barcelona 2, Barcelona 5, and Santa Columa de Montbui—and seven notarial contracts (two from Girona and five from Vic). See Lacave, *Medieval Ketubot*, 31–35, 44–46, 167–72, 176–77, 193–94; AHG Gi-5, vol. 5, fols. 7v–94; AHG Gi-6, vol. 9bis, fols. 12v–13v; ACF, vol. 6, fol. 1784; ACF 4588, fol. 19r; ACF, vol. 4590, fol. 32r; ACF, vol. 4593, fol 16r; ACF, vol. 4606, fols. 5r–8v.
50. The one contract in which a groom provided a *tosefet ketubah* of 2,000 sous, half the value of the 4,000-sou dowry, comes from Vic (ACF, vol. 4590, fol. 32r).
51. A groom from Girona in 1334 granted his wife a *tosefet ketubah* of 1,200 sous while receiving from his bride a dowry of 500 morabatins, or 5,000 sous (AHG Gi-6, vol. 9bis, fols. 12v–13v). Another groom from Vic granted his wife 300 sous, less than one-quarter of her 1,300-sou dowry (ACF, vol. 6, fol. 178r).
52. Ibn Adret, *She'elot u-Teshuvot*, 2.382; Winer, *Women, Wealth, and Community*, 92–95.
53. Maimonides, *Mishneh Torah*, Hilkhot Ishut 12:3.
54. Babylonian Talmud, *Ketubot* 107a–b. For a case from the Middle East about a Jewish woman who supported herself by teaching when her husband failed to provide maintenance for her and their children, see Melammed, "He Said, She Said."
55. Maimonides, *Mishneh Torah*, Hilkhot Ishut 12:2.
56. For Christian women, see de Brocá y Montagut, *Historia del derecho de Cataluña*, 870–72; Vinyoles Vidal and Muntaner i Alsina, "Acreedoras y deudoras, 279; Mikes, "Legislació històrica de la família catalana," 183–85.
57. Ibn Adret, *She'elot u-Teshuvot*, 1.1156, 2.138.
58. AHG Gi-6, vol. 9bis, fol. 33v.
59. Ishbili, *She'elot u-Teshuvot*, 105.
60. Klein, "Widow's Portion," 157–58; Winer, *Women, Wealth, and Community*, 100–102.
61. Assis, *Golden Age*, 132–35; Burns, *Jews in the Notarial Culture*, 43–49; Winer, "Jews in and out of Latin Notarial Culture," 118–20; M. Perry, "*Hatpasah*—Jewish *Translata* Documents," 168.
62. Maimonides, *Mishneh Torah*, Hilkhot Ishut 1:2; Hilkhot Gerushin 1:1.
63. Assis, "Jewish Attitudes," 301–2; Ifft Decker, "Jewish Divorce," 39–41, 45–52; M. Perry, "*Hatpasah*—Jewish *Translata* Documents," 170–74.
64. Bonjueu Saltell stated that he initially made the living-will grant to his son through a Hebrew instrument (*instrumentum ebraycum*) signed on the 23rd of Tammuz, 5085, equivalent to July 3, 1325—about a month before the Girona notarial contracts: AHG Gi-5, vol. 5, fol. 8r. Reina also affirmed that the sum of her dowry had been specified in a Hebrew marriage contract (*in instrumento nuptiali ebrayco*): AHG Gi-5, vol. 5, fol. 9r.
65. Winer, "Jews in and out of Latin Notarial Culture," 114–15, 122–23.
66. Assis, *Golden Age*, 267–68; Klein, *Hebrew Deeds*, 19.
67. M. Perry, "*Hatpasah*—Jewish *Translata* Documents," 170–74.
68. Burns, *Jews in the Notarial Culture*, 30–31; Agresta, "The Doctor and the Notary," 236–40; Ifft Decker, "Jewish Divorce," 47.
69. M. Perry, "*Hatpasah*—Jewish *Translata* Documents," 170–71.
70. For parallels in Venetian Crete, see Lauer, *Colonial Justice*, 130–46.
71. ACF, vol. 4583, fol. 8v; Llop i Jordana, *Vides i veus*, 80–81.
72. Their guardian Vidal Benvenist, who sold the property in 1328, referred to it

as the shared inheritance of his wards Issach and Mireta; see ACB, notaris, vol. 65, fols. 128v–129r.

73. ACF, vol. 4603, fols. 51v, 53r. In 1338, Astrug ceded Preciosa a debt of 1,050 sous owed to their late father, probably part of the process of dividing their joint inheritance: ACF, vol. 4603, fol. 113r.

74. Their father had died by April 1326 (ACF, vol. 4600, fol. 33v); for their mother, Astrugona, as guardian the following year, see ACF, vol. 4600, fol. 48r. The use of the term *tutrix* for Astrugona indicates that she was responsible for a daughter under twelve and/or a son under fourteen; notaries typically employed the term *curator/curatrix* for guardians with wards in their teens. See Winer, *Women, Wealth, and Community*, 56.

75. ACF, vol. 4602, fol. 39v.

76. AHPB, vol. 18/1, fol. 25r–v; Rich Abad, "Able and Available," 77–78.

77. Winer, *Women, Wealth, and Community*, 110–16.

78. Rich Abad, *La comunitat jueva de Barcelona*, 228–32, 297–303; Fumanal Pagès, Colomer Casamitjana, Gutiérrez Ortiz, Redondo Garcia, and Florensa Puchol, "Documentant l'arqueologia."

79. AHPB, vol. 18/1, fol. 25r–v.

80. Ibn Adret, *She'elot u-Teshuvot*, 3.79; Ishbili, *She'elot u-Teshuvot*, 8; Perfet, *She'elot u-Teshuvot*, 413.

81. ACF, vol. 4607, fol. 7r. This register is of uncertain date, but based on the names of individuals, it has been traced to sometime between 1308 and 1315.

82. ACF, vol. 4589, fol. 22r.

83. For Jewish women's use of non-Jewish courts throughout the medieval and early modern Mediterranean, see Dubin, "Jewish Women, Marriage Law"; Zinger, "'She Aims to Harass Him,'" 159–92; Lauer, *Colonial Justice*, 146–51, 154–58.

84. Winer, *Women, Wealth, and Community*, 91–96; Winer, "Marriage, Family," 250–56.

85. See chapter 7; Ifft Decker, "Public Economic Role," 57–58; Ifft Decker, "Between Two Cities," 486–90; Ifft Decker, "Credit and Connections," 17–40.

86. Documents from the late 1280s suggest that Bonmacip and Reina had begun the process of extricating Reina from her marriage to Jucef Darahi of Barcelona: ACF 4589, fols. 19v, 22r. By 1293, she had returned to Vic and started working as a moneylender: ACF 4591, fol. 3r. She had married Astrug Caravida of Girona by 1294, and within a few months, Astrug had begun to refer to himself as a Jew of Vic: ACF 4591, fols. 17r, 19r–v.

87. AHG Gi-5, vol. 20, fols. 16v–17r. For uncle-niece marriages in medieval Egypt, see Goitein, *Mediterranean Society*, 3:26; Krakowski, *Coming of Age*, 213–23.

88. Numbers 27:1–11, 36:1–12.

89. ACB, notaris, vol. 1, fol. 75r.

90. AHG Gi-4, vol. 8, fol. 90v; AHG Gi-5, vol. 17, fol. 70r. For butchers in the medieval Crown of Aragon, see Assis, *Golden Age*, 143–44, 317; Muntané Santiveri, "L'alimentació a l'aljama medieval," 110–16; Rich Abad, *La comunitat jueva de Barcelona*, 63–64.

91. On a number of occasions, Christian men signed agency contracts in which they granted their wives far-reaching authority over their property. In 1345, for example, royal courier Simó Lombard of Barcelona named his wife Francesca as his "designated special and general agent over all my business, goods, and rights, and all matters needing to be looked after, managed, conducted, and administered": ACB, notaris, vol. 220, fols. 16v–17r.

92. Babylonian Talmud, *Kiddushin* 41a–b. For Jewish commercial agency practices in the Islamic world, where Jewish men did not ordinarily appoint their wives as commercial or legal agents, see J. Goldberg, *Trade and Institutions*, 150–61; Cohen, *Maimonides and the Merchants*, 70–113.

93. ACF, vol. 4600, fols. 52v–53r.

94. Goig and Salomó: for joint loan, see ACF, vol. 4602, act dated December 7,

1335. For quitclaims, see ACF, vol. 94/2, fol. 1r–v; ACF, vol. 259, fol. 31v; ACF, vol. 286, fols. 9v, 25r, 146v; ACF, vol. 289, fols. 14v–15r; ACF, vol. 4606, fol. 39v; ACF, vol. 316, fols. 159r–160r. Astrug and Tolsana: for joint loan, see ACF, vol. 4593, fol. 17r. For quitclaims, see ACF, vol. 4595, fol. 96r; ACF, vol. 4596, fols. 18r, 99r; ACF, vol. 4598, fol. 99v; ACF, vol. 286, fol. 29r.

95. Massip i Fonollosa, *Costums de Tortosa*, 4.7.1; 5.1.2, 19; 5.3.4; Winer, *Women, Wealth, and Community*, 32, 35–36.

96. Babylonian Talmud, *Ketubot* 101a–b, *Yevamot* 38a–b; Engel, "Marital Property Rights," 97–101. Although the same distinction remained technically valid in Ashkenaz, local ordinances and customs apparently gave women somewhat more control over property: Tallan, "Medieval Jewish Widows," 67; Grossman, *Pious and Rebellious*, 150–51.

97. AHG Gi-5, vol. 6, fol. 86v.

98. For Vidal as agent, see AHG Gi-5, vol. 9, fols. 9v–10r, 25v, 39v–40r, 51v–52r. For more extensive discussion of this case, see Ifft Decker, "Between Two Cities," 494–95.

99. ACB, notaris, vol. 16, fols. 51v, 169v.

100. Bonadona's first action as a widow: AHG Gi-6, vol. 9bis, fol. 33v. For more on the Caravida family, see Sobrequés Vidal, "Familias Hebreas Gerundenses"; Planas i Marcé, "Els jueus de Girona," 43–44; Roth, "'My Precious Books and Instruments.'"

101. One daughter, Bonafilla, had been widowed by 1327 and remarried by 1334: AHG Gi-5, vol. 7, fols. 97v–98r; AHG Gi-6, vol. 9bis, fol. 33v. By around 1332, Ester had married David Bonjorn of Perpignan, a marriage that ended in a messy divorce; see Roth, "'My Precious Books and Instruments,'" 551. Although a 1339 contract referred to Bonafilla and Ester as their fathers' heirs, their mother apparently received the bulk of the estate in practice: AHG Gi-5, vol. 20, fol. 22r–v.

102. Notably, only Bonadona's support allowed their daughter to pursue her financial interests during her divorce; see Roth, "'My Precious Books and Instruments,'" 559–60. For Catalan Jewish women's reliance on their fathers or husbands to protect their financial interests, see Assis, *Golden Age*, 273–74; Winer, *Women, Wealth, and Community*, 91–94.

103. De Brocá y Montagut, *Historia del derecho de Cataluña*, 870–72; Vinyoles Vidal and Muntaner i Alsina, "Acreedoras y deudoras," 279; Mikes, "Legislació històrica de la família catalana," 183–85.

104. See, for example, the debt collection contracts of Bonadona, widow of the prominent lender Samuel de Piera, in which she stated that she held her husband's goods "pro dote mea et sponsalicio meo": AHPB 18/1, fol. 8r–v.

105. Benedictow, *Black Death*, 278–79, 281; Gyug, "Effects and Extent of the Black Death"; Rodriguez, "Spain," 182, 185–86; Lopez de Meneses, "Una consecuencia de la peste negra," 97–106; Rich Abad, "Able and Available," 71; Einbinder, *After the Black Death*, 117–47.

106. Ibn Adret, *She'elot u-Teshuvot*, 2.290; Lorberbaum, *Politics and the Limits of Law*, 98; Lauer, *Colonial Justice*, 104, 165.

107. Lauer, *Colonial Justice*, 125, 165–66; Klein, *Jews, Christian Society, and Royal Power*, 155–58.

108. Scholars of Italian Jews have argued that dowry inflation gave daughters near-equal shares in the family patrimony: Allegra, "Model of Jewish Devolution," 39, 44, 46, 48; Stow, "Ethnic Amalgamation," 112; Siegmund, "Division of the Dowry," 91; Gasperoni, "Inheritance and Wealth."

109. Klein, *Jews, Christian Society, and Royal Power*, 179–80; Trivellato, *Familiarity of Strangers*, 139–46; Winer, "Marriage, Family," 245–46; Krakowski, *Coming of Age*, 221–23.

110. Ibn Adret, *She'elot u-Teshuvot*, 2.211.

111. Ishbili, *She'elot u-Teshuvot*, 105.

112. Ibn Adret, *She'elot u-Teshuvot*, 6.4.

113. Winer, *Women, Wealth, and Community*, 32–33; Kelleher, *Measure of Woman*, 53–57; Wessell Lightfoot, *Women, Dowries,*

and Agency, 151–88. For elsewhere in Europe: Kirshner, "Wives' Claims Against Insolvent Husbands." Jewish women in early modern Italy pressed similar claims despite Jewish law: Trivellato, *Familiarity of Strangers*, 261–62.

114. Roth, "Regional Boundaries and Medieval Halakhah," 79–81.
115. Ibn Adret, *She'elot u-Teshuvot*, 3.109; Assis, "Jewish Attitudes," 300–301.
116. Ibn Adret, *She'elot u-Teshuvot*, 2.111; 3.15–16.
117. Ibid., 1.957; Schraer, *Stake in the Ground*, 130.
118. Klein, "Widow's Portion," 152.
119. Winer, *Women, Wealth, and Community*, 90–91, 94–95.
120. BT Bava Kamma 102b.
121. Bowman, *Shifting Landmarks*, 170–73.
122. Ishbili, *She'elot u-Teshuvot*, 48.
123. Ibid., 190.
124. Ray, *Sephardic Frontier*, 105–14; Ray, *After Expulsion*, 15–18.

Chapter 3

1. AHG Gi-4, vol. 12, fols. 55v–56r.
2. Emery, *Jews of Perpignan*, 128–30; Burns, *Jews in the Notarial Culture*, 9–10.
3. Wray, *Communities and Crisis*, 196.
4. The cleric Pere de Terrades came from Cogolls, about 30 kilometers from Canet d'Adri; the other witness, Ferrer d'Aguila, came from Fornells de la Selva, which lay about 20 kilometers from Canet d'Adri on the other side of Girona.
5. Cossar, *Clerical Households*, 7–8.
6. Carreras i Candi, "Desenrotllament de la institució notarial," 751–53; Baiges i Jardí, "El notariat català," 133–35; Brundage, *Medieval Origins*, 397–99; Cossar, *Clerical Households*, 22–23.
7. Baiges i Jardí, "El notariat català," 142; Blasco Martínez, "El notariado en Aragón," 199–200; Conde y Delgado de Molina, "Notaries i conflictes entre notaris," 11; Ginebra i Molins, "Les escrivanies eclesiàstiques," 89–91.
8. Baiges i Jardí, "El notariat català," 146; Blasco Martínez, "El notariado en Aragón," 205–7.
9. Baiges i Jardí, "El notariat català," 148; Blasco Martínez, "El notariado en Aragón," 207–10; Brundage, *Medieval Origins*, 402–3.
10. Blasco Martínez, "El notariado en Aragón," 207–8; Brundage, *Medieval Origins*, 400–401.
11. Baiges i Jardí, "El notariat català," 147; Blasco Martínez, "El notariado en Aragón," 205; Burns, *Jews in the Notarial Culture*, 43–49; Winer, "Jews in and out of Latin Notarial Culture," 118–20.
12. Brundage, *Medieval Origins*, 404–5.
13. Guilleré, *Diner, poder, i societat*, 71, 77.
14. Ferrer i Mallol, "L'instrument notarial," 41–68; Baiges i Jardi and Piñol Alabart, "Notariat, comerç, i cultura escrita," 1828–1833.
15. Denjean, "Crédit et notariat," 188–91; Smail, *Legal Plunder*, 107–9.
16. Pagarolas i Sabaté, "Notariat i cultura," 338.
17. To Figueras, "Las funciones sociales del notariado," 174–75; Reyerson and Salata, *Medieval Notaries*, 12; Milton, *Market Power*, 39.
18. Smail, *Imaginary Cartographies*, 68–71; Wray, *Communities and Crisis*, 158–71; Mosher Stuard, "Where Notaries Provided Legal Services," 270–71. Italian notaries also maintained offices, which came to serve as archival repositories for completed registers; see Meyer, "Hereditary Laws and City Topography," 228–30.
19. Bartomeu de Miramat, a notary active in Barcelona from 1335 to 1346, was more conscientious than many of his colleagues about specifying a location but still limited himself to identifying a parish. For example, he indicated that a May 1346 marriage contract was concluded in the couple's home parish of Santa Eulàlia del Papiol, just outside Barcelona: AHPB, vol. 10/3, fol. 93r.
20. AHG Gi-5, vol. 6, fols. 97r–99r.
21. AHG Gi-5, vol. 12, fol. 41v.
22. Notaries functioned as brokers, bringing together creditors and debtors, in early modern France. See Hardwick, *Practice*

of Patriarchy, 37–41; Hoffman, Postel-Vinay, and Rosenthal, "Information and Economic History."

23. ACB, notaris, vol. 31, fols. 98r–106v.
24. Carreras i Candi, "Desenrotllament de la institució notarial," 753; Pagarolas i Sabaté, "Notariat i cultura," 341–45.
25. Pagarolas i Sabaté, "Notariat i cultura," 345–46; Pagarolas i Sabaté, "Gènesi i evolució dels registres notarials," 166–67.
26. Baiges i Jardí, "El notariat català," 136; Pagarolas i Sabaté, "Notariat i cultura," 343; Ferrer i Mallol, "L'instrument notarial," 41. For Italy, see Meyer, "Hereditary Laws and City Topography," 225–26.
27. AHG Gi-4, vol. 12, fols. 55v–56r: Astrug de Pedracissa, Jew of La Bisbal; Ponc Malarç, draper of Girona; Ramon Gerald, draper of Girona; Mosse d'Escola, Jew of Girona; Barzelay des Mestre, Jew of Girona; Guillem Vives, canon of Girona; Ramon de Canova of Girona; Pere Sabater of Sant Sadurní; Guillem d'Abadia, draper of Girona; Ramon Tremir, apothecary of Girona; Bonanata, daughter of Pere Joan of Sant Vicenç de Canet d'Adri; Pere, husband of Bonanata; Bonadona, widow of Astrug Caravida, Jew of Girona; Bonanat de Llemena, draper of Girona; Pere de Terrats, cleric of Cogolls; Ferrer de Margarit of Fornells de Selva; Berenguer de Vall of Hostalet; Guillem de Bosch of Hostalet; Guillem d'Olivela of Hostalet; Guillem de Sant Martí, draper of Girona; Berenguer de Sant Martí, draper of Girona; Berenguer Amall, cleric of Girona.
28. Farmer, *Surviving Poverty*, 2.
29. Ollich i Castanyer, "Les taxes dels notaris," 412–14; Baiges i Jardí, "El notariat català,"153–54; Blasco Martínez, "El notariado en Aragón," 213–15.
30. Bernardi, "En marge des contrats."
31. Smail, *Imaginary Cartographies*, 65–73.
32. Obradors-Suazo, "Making the Citizen," 27–33.
33. McDowell, "Place and Space," 12.
34. Hanawalt, "Medieval English Women," 22; Hutton, "Women, Men, and Markets," 415–30.
35. Hanawalt, "Medieval English Women," 24–26.
36. Ibid., 22–23.
37. Hutton, "Women, Men, and Markets," 410, 419–21.
38. ACF, vol. 9, fol. 67r.
39. For a discussion of this problem, see Wray, *Communities and Crisis*, 196.
40. Vinyoles, *Les barcelonines*, 83–85; Ferrer i Mallol, "L'instrument notarial," 46–50.
41. ACB, notaris, vol. 74, fols. 49r–60r, 179v–182r.
42. In Barcelona, 127 of 145 grooms (87.6%), 111 of 130 in Girona (85.4%), and 557 of 699 in Vic (79.7%) acted alone when signing their *capítols matrimonials*. In contrast, 91 of 145 brides in Barcelona (62.8%), 102 of 130 in Girona (78.5%), and 536 of 699 in Vic (76.7%) signed alongside one or more family members, who typically accepted at least partial responsibility for the payment of the dowry. See Ifft Decker, "Gender, Religious Difference," 74.
43. Kevin Mummey noted the same in Mallorca: Mummey, "Measuring the Margins," 114.
44. AHG Gi-4, vol. 4, fol. 82v. For other contracts involving the couple in which Berenguera is mentioned by name: AHG Gi-5, vol. 11, fol. 32v; AHG Gi-5, vol. 38, fols. 27r–28r; AHG Gi-6, vol. 23, fol. 21r–v.
45. AHG Gi-7, vol. 3, fols. 86v–87r, 93v.
46. ACF, vol. 10, fols. 141r–142r.
47. Women are better represented in agency contracts than in many other types of transactions. Women appointed 18% of agents in Barcelona (57 of 316), 9% in Girona (9 of 100), and 13.4% in Vic (39 of 290). In the larger sample of women's contracts, it is striking that although credit is one of the best-represented businesses in notarial documentation, women appointed agents far more often than they extended loans. In Barcelona, there were 43 women creditors

compared to 212 women appointing agents (Barcelona is a rare case in which the general sample has more agency than credit contracts, but the disparity is narrower: 183 credit contracts and 316 agency contracts). In Girona, there were 69 women creditors and 70 women appointing agents (a less drastic disparity but striking, given that in the general sample there are more than twice as many loans as agency contracts), and in Vic, 86 women creditors but 131 women appointing agents.

48. Women appointed male agents in 98.6% of contracts in Barcelona (209 of 212), 100% of women's 70 agency contracts in Girona, and 97.7% (128 of 131) of contracts in Vic.
49. ACB, notaris, vol. 53, fol. 11r.
50. AHG, Gi-6, vol. 4, fol. 137r.
51. Women sellers also outnumbered women buyers and lessors in Marseille, London, and Ghent. See Reyerson, "Land, Houses and Real Estate Investment," 44, 58–59; Hanawalt, *Wealth of Wives*, 164–65; Hutton, *Women and Economic Activities*, 61–65.

Chapter 4

1. Emery, *Jews of Perpignan*, 27–38; Assis, *Golden Age*, 238–39; Meyerson, *Jews in an Iberian Frontier Kingdom*, 46–49; Klein, *Jews, Christian Society, and Royal Power*, 164–73; Mell, *Myth of the Medieval Jewish Moneylender*, 1:198–216.
2. AHG Gi-6, vol. 9bis, fol. 33v.
3. Ishbili, *She'elot u-Teshuvot*, 139.
4. Astrug Caravida extended 119 extant loans between April 7, 1321 (AHG Gi-8, vol. 1, fol. 2r) and March 8, 1334 (AHG Gi-5, fols. 28, fol. 137r). His largest loan was for 3,400 sous: AHG Gi-5, vol. 15, fol. 130v.
5. Their daughter Bonafilla had married her first husband, Samuel Astrug, by the mid-1320s, and by her father's death in 1334 she had married her second husband (AHG Gi-5, vol. 7, fols. 97v–98r; AHG Gi-6, vol. 9bis, fol. 33v). Their daughter Ester had married David Bonjorn of Perpignan by 1332 and would not begin to seek a divorce until 1337; see Roth, "'My Precious Books and Instruments,'" 550–53. The girls formally inherited from their father, but the premortem donation writ had presumably put the bulk of the estate under the control of their mother: AHG Gi-5, vol. 20, fol. 22r–v.
6. After her first debt collection in 1334, she first extended a new loan on June 12, 1336 (AHG Gi-7, vol. 3, fol. 47v), and extended her last new loan on December 18, 1338 (AHG Gi-4, vol. 8, fol. 36r–v). She collected on a loan for the last time on January 17, 1340 (AHG Gi-6, vol. 22, fols. 73v–74r).
7. The same was true in Perpignan: Winer, *Women, Wealth, and Community*, 103.
8. Ifft Decker, "Gender, Religious Difference," 170–72.
9. Roth, "'My Precious Books and Instruments,'" 558–60.
10. Rich Abad, *La comunitat jueva de Barcelona*, 52–54; Mora, "Un recorregut per la història d'antic call," 89–90; Sagrera and Sureda, "Comunitat jueva i espais urbans," 35–45; Agresta, "'Unfortunate Jews,'" 325–26; Rubin, *Cities of Strangers*, 56–59.
11. Daileader, *True Citizens*, 148–51; Klein, *Jews, Christian Society, and Royal Power*, 193; T. Barton, *Contested Treasure*, 115–17; Rubin, *Cities of Strangers*, 57.
12. Assis, "Jewish Attitudes," 294–95; Assis, *Golden Age*, 145–60; Klein, *Jews, Christian Society, and Royal Power*, 45–50; T. Barton, *Contested Treasure*, 91–93.
13. Rowe, *The Jew, the Cathedral*, 118–34, 165–78, 225–32; Haskell, *Mystical Resistance*, 108–9, 115–33.
14. Rubin, *Corpus Christi*, 243–71; Muir, "Eye of the Procession"; Merback, "Living Image of Pity," 160–65; Brown, "Perceptions of Relics," 190–94; Arlinghaus, "Myth of Urban Unity," 224–28; MacEvitt, "Processing Together," 456–57; R. Perry, "Medieval Inchinata Procession at Tivoli," 48–58.

15. AHCB, Llibres del Consell, vol. 7, fol. 38r.
16. Rubin, *Cities of Strangers*, 62–66.
17. Meyerson, *Jews in an Iberian Frontier Kingdom*, 60.
18. AHCB, Llibres del Consell, vol. 1, fols. 93v–94r.
19. Nirenberg, *Communities of Violence*, 200–230.
20. Agresta, "'Unfortunate Jews,'" 330–39.
21. Fourth Lateran Council, Canon 68, in García y García, *Constituciones concilii quarti lateranensis una cum commentariis glossatorum*, 107; Cutler, "Innocent III," 111–16; Nirenberg, *Communities of Violence*, 133; Assis, *Golden Age*, 30, 284; Toaff, *Love, Work, and Death*, 173–79; Meyerson, *Jews in an Iberian Frontier Kingdom*, 75–76; Ray, *Sephardic Frontier*, 157–60; Alvarez Perez, "Next-Door Neighbors," 315; Rubin, *Cities of Strangers*, 61–62.
22. AHCB, Llibres del Consell, vol. 1, fols. 93v–94r; AHCB, Llibres del Consell, vol. 2, fols. 41v–42r; AHCB, Llibres del Consell, vol. 7, fol. 24v.
23. Pagarolas i Sabaté, "Notariat i cultura," 338; To Figueras, "Las funciones sociales del notariado," 174–75; Reyerson and Salata, *Medieval Notaries*, 12; Milton, *Market Power*, 39.
24. AHG Gi-4, vol. 12, fols. 55v–56r.
25. Assis, *Golden Age*, 46; Meyerson, *Jews in an Iberian Frontier Kingdom*, 76; Ray, "Images of the Jewish Community," 202.
26. The one exception to this tendency—which is in itself revealing—is the notarial practice of identifying converts with the term *baptizatus/a*. A woman named Sança was identified as *baptizata* in her 1334 manumission contract: ACB, vol. 93, fol. 128r. I found no obvious examples of Jewish converts to Christianity in the pre-1350 records, but after the 1391 mass conversions, the notaries often specified New Christians' convert identity in this matter. In 1392, for example, the convert Pere de Banyoles was described as "now newly baptized by the grace of God": AHG, Gi-5, vol. 435, fol. 58r–v.
27. Smail, *Imaginary Cartographies*, 195–203, 208–10.
28. ACB, notaris, vol. 46, fol. 77v.
29. AHG Gi-4, vol. 12, fol. 55v.
30. "Instrumenta christianica vel ebrayca": Arxiu de la Corona d'Aragó, Cancilleria, reg. 37, fol. 26v; published in Burns, *Jews in the Notarial Culture*, 151–52.
31. Burns, *Jews in the Notarial Culture*, 46, 151.
32. Ifft Decker, "Jewish Divorce," 49–52.
33. Rena Lauer witnessed a similar phenomenon in cases involving Jewish litigants that went before the Venetian courts of Crete: Lauer, *Colonial Justice*, 139–46.
34. On this imagery, see Lipton, *Dark Mirror*, 175–77. The notary responsible for the register probably drew the caricature himself: Cossar, *Clerical Households*, 29–31.
35. ACF, vol. 4603, cover.
36. Reference in this volume to Salomó Vidal as lender: ACF 4603, fol. 86v. Loan extended by his wife Goig: ACF 4603, fol. 84r.
37. Patton, *Art of Estrangement*, 59–61.
38. Lipton, "Isaac and Antichrist in the Archives."
39. Cossar, *Clerical Households*, 29.
40. Winer, "Jews in and out of Latin Notarial Culture," 114–15, 122–24.
41. Assis, *Golden Age*, 132–35; Burns, *Jews in the Notarial Culture*, 43–49; Winer, "Jews in and out of Latin Notarial Culture," 118–20; M. Perry, "*Hatpasah*—Jewish *Translata* Documents," 168.
42. M. Perry, "*Hatpasah*—Jewish *Translata* Documents," 181.
43. Credit arrangements between Christian debtors and Jewish creditors were recorded in 501 of 813 (61.6%) Barcelona contracts involving Jews, 5,431 of 6,366 (85.3%) Girona contracts involving Jews, and 3,232 of 3,601 (89.8%) of contracts from the general Jewish sample in Vic.
44. Emery, *Jews of Perpignan*, 17–25; Assis, *Golden Age*, 206–7, 238–39, 251–52; Assis,

Jewish Economy, 15–16; Toaff, *Love, Work, and Death*, 195–233; Meyerson, *Jews in an Iberian Frontier Kingdom*, 15–45; Ray, *Sephardic Frontier*, 55–71; Bensch, "Jewish Merchant in Romania"; Soifer Irish, *Jews and Christians*, 59–63; Mell, *Myth of the Medieval Jewish Moneylender*, 2:113–46; Schraer, *Stake in the Ground*, 198–235.

45. Assis, *Jewish Economy*, 15–27; Meyerson, *Jews in an Iberian Frontier Kingdom*, 180–84; Denjean, *Le loi de lucre*, 171–75; Winer, "Jews in and out of Latin Notarial Culture," 123.
46. Shatzmiller, *Shylock Reconsidered*, 9–20; Denjean, *Le loi de lucre*, 274–79.
47. Girondi, *Derashot ha-Ran*, 11; ibn Adret, *She'elot u-Teshuvot*, 2.134, 292; Assis, "Jewish Attitudes," 297–99.
48. Assis, "Jewish Attitudes," 300–301; Assis, *Golden Age*, 145–54; Ifft Decker, "Jewish Divorce," 45–52.
49. Klein, *Hebrew Deeds*, 19.
50. ACF 4595, fols. 61v–62r; Ifft Decker, "Jewish Divorce," 45–48.
51. Smail, *Imaginary Cartographies*, 14.
52. See, for example, the 1306 will of Astruga, wife of Jucef Abraham of Puigcerdà, in Burns, *Jews in the Notarial Culture*, 178–79.
53. Docs. 35, 36, and 38 in Burns, *Jews in the Notarial Culture*, 177–82. Unfortunately, the notary who copied the 1267 will of Goig, wife of David Canviador of Vic, failed to include the witness list: ACF, vol. 4583, fol. 8r.
54. Meyerson, *Jews in an Iberian Frontier Kingdom*, 112–16; Cohen, *Poverty and Charity*, 35–44, 51–70; Mell, *Myth of the Medieval Jewish Moneylender*, 1:174–87.
55. AHG Gi-4, vol. 12, fols. 55v–56r.
56. Nirenberg, *Communities of Violence*, 141; Ray, *Sephardic Frontier*, 165–74; Furst, "Captivity, Conversion, and Communal Identity," 202–11; S. Barton, *Conquerors, Brides, and Concubines*, 45–75; Safran, *Defining Boundaries*, 128–33, 139–40.
57. AHG Gi-5, vol. 45, fols. 132r–133v.
58. López de Meneses, "Una consecuencia de la peste negra," 97–106, 127–29; Gyug, "Effects and Extent of the Black Death"; Guilleré, "La peste noire," 106, 115–22, 140; Benedictow, *Black Death*, 80, 278–81; Rodriguez, "Spain," 182; Rich Abad, "Able and Available," 71–73; Einbinder, *After the Black Death*, 118–22.
59. AHG Gi-5, vol. 45, fol 69r–v, 90v–91r, 113r–v, 115v–116r, 116v, 117r, 117v–118r, 129v–130v, 131r; AHG Gi-6, vol. 45, fols. 124v–125r.
60. Ifft Decker, "Between Two Cities," 497–98.
61. In 1349, she hired a wet nurse for her infant daughter Druda: AHG Gi-6, vol. 45, fol. 42r–v. On wet-nursing, see Baumgarten, *Mothers and Children*, 119–53; Winer, "Conscripting the Breast," 177.
62. Meyerson, *Jews in an Iberian Frontier Kingdom*, 179–80.
63. Jordan, "Jews on Top," 48–52.
64. Shatzmiller, *Shylock Reconsidered*, 71–72, 104–18; Ifft Decker, "Jewish Women, Christian Women," 174–76.
65. Nirenberg, *Communities of Violence*, 13–14; Meyerson, *Jewish Renaissance*, 65–108.

Chapter 5

1. ACB, notaris, vol. 68, fols. 19v–22r, 24v–26r. On *societas* agreements: Reyerson, *Business, Banking, and Finance*, 10, 16–17.
2. Twelve women made thirteen investments (one woman made two separate investments) out of a total of twenty-eight. They contributed 1,654 pounds out of a total of 4,625 pounds and 5 sous.
3. Reyerson, *Business, Banking, and Finance*, 19–24; J. Goldberg, *Trade and Institutions*, 193–209.
4. ACB, notaris, vol. 68, fol. 24v.
5. ACB, notaris, vol. 52, fols. 16v–18r, 42r–46r.
6. Jaume Carbó consented to part of the grant Valença made to her nephew Peret Corretger in 1323, suggesting that he had received Sibil·la's share of the property as part of her dowry:

ACB, notaris, vol. 57, fols. 25r–27v. In a subsequent contract, Valença also granted her nephew the sum owed to her as her inheritance from her mother and her other brother Bernat, and she explained that she and Sibil·la jointly held property as collateral for these inheritance debts: ACB 57, fols. 27v–28v.

7. ACB, notaris, vol. 52, fols. 51r–52v, 53r–54v.
8. ACB, notaris, vol. 20, fol. 97r.
9. ACB, notaris, vol. 57, fols. 25r–28v; ACB, notaris, vol. 75, fols. 35r–37r.
10. Vinyoles, *Les barcelonines*, 35–50; Bennett, *Ale, Beer, and Brewsters*, 77–97; Farmer, *Surviving Poverty*, 117–31, 134; Bennett, *History Matters*, 72–79; Comas, Muntaner, and Vinyoles, "Elles no només filaven," 19–45; Farmer, *Silk Industries*, 106–36. For an exception, see Howell, *Women, Production, and Patriarchy*, 27–33.
11. Howell, *Women, Production, and Patriarchy*, 27–33; Farmer, "Merchant Women"; Comas, Muntaner, and Vinyoles, "Elles no només filaven," 25–31, 36–37; Hanawalt, *Wealth of Wives*, 6; Vinyoles Vidal and Muntaner i Alsina, "Acreedoras y deudoras," 279–80. For exceptions to this tendency, see Reyerson, "Women in Business"; Hutton, *Women and Economic Activities*, 35–58.
12. Mummey, "Measuring the Margins," 123.
13. AHCB, Llibres del Consell, vol. 10, fols. 20r, 24r–v, 27v–29r, 34v; vol. 11, fols. 23r–24r.
14. Maimonides, *Mishneh Torah*, Hilkhot Ishut 12:3. For a case from Egypt in which a husband wished to prevent his wife from working as a teacher, see Melammed, "He Said, She Said," 21–22, 28–29.
15. Grossman, *Pious and Rebellious*, 111–12; Melammed, "Jewish Woman in Medieval Iberia," 267; Rich Abad, "Able and Available," 79–82.
16. Klapisch-Zuber, "Women Servants in Florence," 59.
17. Vinyoles, *Les barcelonines*, 40–43; Klapisch-Zuber, *Women, Family, and Ritual*, 165–78; Klapisch-Zuber, "Women Servants in Florence"; Kowaleski, "Women's Work," 153–54; Chojnacka, *Working Women*, 14–22; Winer, *Women, Wealth, and Community*, 144–48; Wessell Lightfoot, *Women, Dowries, and Agency*, 116–21.
18. Wessell Lightfoot, *Women, Dowries, and Agency*, 56–57.
19. Winer has suggested that in at least one case from Perpignan in which a widow placed her daughter in domestic service, she acted out of financial desperation: Winer, *Women, Wealth, and Community*, 65.
20. Mosher Stuard, "To Town to Serve," 44–45; Winer, *Women, Wealth, and Community*, 144; Blumenthal, *Enemies and Familiars*, 82–87; Phillips, *Slavery in Medieval and Early Modern Iberia*, 103–4; Barker, *That Most Precious Merchandise*, 48–59.
21. Klapisch-Zuber, "Women Servants in Florence," 60; Blumenthal, *Enemies and Familiars*, 82–83; Phillips, *Slavery in Medieval and Early Modern Iberia*, 104; Barker, *That Most Precious Merchandise*, 72–74.
22. Klapisch-Zuber, "Women Servants in Florence," 68; Reyerson, "Women in Business," 121; Kowaleski, "Women's Work," 153; Klapisch-Zuber, *Women, Family, and Ritual*, 173–74; P. Goldberg, *Women, Work, and Life Cycle*, 168–73, 229–32; Winer, *Women, Wealth, and Community*, 57, 65; Wessell Lightfoot, *Women, Dowries, and Agency*, 117–20.
23. Domestic servants identified themselves only as their fathers' daughters in 9 of 11 contracts from Vic (81.8%), 26 of 28 from Barcelona (92.9%), and 25 of 26 from Girona (96.2%). Often their parents entered them into service.
24. The majority of women entering domestic service in Barcelona—17 of 28 (60.7%)—came from small villages, while another four (14.3%) came from smaller cities, including Puigcerdà,

Sabadell, and Girona. In Girona, in contrast, local urban servant girls were evenly matched with rural girls from parishes outside the city (13 of each), whereas in Vic, girls from the city outnumbered those from rural areas (6 urban women; 3 rural women; 2 of unknown background).

25. Wessell Lightfoot, *Women, Dowries, and Agency*, 20–21; Chojnacka, *Working Women*, 86.
26. Klapisch-Zuber, "Women Servants in Florence," 73–74; Kowaleski, "Women's Work," 153–54; Kowaleski, *Local Markets and Regional Trade*, 169; Winer, *Women, Wealth, and Community*, 144–48.
27. ACB, notaris, vol. 13, fols. 112v–113r.
28. Six of eight Christian wet nurses in Barcelona (75%), three of four in Girona (75%), and one of two in Vic (50%) were married; their husbands normally either granted permission or concluded the contract on their behalf.
29. Klapisch-Zuber, *Women, Family, and Ritual*, 159–60; Winer, "Conscripting the Breast," 175–76; Winer, "The Mother and the *Dida*," 60.
30. ACB, notaris, vol. 13, fol. 110v; AHG Gi-5, vol. 52, fol. 78v; see also Winer, "The Mother and the *Dida*," 58–59; Blumenthal, "'With My Daughter's Milk,'" 102–6.
31. Blumenthal, *Enemies and Familiars*, 80–93; Barker, *That Most Precious Merchandise*, 77–80.
32. Winer, *Women, Wealth, and Community*, 139–42.
33. ACB, notaris, vol. 3, fol. 47r–v.
34. AHG Gi-5, vol. 1, fols. 88v–89r.
35. Mosher Stuard, "To Town to Serve," 44–47; Winer, *Women, Wealth, and Community*, 148–56; Winer, "Conscripting the Breast," 166–72; Blumenthal, *Enemies and Familiars*, 147–48; Phillips, *Slavery in Medieval and Early Modern Iberia*, 106; Barker, *That Most Precious Merchandise*, 82, 107–8.
36. ACB, notaris, vol. 16, fol. 122v.
37. ACB, notaris, vol. 16, fols. 140v–141r.
38. Blumenthal, *Enemies and Familiars*, 70–76.
39. Women acting independently concluded contracts with 64.3% of female servants in Barcelona and 38.5% in Girona. While women in Vic never contracted domestic servants alone, they acted alongside their husbands to hire 45.5% of women servants.
40. Klapisch-Zuber, *Women, Family, and Ritual*, 143–44, 159–62; on Catalonia.
41. Women independently hired three of eight wet nurses in Barcelona, while a married couple hired a fourth: ACB, notaris, vol. 13, fol. 110v; ACB, notaris, vol. 232, fol. 16r; AHPB 16/4, fol. 13r; ACB, notaris, vol. 24, fol. 35r–v. In Girona, women hired two of four wet nurses: AHG Gi-5, vol. 6, fol. 65r; AHG Gi-5, vol. 52, fol. 78v. A married couple jointly employed their child's wet nurse in one of the two wet-nursing contracts from Vic: ACF, vol. 224, fol. 60r. See also Winer, "The Mother and the *Dida*," 57, 64–67; Winer, "Conscripting the Breast," 168–69.
42. Bennet, *History Matters*, 59–60.
43. See also Lavezzo, "Antisemitism and Female Power."
44. Evidence from Mallorca includes more examples of women buying as well as selling slaves: Mummey, "Measuring the Margins," 113–18.
45. ACB, notaris, vol. 13, fols. 115v–116v.
46. Anna Rich Abad had similar findings in her work on Barcelona after 1348: Rich Abad, *La comunitat jueva de Barcelona*, 178–84.
47. Ibn Adret, *She'elot u-Teshuvot*, 1.205; Girondi, *Derashot ha-Ran*, 68; Assis, "Sexual Behavior," 38; Grossman, *Pious and Rebellious*, 136–38.
48. Baumgarten, *Mothers and Children*, 134–44.
49. Winer, *Women, Wealth, and Community*, 135. This practice was also common in modern European Jewish communities: Kaplan, *Making of the Jewish Middle Class*, 155.
50. Ibn Adret, *She'elot u-Teshuvot*, 4.310.

51. AHG Gi-4, vol. 26, fol. 44v; AHG Gi-6, vol. 45, fol. 42r–v.
52. AHG Gi-6, vol. 14, fol. 11r–v.
53. AHG Gi-5, vol. 20, fols. 16v–17r.
54. Winer, *Women, Wealth, and Community*, 143.
55. ACF 4583, fol. 14v.
56. ACF 9, fol. 228r. On the cost-effectiveness of female domestic slavery, see Blumenthal, *Enemies and Familiars*, 86–87.
57. Winer, *Women, Wealth, and Community*, 143. Notably, inventories from Marseille rarely reported slaves as assets, although slaves appeared more regularly in inventories from Valencia and Sicily. See Smail, *Legal Plunder*, 67.
58. ACF 15, fol. 89r. For more on Goig, see chapter 7.
59. Smail, *Legal Plunder*, 113–15.
60. Farmer, *Surviving Poverty*, 47, 130–31.
61. Comas, Muntaner, and Vinyoles, "Elles no només filaven," 27–29, 31–35.
62. ACF 274, fol. 109r. Married couples also shared textile workshops in Ghent: Hutton, *Women and Economic Activities*, 106–12.
63. For example, Elisenda, widow of the carder Bernat Rubiol of Girona, who in 1324 bought raw wool on credit: AHG Gi-5, vol. 26, fol. 62r.
64. Vinyoles, *Les barcelonines*, 36–39.
65. ACF, vol. 3310, fols. 46v–47r.
66. Howell, "Women, the Family Economy," 200–216; Howell, *Women, Production, and Patriarchy*, 144–47, 162; Hanawalt, *Wealth of Wives*, 174, 177–80; Farmer, "Merchant Women"; Hutton, *Women and Economic Activities*, 106–15; Reyerson, *Women's Networks*, 106; Farmer, *Silk Industries*, 106–35.
67. Kathryn Reyerson has discussed in detail a woman who entered into a formal commercial partnership with her sons: Reyerson, *Mothers and Sons, Inc.*, 129–47.
68. For parallels elsewhere in Europe: Reyerson, "Women in Business," 121; Kowaleski, "Women's Work," 152; P. Goldberg, *Women, Work, and Life Cycle*, 124–27; Kowaleski, *Local Markets and Regional Trade*, 154; Hutton, *Women and Economic Activities*, 112–13; Farmer, *Silk Industries*, 130–31.
69. Guilleré, *Diner, poder, i societat*, 34–36.
70. AHG Gi-4, vol. 14, fols. 93v, 134r; AHG Gi-5, vol. 38, fols. 126v, 137v; AHG Gi-4, vol. 12, fol. 114v.
71. They formed a *societas* for four years with 886 pounds, 16 sous, and 9 pence in capital: AHG Gi-6, vol. 16, fols. 99v–101v.
72. AHG Gi-5, vol. 34, fols. 6v, 35v, 41v, 42r, 43r, 75r; AHG Gi-5, vol. 20, fol. 28r–v, 35r, 47r, 47v, 75r, 75v, 114r.
73. Kowaleski, "Women's Work," 152–53; P. Goldberg, *Women, Work, and Life Cycle*, 118–24; Kowaleski, *Local Markets and Regional Trade*, 153; Hutton, *Women and Economic Activities*, 112; Farmer, *Silk Industries*, 135–36, 145–48.
74. Ogilvie, *Bitter Living*, 165–67.
75. Women acting alone received very few *commenda* investments: 6 of 263 in Barcelona (2.3%), 5 of 240 in Girona (2.1%), and 4 of 436 in Vic (1%): Ifft Decker, "Gender, Religious Difference," 277. Other scholars have obtained similar results: Reyerson, "Women in Business," 130; Reyerson, *Business, Banking, and Finance*, 18, 23; Comas, Muntaner, and Vinyoles, "Elles no només filaven," 21–31.
76. ACB, notaris, vol. 36, fol. 179r–v.
77. Comas, Muntaner, and Vinyoles, "Elles no només filaven," 38.
78. ACB, notaris, vol. 96, fol. 24v.
79. Ifft Decker, "Public Economic Role," 62–63.
80. Rich Abad, *La comunitat jueva de Barcelona*, 154–56, 162–63; Rich Abad, "Able and Available," 80–81. Jews also worked in the silk industry in Paris: Farmer, *Silk Industries*, 153–57.
81. "Ratione serici crudi quod a vobis emimus habuimus et recepimus ad opus dictorum nostrorum officiorum sederie et tincturerie": ACB, notaris, vol. 46, fol. 77v.
82. ACB, notaris, vol. 16, fols. 51v, 169v.

83. Vinyoles, *Les barcelonines*, 48; Comas, Muntaner, and Vinyoles, "Elles no només filaven," 36. In England, women dominated the brewing trade until the fifteenth century: Bennett, "Village Ale-Wife," 24–28; Kowaleski, "Women's Work," 151; P. Goldberg, *Women, Work, and Life Cycle*, 111–18; Kowaleski, *Local Markets and Regional Trade*, 133–36; Bennett, *Ale, Beer, and Brewsters*, 14–36.
84. ACF 43, fol. 51r. For a similar example in Perpignan, see Winer, *Women, Wealth, and Community*, 41.
85. ACF 11, fol. 4r.
86. Nicholas, "Child and Adolescent Labor," 1122–24; S. Epstein, "Craft Guilds, Apprenticeship," 690–92.
87. Women artisans contracted girl apprentices in 9 of 10 contracts in Vic, 40 of 42 in Girona, and all 15 in Barcelona. Girls apprenticed with women or married couples in 18 of 30 contracts in Vic, 41 of 46 in Girona, and 15 of 17 in Barcelona: Ifft Decker, "Gender, Religious Difference," 286. On the gendered challenges women faced in managing boy apprentices, see Karras, *From Boys to Men*, 124–25. Girls also normally apprenticed with women in Montpellier: Reyerson, *Women's Networks*, 87–88.
88. ACF 289, fol. 42r. In England, similarly, male brewers often represented the family business publicly, though their wives performed most of the actual labor of brewing: Bennett, *Ale, Beer, and Brewsters*, 67–72.
89. Reyerson, *Women's Networks*, 76–77.
90. ACB, notaris, vol. 58, fols. 134r–135r; ACB, notaris, vol. 132, fol. 28r.
91. In Barcelona, parents or guardians acted on behalf of 6 of 17 female apprentices (35.3%), while another 2 acted with their fathers' consent. More dramatically, parents or guardians entered 38 of 44 girls into apprenticeships in Girona (86.4%), and 30 of 31 (96.8%) in Vic.
92. Reyerson, *Women's Networks*, 80–82.
93. In Barcelona, 10 of 15 mistresses (66.7%) were married, as were 29 of 42 (69%) in Girona. Only 4 of 10 independent mistresses in Vic (40%) were married, but girls apprenticed with married couples acting jointly in another 9 contracts.
94. E.g., AHPB 18/1, fols. 19v–20r; Rich Abad, *La comunitat jueva de Barcelona*, 156–59, 165.
95. Shatzmiller, *Shylock Reconsidered*, 72–79; García Marsilla, *Vivir a crédito*, 129; Denjean, *Le loi de lucre*, 4; Soldevila i Temporal, *Crèdit i endeutament*, 13, 18, 54, 107; Smail, *Legal Plunder*, 130–34.
96. Shatzmiller, *Shylock Reconsidered*, 9–14; Smail, *Consumption of Justice*, 148–57; Meyerson, *Jews in an Iberian Frontier Kingdom*, 184–85; Smail, *Legal Plunder*, 160–73.
97. Reyerson, *Business Banking, and Finance*, 62; Shatzmiller, *Cultural Exchange*, 18–19, 22–44; Smail, *Legal Plunder*, 75, 116–23.
98. Ray, *Sephardic Frontier*, 40–42, 51–53, 61; Schraer, *Stake in the Ground*, 149–66.
99. Women acting independently extended 10 of 163 loans in Barcelona (6.1%), 16 of 157 in Girona (10.2%), and 20 of 617 in Vic (3.2%).
100. García Marsilla, *Vivir a crédito*, 39–43; Gaulin, "Affaires privées," 81–84; Denjean, "Crédit et notariat," 188–89.
101. Denjean, *Le loi de lucre*, 16, 100–104.
102. AHG Gi-4, vol. 4, fol. 82v.
103. Milton, *Market Power*, 75–76.
104. ACF, vol. 9, fols. 117v, 124r, 159r, 174r.
105. Jordan, *Women and Credit*, 24–26; Smail, *Consumption of Justice*, 133–59; Reyerson, *Women's Networks*, 97–99.
106. For parallels elsewhere in the medieval and early modern Mediterranean, see Chojnacka, *Working Women*, 50–80; Reyerson, *Women's Networks*, 19–27, 100; Krakowski, *Coming of Age*, 62–67. In contrast, women in Ghent mostly extended loans to non-relatives as capital investments; see Hutton, *Women and Economic Activities*, 97–101.
107. AHG Gi-5, vol. 17, fol. 38r.
108. ACB, notaris, vol. 33, fols. 121v–122v; AHG Gi-5, vol. 11, fol. 47v; ACF, vol. 97/2, fol. 93r–v.

109. In the larger sample of women's transactions, widows extended 19 of 40 women's loans in Barcelona (47.5%), 28 of 67 in Girona (41.8%), and 28 of 86 in Vic (32.6%): Ifft Decker, "Gender, Religious Difference," 201. Women of unknown marital status—a category that probably encompasses both single women and some wives and widows who did not identify themselves in relation to their living or deceased husbands—extended another 8 of 40 loans in Barcelona (20%), 19 of 67 in Girona (28.4%), and 39 of 86 in Vic (45.3%). Widows typically accounted for the bulk of women's independent transactions throughout the western Mediterranean: Reyerson, *Business, Banking, and Finance*, 74; Winer, *Women, Wealth, and Community*, 33, 40–41. Single women often faced poverty but enjoyed economic independence: Wiesner, "Having Her Own Smoke," 199–207; Chojnacka, "Singlewomen," 221–25; Froide, "Marital Status," 243–52.

110. ACB, notaris, vol. 3, fol. 92r.

111. AHG Gi-5, vol. 9, fol. 94v. For more on the Renau family, see Guilleré, *Diner, poder, i societat*, 81–84, 108–9.

112. For Brunissenda acting as coexecutor with her son-in-law Eymeric dela Via and fellow Girona elite Bernat de Bordils, see AHG Gi-5, vol. 28, fols. 16r, 125r–v; AHG Gi-5, vol. 43bis, fol. 19r; AHG Gi-6, vol. 13, fols. 20v–21r; AHG Gi-8, vol. 1bis, fol. 1v.

113. In 1328, for example, Francesca, wife of the sailor Ramon Palau of Barcelona, collected on a loan of 108 sous 6 pence owed to her absent husband: ACB, notaris, vol. 92, fol. 54v. Susan McDonough argues that wives of sailors, merchants, and shipowners in Marseille often represented their husbands, who frequently left town on business: McDonough, *Witnesses, Neighbors, and Community*, 39.

114. ACB, notaris, vol. 92, fol. 29r.

115. Smail, *Legal Plunder*, 93–124.

116. AHPB, vol. 18/1, fol. 62r; AHPB, vol. 19/8, fol. 89r–v.

117. In Vic, women acting independently collected on 22 of 519 repaid loans (4.2%), whereas groups including women collected on 58 loans (11.2%). In contrast, women acting alone collected on 21 of 239 loans in Barcelona (8.8%), while groups including women collected on only 8 loans (3.3%), and in Girona women acting independently collected on 18 of 189 loans (9.5%), but only one group including a woman collected on a loan (0.5%): Ifft Decker, "Gender, Religious Difference," 201. While Christian women more often borrowed money than lent it in Catalonia and Montpellier, the opposite was true in Ghent; see Reyerson, *Business, Banking, and Finance*, 67, 76; Hutton, *Women and Economic Activities*, 82, 87.

118. ACF, vol. 259, fol. 117v.

119. Groups including women only received 10 of 165 loans in Barcelona (6.1%), but 136 of 615 loans in Vic (22.1%) and 82 of 259 in Girona (31.7%): Ifft Decker, "Gender, Religious Difference," 190.

120. ACB, notaris, vol. 94, fol. 97r–v.

121. ACB, notaris, vol. 7, fol. 93r.

122. Chabot, "Widowhood and Poverty"; Smail, *Legal Plunder*, 93–124.

123. In 1328, Dolça Balbos, widow of Pere Sabater of Carrer de Sant Pere of Vic, borrowed 30 sous from the priest Bernat Andreu of Santa Maria d'Olot "on account of the hunger and thirst which I sustain in the illness from which I now suffer, and for my other needs" (propter famem et sitim quas sustineo in infirmitate quam nunc patior et ad alia mea necessaria): ACF, vol. 105/1, fol. 6v.

124. Assis, *Jewish Economy*, 15–16; Ray, *Sephardic Frontier*, 56; Denjean, *Le loi de lucre*, 2; Mell, *Myth of the Medieval Jewish Moneylender*, 2:3–112.

125. Assis, *Jewish Economy*, 15–27; Meyerson, *Jews in an Iberian Frontier Kingdom*, 176–79; Denjean, *Le loi de lucre*, 177; Winer, "Jews in and out of Latin Notarial Culture," 116.

126. Mell, *Myth of the Medieval Jewish Moneylender*, 1:1–17, 199–208.

127. Baer, *History of the Jews*, 1:79–85, 197–212; Assis, *Golden Age*, 206–7, 238–39, 251–52; Meyerson, *Jews in an Iberian Frontier Kingdom*, 15–45; Meyerson, *Jewish Renaissance*, 109–37; Ray, *Sephardic Frontier*, 55–71; Bensch, "Jewish Merchant in Romania"; Soifer Irish, *Jews and Christians*, 59–63; Schraer, *Stake in the Ground*, 198–235.

128. In 1318, for example, Vic had ten taxpaying Jewish households: Llop Jordana, *Vides i veus*, 246. Between 1310 and 1320, thirty-nine Jews extended at least one loan, and thirteen extended five or more. Households may have been multigenerational, and many had multiple lenders—the top thirteen lenders represent at most nine households, as in four cases both husband and wife worked as creditors. These numbers suggest that in Vic, most Jewish households solvent enough to pay taxes had at least one member working at least part time as a moneylender.

129. Lipton, "Where Are the Gothic Jewish Women?," 141–42, 155–56; Patton, *Art of Estrangement*, 59–61, 88–96; Lipton, *Dark Mirror*, 201–37. For an exceptional depiction of a Jewish woman moneylender from England, see Lipton, "Isaac and Antichrist in the Archives," 8–11, 21–22.

130. Jordan, "Jews on Top," 53; Tallan, "Medieval Jewish Widows," 66; Einbinder, "Pucellina of Blois"; Grossman, *Pious and Rebellious*, 120; Keil, "Public Roles of Jewish Women," 320–21; Hoyle, "Bonds That Bind," 123; Bartlet, *Licoricia of Winchester*, 63–77.

131. The individual contracts preserved in loose parchments in the Arxiu Capitular de Barcelona contain hundreds of new Jewish loans dating between 1250 and 1291, but only one extended by a woman (ACB, pergamins, 1–6–1791). The extant notarial registers, dating from 1292, have fewer references to Jews than the surviving documentation from Girona or Vic; certain notaries, whose registers have largely not survived, may have specialized in Jewish business.

132. Reyerson, *Business, Banking, and Finance*, 73–74; Courtemanche, "Les femmes juives," 550; Assis, *Jews of Santa Coloma de Queralt*, 36–37; Denjean, *Juifs et Chrétiens*, 96–103; Winer, *Women, Wealth, and Community*, 87–88; Blasco Martínez, "Queen for a Day," 91–92; Ifft Decker, "Jewish Women, Christian Women," 166.

133. Claude Denjean, in contrast, argues that Jewish women were more economically active than Christian women: Denjean, *Juifs et Chrétiens*, 103. Rebecca Winer found that Jewish wives acted independently more often than Christian wives, but she also contends that Christian widows had more authority as independent guardians: Winer, *Women, Wealth, and Community*, 97–99, 115–16.

134. Married women extended only 6 of Jewish women's 72 loans in Girona (8.3%), while women of unknown marital status accounted for another 6 loans. Widows made the remaining 60 loans (83.3%). In contrast, Denjean and Winer found that Jewish wives played a more economically active role than Christian wives: Denjean, *Juifs et Chrétiens*, 103; Winer, *Women, Wealth, and Community*, 97. However, Winer emphasizes that Jewish widows undoubtedly played a more prominent role in commerce than wives in Perpignan, as in Barcelona and Girona (99–103).

135. On Jewish married couples in shared family businesses, see Winer, *Women, Wealth, and Community*, 98–99; Ifft Decker, "Public Economic Role," 58–63.

136. ACB, notaris, vol. 97, fol. 10r.

137. ACB, pergamins, 1–6–1896.

138. Latin: "nomine meo et dicti mariti mei."

139. Vidal had loaned Berenguer 70 sous in February of 1274. The loan should have yielded closer to 30 sous in interest (as

opposed to 26 sous), but Jewish lenders often agreed to charge interest only after a grace period of a few months. In a contract from May 15, 1349, for example, the Jewish creditor agreed not to charge interest if the debtor repaid within a month but charged the standard rate of 20% per annum after that date: ACB, notaris, vol. 221, fol. 102v.

140. Latin: "quod dictus maritus meus ratifficabit, approbabit, et laudabit vobis predictam solucio."

141. Reyerson, *Business, Banking, and Finance*, 62; Denjean, "Crédit et notariat," 194; Smail, *Legal Plunder*, 124–28.

142. Bonafilla, three witnesses (one Christian and two Jewish), the notary, and the scribe signed in Latin, while Bonafilla and one of the Jewish witnesses signed in Hebrew. Bonafilla did not physically sign in Hebrew; the text states that she orally consented and the witness, Roven Jaffia, signed on her behalf. While some Jewish women may have read Hebrew, few learned to write it. Although Elka Klein suggests that signing through a witness also provided a form of protection—plausible deniability if their husbands questioned their actions, for example—the complete absence of any signatures by women, regardless of their role in the transaction or claim to the property in question, suggests a lack of writing skills. See Klein, "Public Activities," 51–52; Planas Marcé, "'Only That Which I Have Lost,'" 108–9; Winer, "Jews in and out of Latin Notarial Culture," 120–21.

143. Ifft Decker, "Jewish Women, Christian Women," 171–74.

144. Lopez, *Commercial Revolution*, 76–77; Pryor, "Mediterranean Commerce"; Madurell Marimón and García Sanz, *Comandas comerciales barcelonesas*, 62–79; Reyerson, *Business, Banking, and Finance*, 9–14; Bensch, *Barcelona*, 221–32; Reyerson, *Art of the Deal*, 17–46.

145. Reyerson, *Business, Banking, and Finance*, 87–91.

146. Women acting independently extended 10 of 163 loans in Barcelona (6.1%) and 16 of 157 in Girona (10.2%). In comparison, they made 18 of 263 *commenda* investments in Barcelona (6.8%) and 23 of 148 in Girona (15.5%). The women-only sample also highlights the importance of *commenda* investments in women's economic strategies: in Girona, new *mutuum* loans outnumbered *commenda* contracts in the general sample, but women were more than twice as likely to make *commenda* investments (153 contracts) as *mutuum* loans (67). The general sample from Barcelona included slightly more *commenda* investments (263) than *mutuum* loans (173), but in the women-only sample, women made nearly five times as many *commenda* investments (194) as *mutuum* loans (40).

147. Women acting independently made 20 of 617 new loans in Vic (3.2%) and 17 of 436 *commenda* investments (3.9%). However, in the women-only sample, *mutuum* loans extended by women (86) dramatically outnumbered women's *commenda* investments (25).

148. Reyerson, *Business, Banking, and Finance*, 17, 22–23; Reyerson, "Women in Business," 129–32; Angelos, "Women in Genoese Commenda Contracts," 300; Winer, *Women, Wealth, and Community*, 33–34, 40–41. Women remained involved in investment in fifteenth-century Barcelona; see Vinyoles Vidal and Muntaner i Alsina, "Acreedoras y deudoras," 291.

149. Madurell Marimón and García Sanz, *Comandas comerciales barcelonesas*, 23–28, 126–28; Bensch, *Barcelona*, 231–32.

150. González de Lara, "Secret of Venetian Success," 252.

151. On popular commercial destinations for voyages from Barcelona, see Madurell Marimón and García Sanz, *Comandas comerciales barcelonesas*, 21–28, 34–39; Bensch, *Barcelona*, 221–32.

152. ACB, notaris, vol. 68, fol. 25r.

153. ACB, notaris, vol. 92, fols. 55v, 90v.
154. ACB, notaris, vol. 92, fol. 139v.
155. ACF, vol. 317, fol. 276r.
156. E.g., AHG Gi-6, vol. 2, fol. 11v.
157. Pryor, "Origins of the *Commenda* Contract," 26–29; J. Goldberg, *Trade and Institutions*, 125.
158. Assis, "Els jueus de Barcelona," 35–37, 41–49; Bensch, "Jewish Merchant in Romania," 137–48; Polonio Luque, "Jueus i conversos."
159. Green, "Conversing with the Minority," 105–6.
160. Ibid., 110.
161. Jordan, "Jews on Top," 50–55; Jordan, *Women and Credit*, 25–27.
162. Hoyle, "Bonds That Bind," 122–24.
163. Farmer, *Surviving Poverty*, 136–43.
164. Reyerson, *Women's Networks*.
165. Mummey, "Measuring the Margins," 115–18.
166. Reyerson, *Women's Networks*, 67–90.
167. Women debtors received 5.6% (3 of 54) of women's loans in Barcelona, 10.4% (7 of 67) in Girona, and 8.1% (7 of 86) in Vic.
168. Women debtors in Barcelona received 6.7% of all Christian loans (11 of 163), compared with 5.6% of women's loans (3 of 54).
169. Women debtors received 2.5% of all Christian loans in Girona (4 of 157) and 3.9% of Christian loans in Vic (24 of 617), compared with 10.4% of women's loans in Girona (7 of 67) and 8.1% in Vic (7 of 86).
170. ACF 286, fol. 112r–v.
171. Christian women acting alone received 1.7% (16 of 924) of Jewish women's loans in Vic and 2.5% (2 of 81) in Girona.
172. Christian women acting alone received 2.1% of all Jewish loans in Vic (55 of 2,663), compared with 1.7% (16 of 924) of Jewish women's loans.
173. Christian women acting alone received 1.7% of all Jewish loans in Girona (56 of 3,221), compared with 2.5% (2 of 81) of Jewish women's loans.
174. Courtemanche, "Les femmes juives," 553; Ifft Decker, "Jewish Women, Christian Women," 169, 171.
175. Christian women acting alone received 6.1% of all Jewish loans in Barcelona (16 of 261), compared with 15.6% (5 of 32) of Jewish women's loans.
176. Guild regulations elsewhere in Europe actively worked to keep women from competing with men; see Ogilvie, "Guilds, Efficiency, and Social Capital," 304–7. The Jewish community of Barcelona may have similarly sought to keep Jewish women creditors from remaining as competitors when they were no longer needed; indeed, most Jewish women creditors disappeared from the market in the early 1350s. See Rich Abad, "Able and Available," 79.
177. ACB, notaris, vol. 68, fol. 25v. The siblings are identified as such in a 1332 contract in which they acted jointly as testamentary exeuctors for their late brother Berenguer, alongside another brother, Galceran: ACB, notaris, vol. 72 fols. 6r–10r.
178. Jaume as merchant: ACB, notaris, vol. 57, fol. 112r–v.
179. AHCB, Manuals, vol. 1, fol. 70r, vol. 2, fol. 35r.
180. ACB, notaris, vol. 52, fol. 20r–v; ACB, notaris, vol. 20, fol. 97r. In Genoa, testators chose in-laws as executors nearly as often as close blood relatives: S. Epstein, *Wills and Wealth*, 223–26.
181. ACB, notaris, vol. 57, fols. 25r–27v; ACB, notaris, vol. 75, fols. 35r–37r.
182. It was common throughout the western Mediterranean for women to transfer inherited wealth back to men of their natal families: Courtemanche, *La richesse des femmes*, 168–81; Chojnacki, *Women and Men*, 127–30; Kuehn, *Heirs, Kin and Creditors*, 128, 130.
183. AHG Gi-4, vol. 14, fol. 31r; AHG Gi-6, vol. 16, fol. 108r; AHG Gi-5, vol. 35, fols. 16v–17r; AHG Gi-6, vol. 25, fol. 75r–v.
184. See chapter 2.
185. AHG Gi-6, vol. 34, fols. 100v–102r AHG Gi-6, vol. 39, fol. 94r.
186. Hutton, *Women and Economic Activities*, 98–99.
187. Krakowski, *Coming of Age*, 62–67, 294.

Chapter 6

This chapter was published in an earlier form as "Minding Manors: Gender, Acculturation, and Jewish Women's Landholding in Medieval Catalonia," *Hispania Judaica Bulletin* 14 (2019): 15–38.

1. ACB, pergamins, 1–1–31.
2. Klein, *Jews, Christian Society, and Royal Power*, 130–32, 136, 169, 213–14.
3. Ibid., 78–95.
4. ACB, pergamins, 4–42–311; Klein, *Jews, Christian Society, and Royal Power*, 178–79, 206.
5. Baucells i Reig, *Vivir en la edad media*, 2:1533–38.
6. Reyerson, "Land, Houses and Real Estate Investment," 40–41.
7. Bensch, *Barcelona*, 306.
8. The use of morabatins for many rents probably represents an attempt to fix rents in a gold coinage that enjoyed a higher degree of standardization. In Catalonia and Valencia, the buying and selling of rents was an important form of commerce, which eventually transformed into a credit instrument or annuity: García Marsilla, *Vivir a crédito*, 163–75, 178–84.
9. Kelleher, *Measure of Woman*, 57–60; Kelleher, "Later Medieval Law," 138–43; Mummey, "Measuring the Margins," 118–19.
10. In Barcelona, both Jews and Christians typically signed parchment contracts when they incurred a debt or relinquished rights. Jews typically signed in Hebrew: Winer, "Jews in and out of Latin Notarial Culture," 130–32. Scholars have found no examples of Jewish women signing their own names in Hebrew. Although some may have known how to read, they probably did not know how to write. Writing was a separate skill from reading, and even Jewish men—typically better educated than Jewish women—could often sign their names but nothing more. Instead, Jewish women asked Jewish men—who usually also acted as witnesses—to physically sign on their behalf: Planas Marcé, "'Only That Which I Have Lost,'" 108–9; Winer, "Jews in and out of Latin Notarial Culture," 120–21. Alternatively, Elka Klein suggested that signing through a witness provided a form of protection to women: Klein, "Public Activities," 51–52. However, the absence of any women's Hebrew signatures, regardless of their role in the transaction or claim to the property in question, requires us to consider the possibility that they did not have the opportunity to learn writing skills.
11. ACB, pergamins, 1–1–32.
12. Klein, *Jews, Christian Society, and Royal Power*, 84, 202, 214.
13. ACB, pergamins, 1–1–33.
14. ACB, pergamins, 1–1–34.
15. Klein, "Public Activities," 59.
16. Hughes, "From Brideprice to Dowry," 281–83.
17. Reyerson, "Land, Houses, and Real Estate Investment," 43–44, 48, 77–81.
18. Courtemanche, *La richesse des femmes*, 104–5, 112–15; Winer, *Women, Wealth, and Community*, 26–27.
19. Dillard, *Daughters of the Reconquest*, 76–77.
20. McMillin, "House on Sant Pere Street"; Reyerson, *Women's Networks*, 29–40.
21. On the use of this dichotomy in scholarship on northern European women, see, e.g., Simons, *Cities of Ladies*, 8–10.
22. Hanawalt, *Wealth of Wives*, 164–65.
23. Bennett, *Women in the Medieval English Countryside*, 164–68.
24. Hutton, *Women and Economic Activities*, 61–70.
25. Skinner, *Women in Medieval Italian Society*, 141–45, 191–92.
26. Klapisch-Zuber, *Women, Family, and Ritual*, 213–14; Kuehn, *Law, Family, and Women*, 101–26.
27. Chojnacki, *Women and Men*, 76–88; Bellavitis, *Famille, genre, transmission*, 58–62; Fregulia, "Widows, Legal Rights."
28. Vinyoles, *Les barcelonines*, 85; Pérez Molina, *Las mujeres ante la ley*, 172–80; Wessell Lightfoot, *Women, Dowries, and Agency*, 78–83.

29. Poska, *Women and Authority*, 45–50; Coolidge, *Guardianship, Gender, and the Nobility*, 77–87.
30. Massip i Fonollosa, *Costums de Tortosa*, 6.4.2, 13–14, 22–24; 6.10. Bensch, *Barcelona*, 245–46, 253; To Figueras, *Família i hereu*, 111–12, 117–19, 122–23.
31. Kelleher, *Measure of Woman*, 51–52.
32. Courtemanche, *La richesse des femmes*, 121–27; Mosher Stuard, "Burdens of Matrimony," 65–68; Bensch, *Barcelona*, 270–72; Skinner, *Women in Medieval Italian Society*, 196; Winer, *Women, Wealth, and Community*, 32–33; Bermejo, "Law, Women, and Marriage," 330–41.
33. Massip i Fonollosa, *Costums de Tortosa*, 4.21, 23, 28; 4.22.2, 4.
34. Aquinas, *Summa Theologica*, Part II, Q. LXXVIII, A. I.
35. Bensch, *Barcelona*, 268–69; Winer, *Women, Wealth, and Community*, 34–37; Kelleher, *Measure of Woman*, 52–53.
36. Massip i Fonollosa, *Costums de Tortosa*, 4.22.5; Winer, *Women, Wealth, and Community*, 26–27.
37. Kuehn, *Heirs, Kin, and Creditors*, 32–33.
38. Bonnassie, *La Catalogne*, 1:263; Bowman, *Shifting Landmarks*, 39–40, 47–50.
39. ACB, notaris, vol. 21, fols. 28r–29r.
40. ACB, notaris, vol. 17, fols. 8r–9v.
41. Agnes de Bossones, an elite woman of Montpellier, similarly sought to maintain and expand a fortune in landed wealth: Reyerson, *Women's Networks*, 29–30, 39.
42. Winer, *Women, Wealth, and Community*, 27.
43. ACB, notaris, vol. 17, fols. 8r–9v.
44. AHG Gi-8, vol. 23, fol. 22r.
45. AHG Gi-8, vol. 23, fol. 142v.
46. AHG, Gi-4, vol. 2, fols. 49v–50r; AHG, Gi-8, vol. 23, fols. 124r–125r, vol. 1bis, fol. 20v.
47. AHG, Gi-8, vol. 1bis, fol. 20v.
48. ACB, notaris, vol. 52, fols. 16v–18r.
49. ACB, notaris, vol. 52, fols. 42r–46r.
50. ACB, vol. 20, fol. 97r.
51. ACB, notaris, vol. 68, fol. 24v.
52. Raimunda, widow of En Pere de Camerada, an active widowed guardian of Perpignan, similarly relied occasionally on male relatives as agents, although she often acted decisively and alone: Winer, *Women, Wealth, and Community*, 61–62.
53. ACB, notaris, vol. 28, fols. 24v–25r; ACB, notaris, vol. 31, fols. 168v–170r, 176v–178v, 186v–190r; ACB, notaris, vol. 33, fols. 109r–110v.
54. ACB 20, fol. 130v; ACB 33, fols. 83v–84r; ACB 48, fols. 22r, 41v–42r. For women's guardianship, see Winer, *Women, Wealth, and Community*.
55. ACB, notaris, vol. 20, fol. 32v. On the Marquet family, see Ferrer i Mallol, "Una família de navegants," 137–267.
56. For example, a 1339 contract in which a widowed guardian of her minor children sold a piece of land with a vineyard, which she held from Blanca: ACB 113, fols. 157–59v.
57. ACB 28, fols. 35r–36r.
58. Bensch, *Barcelona*, 304–5; Winer, *Women, Wealth, and Community*, 26–27; Smail, *Legal Plunder*, 59–66; Reyerson, *Women's Networks*, 29–30.
59. Ruiz Domenec, "Urban Origins of Barcelona," 267–70, 281–82; Bensch, *Barcelona*, 304–13.
60. That is, 918 of 3856 contracts (23.8%).
61. In Barcelona, 289 of 1807 contracts (16.0%) deal with real estate. In Girona, 298 of 2458 contracts (12.1%) record real estate transactions.
62. Reyerson, "Land, Houses and Real Estate Investment," 73; Bensch, *Barcelona*, 306–7.
63. ACB, notaris, vol. 1, fols. 85v–87r, 105r–106r.
64. Reyerson, "Land, Houses and Real Estate Investment," 73–74; Bensch, *Barcelona*, 306–9.
65. Bensch, *Barcelona*, 307.
66. Reyerson, "Land, Houses and Real Estate Investment," 78–80.
67. AHCB, Consell de Cent, Manuals, vol. 2, fol. 87r–v.
68. The same year, Benvinguda, wife of Bertran Cabrera of Barcelona, and her husband sold houses in Carrer de Sant

Pau, in the suburbs of Barcelona, which Benvinguda had inherited from her late father. They held the houses from the canons of Barcelona, for an annual rent of 2 maravedis (about 15 sous), and sold them for 35 pounds: ACB, notaris, vol. 98, fols. 1r–6v.

69. ACB, notaris, vol. 27, fols. 18v–20r.
70. Women acted independently in 68 of 147 real estate sales involving women in Barcelona (46.3%), 60 of 186 in Girona (32.3%), and 80 of 561 in Vic (14.3%).
71. In Barcelona, 68.1% of male sellers sold property alone, compared to 46.3% of women sellers; in Girona, 47.9% of men sold property alone, versus 32.2% of women. Men were least likely to act independently in Vic, where only 38.3% of male sellers acted independently (but only 14.3% of women acted independently). In the smaller random sample of registers where I considered all contracts, independent male sellers appear at least four times as often as independent female sellers (96 to 20 in Barcelona; 69 to 8 in Girona; 158 to 29 in Vic).
72. Bensch, *Barcelona*, 304–6.
73. In Barcelona, 116 of 164 (70.7%) of properties were sold by individuals acting independently.
74. ACF, vol. 32, fol. 105v.
75. Bowman, *Shifting Landmarks*, 51.
76. ACF, vol. 60, fols. 29v–30r; ACF, vol. 213/2, fol. 22r.
77. ACF, vol. 90, fol. 6v; ACF, vol. 259, fol. 40r–v; ACF, vol. 317, fol. 63v.
78. Mixed-gender family groups sold property in 29 of 164 contracts in Barcelona (17.6%), 63 of 154 in Girona (40.9%), and 229 of 451 in Vic (50.8%). In comparison, groups of this type leased out property in only 6 of 116 contracts in Barcelona (5.2%), 22 of 142 in Girona (15.5%), and 82 of 453 in Vic (18.1%).
79. Bennett, *Women in the Medieval English Countryside*, 167–68; Winer, *Women, Wealth, and Community*, 58–61; Smail, *Legal Plunder*, 145–53.
80. For example, ibn Adret, *She'elot u-Teshuvot*, 6.4.
81. Ibid., 1.949. See also Klein, "Widow's Portion," 155–56.
82. Roth, "Regional Boundaries and Medieval Halakhah," 76, 82.
83. ACB, pergamins, 1–2–1362.
84. In the Hebrew deeds from Barcelona collected and translated by Elka Klein, women or groups including women sold five of eight properties (62.5%); married couples made two of these five sales. See Klein, *Hebrew Deeds*, docs. 1, 3; pp. 22–24; 32–34.
85. Ibn Adret, *She'elot u-Teshuvot*, 1.957.
86. Massip i Fonollosa, *Costums de Tortosa*, 4.21, 23, 28; 4.22.2, 4; Bonnassie, *La Catalogne*, 1:263; Bowman, *Shifting Landmarks*, 39–40, 47–50.
87. Klein, "Widow's Portion," 153.
88. E.g., ACB, pergamins, 1–6–701, 1–6–507; AHG Gi-6, vol. 35, fols. 108r–109r.
89. E.g., AHG Gi-5, vol. 1, fol. 34r.
90. ACB, pergamins, 1–6–2874.
91. E.g., ACB, notaris, vol. 8, fols. 174–19r.
92. ACB, pergamins, 4–42–311. For their father's Hebrew will, surviving in two copies, see ACB Hebreus 24ab, 25; Millàs i Vallicrosa, *Documents hebraics de jueus catalans*, docs. 25, 26. I also discuss this case in Ifft Decker, "Minding Manors," 31–33.
93. Klein, "Splitting Heirs," 49–50; ACB, pergamins, 4–42–311 (sale); ACB, pergamins, 1–6–4017 (quitclaim for sale price).
94. ACB, pergamins, 4–42–311; ACB, pergamins, 1–6–156.
95. Klein, "Splitting Heirs," 58–59.
96. Ibid., 59.
97. Asher ben Yehiel, *She'elot u-Teshuvot*, 34.2, ibn Adret, *She'elot u-Teshuvot*, 5.237.
98. Ifft Decker, "Jewish Divorce," 49–52.
99. Women as sellers: ACB, pergamins, 1–6–3980; 1–6–701, 1–2–1362, 1–1–31. Women provide consent: 4–42–311; 1–1–1357.
100. In comparison, 46.3% of Christian women's sales in Barcelona and 32.2%

in Girona involved women acting independently.

101. Ifft Decker, "Credit and Connections," 20–21.
102. Schraer, *Stake in the Ground*, 180–97, 234–35.
103. Klein, *Hebrew Deeds*, 21–91.
104. Meyerson, *Jews in an Iberian Frontier Kingdom*, 15–30; Ray, *Sephardic Frontier*, 38–53; Schraer, *Stake in the Ground*, 58–119.
105. Jews transacted with Christians in 16 of 25 Jewish real estate contracts from Barcelona (64.0%) and 39 of 57 from Girona (68.4%).
106. Assis, *Golden Age*, 210–31.
107. Ibid., 207–9; Nirenberg, *Communities of Violence*, 203–14.
108. Assis, *Golden Age*, 200; Schraer, *Stake in the Ground*, 73–75.
109. ACB, notaris, vol. 44, fols. 202r–203r.
110. AHG Gi-5, vol. 1, fol. 34r.
111. Llop i Jordana and Ollich i Castanyer, "Els espais de la comunitat jueva," 69–70; Llop i Jordana, *Vides i veus*, 42–43.
112. ACB, pergamins, 4–42–311.
113. AHG, Gi-5, vol. 26, fols. 91v–92r.
114. ACB, pergamins, 1–1–1357.
115. See chapter 2.
116. Klein, "Splitting Heirs," 53, 59–60.
117. In 1327, Bondia Enoch, son of Enoch Caravida of Girona, sold property alongside his widowed mother and his sisters, Bonadona and Reina: AHG Gi-5, vol. 7, fol. 9r–v. In 1328, Issach Gracià sold property in Barcelona that, the contract specifies, he had jointly inherited with his minor sister Mireta: ACB, notaris, vol. 63, fols. 115r–121r, ACB, notaris, vol. 65, fols. 128v–129r.
118. Ishbili, *She'elot u-Teshuvot*, 8.
119. See chapters 3 and 4.
120. Klein, "Public Activities," 56–57; Winer, *Women, Wealth, and Community*, 97–98; Ifft Decker, "Between Two Cities," 488–90, 494–95.
121. AHPB 18/1, fols. 17v–18r.
122. Benedictow, *Black Death*, 80–81, 281; Rodriguez, "Spain," 182; Lopez de Meneses, "Una consecuencia de la peste negra," 97–106; Rich Abad, "Able and Available," 71.
123. For Bonadona's one loan collection, see AHG, Gi-5, vol. 6, fol. 86v. Bonadona's contract appointing Vidal as her agent has not survived, but Vidal referred to it, providing the notary and date, when he collected on a loan owed to the late Bramon de Torroella in June of 1330. See AHG Gi-5 9, fols. 9v–10r.
124. AHG Gi-5, vol. 37, fol. 7r–v.
125. ACB, notaris, vol. 65, fols. 44r–45v.
126. ACB 44, fols. 202r–203r.
127. Maimonides, *Mishneh Torah*, Hilkhot Nachalot 1:1–5.
128. ACB 221, fols. 23v–25v.
129. Klein, "Splitting Heirs," 52–53.
130. ACB, pergamins, 1–2–1362.
131. ACB, pergamins, 1–6–2874.
132. Maimonides, *Mishneh Torah*, Hilkhot Nachalot 1:8.
133. Bonadona, widow of Astrug Caravida of Girona, stated in numerous contracts that her husband had made her a *donatio* (donation, grant, or gift) or *donatio inter vivos* (living-will grant) of all his debts, using a Hebrew contract: AHG Gi-5, vol. 38, fol. 110r–v. For an extensive study of a Jewish testator who used a Latinate will to name his wife as heir, disinheriting his convert brother in the process, see Agresta, "The Doctor and the Notary."
134. AHG Gi-5, vol. 3, fol. 18r–v.
135. ACB, notaris, vol. 96, fols. 19v–22v. The town is today known as Vilagrassa, located in the province of Urgell.
136. ACF 5, fols. 104r–105r.
137. ACB, notaris, vol. 7, fols. 108r–110r, 137v–138r.
138. ACB, notaris, vol. 23, fol. 47r–v.

Chapter 7

A portion of this chapter was published in an earlier form as "Credit and Connections: Jewish Women Between Communities in Vic, 1250–1350." Reproduced from *Women and Community in Medieval and Early Modern Iberia*, edited by Michelle Armstrong-Partida,

Alexandra Guerson, and Dana Wessell Lightfoot, by permission of the University of Nebraska Press. Copyright 2020 by the Board of Regents of the University of Nebraska.

1. ACF, vol. 4591, fol. 3r.
2. Bonmacip extended 295 new loans over the course of a career that lasted from 1264 (ACF, vol. 4582, fol. 3r) to 1311 (ACF 4594, fol. 8v). He had married his wife Reina by December 1266, when the couple jointly sold barley on credit to two Christians (ACF, vol. 4583, fol. 1v). Reina the elder extended her first independent extant loan in February 1267 (ACF, vol. 4583, fol. 4r), and her last in April 1305 (ACF, vol. 4592, fol. 54r).
3. Ifft Decker, "Credit and Connections," 22–24; Llop i Jordana, *Vides i veus*, 79–81.
4. Ifft Decker, "Credit and Connections," 25.
5. Contract in which Jucef referred to Bonmacip as his father-in-law: ACF, vol. 20, fol. 69v.
6. ACF, vol. 4589, fol. 19v.
7. ACF, vol. 4589, fol. 22r.
8. Regné, *History of the Jews in Aragon*, doc. 1338, 242; Llop i Jordana, *Vides i veus*, 94.
9. Assis, *Golden Age*, 260–61, 273–74; Ifft Decker, "Jewish Divorce," 53; Roth, "'My Precious Books and Instruments,'" 551–53.
10. Bonmacip died sometime between July 1311, when he extended his last extant loan, and May 1314, when Reina first referred to herself as his sole universal heir: ACF, vol. 4595, fol. 73r.
11. Sobrequés Vidal, "Familias Hebreas Gerundenses," 85–98.
12. Ifft Decker, "Between Two Cities," 489.
13. The data on Jewish divorce and remarriage in medieval Catalonia are too sparse to allow firm conclusions, but Catalan rabbis expressed little concern about either divorce or the remarriage of divorcées: Ifft Decker, "Jewish Divorce," 39–41. In the eastern Mediterranean, divorced brides contracted 20% of new marriages: Goitein, *Mediterranean Society*, 3:274.
14. First appearance of Astrug Caravida in Vic in September 1294, when he referred to himself as a "Jew of Girona, now an inhabitant of Vic": ACF, vol. 4591, fol. 15r. First reference to Astrug as the son-in-law of Bonmacip: ACF, vol. 4591, fol. 17r. First reference to Astrug Caravida as a "Jew of Vic": ACF, vol. 4591, fol. 19r–v. See also Ifft Decker, "Between Two Cities," 489. He is distinct from, but possibly related to, the previously referenced Astrug Caravida of Girona, whose widow Bonadona became an active creditor in the 1330s.
15. Reina extended 40 extant new loans between 1293 and 1310, while Astrug extended 71 loans over approximately the same period. The total volume of Reina's cash loans was 2,937 sous; the total volume of Astrug's was 4,605.2 sous. Reina extended an average loan of 73 sous and a median loan of 55.5 sous; her smallest loan was for 15 sous, while her largest was for 550 sous. Astrug extended an average loan of 65 sous and a median loan of 40 sous; his loans ranged between 7 sous and 1,100 sous. However, given the low rates of survival of notarial registers, these loans probably represent only a fraction of their total business. Based on the values of their extant loans, Reina's credit transactions accounted for 38.9% of the couple's total income from moneylending. Intriguingly, wives contributed 38% of household income, on average, in the United States in 1988. See Kristin Smith, *Recessions Accelerate Trend of Wives as Breadwinners*, Carsey Institute, Issue Brief no. 56 (Fall 2012), http://scholars.unh.edu/cgi/viewcontent.cgi?article=1180&context=carsey.
16. She first referred to herself as "Reina, wife of Astrug Caravida" in February 1296, with a loan of 34 sous to Berenguera, widow of Bartomeu de Gurri, and her daughter Bartomeua: ACF 4591, fol. 31v.

17. On the Jewish community in this decade, see Llop i Jordana, *Vides i veus*, 71–75.
18. See chapter 5; Winer, *Women, Wealth, and Community*, 87–88; Ifft Decker, "Jewish Women, Christian Women," 166; Ifft Decker, "Public Economic Role," 50–51.
19. Winer, *Women, Wealth, and Community*, 99–103; Ifft Decker, "Public Economic Role," 50–58; Ifft Decker, "Jewish Women, Christian Women," 166–67; and chapter 5. Cf. Denjean, *Juifs et Chrétiens*, 98–103.
20. Llop i Jordana, *Vides i veus*, 121.
21. Baer, *History of the Jews*, 1:79–85, 197–212; Assis, *Golden Age*, 206–7, 238–39, 251–52; Toaff, *Love, Work, and Death*, 195–214; Meyerson, *Jews in an Iberian Frontier Kingdom*, 15–45; Meyerson, *Jewish Renaissance*, 109–37; Ray, *Sephardic Frontier*, 55–71; Bensch, "Jewish Merchant in Romania"; Soifer Irish, *Jews and Christians*, 59–63; Mell, *Myth of the Medieval Jewish Moneylender*, 1:198–216; 2:120–38; Llop i Jordana, *Vides i veus*, 119–21; Schraer, *Stake in the Ground*, 198–235.
22. Ifft Decker, "Public Economic Role," 56–57; Llop i Jordana, *Vides i veus*, 79–81; Ifft Decker, "Credit and Connections," 22–24.
23. Loan extended by David Canviador: ACF 6, fol. 32v. On David's profession: Llop i Jordana, *Vides i veus*, 80. On moneychangers: Guilleré, *Diner, poder, i societat*, 73, 77–78, 101–3.
24. Goig's first extant loan dates from July 1252: ACF, vol. 6, fol. 4v. She extended 24 extant loans in the 1250s, 32 in the 1260s, and 26 in the 1270s; she also extended 6 loans of indeterminate date, probably from the 1260s or 1270s. Perhaps because of her age, she gradually exited the credit market in the 1280s, when she made only 5 extant loans. She also extended a new loan in 1310 after a long period of inactivity.
25. Goig's daughter-in-law, also named Goig, wife of Astrug David, extended 12 loans between 1285 and 1306, while the younger Goig's daughter-in-law, Reina, widow of Bonjueu Canviador, extended 21 loans between 1310 and 1317. Her own daughters never played a major role as creditors, and despite her own history as a successful businesswoman, Goig all but disinherited them: ACF, vol. 4583, fol. 8v; discussed in chapter 2.
26. Married couples extended only 12 loans, whereas women acting alone extended 924, and other types of groups including women extended 62. However, married couples collected on loans together on 23 occasions—despite the fact that new loans dramatically outnumbered repayment contracts in the extant documentation: my sample yielded 71 loan repayment contracts, as compared with 2,663 new loans. See also Llop i Jordana, *Vides i veus*, 30.
27. Joint loan: ACF, vol. 4593, fol. 17r. Tolsana's first independent loan: ACF, vol. 4594, fol. 3r. See also Ifft Decker, "Credit and Connections," 28.
28. ACF, vol. 4595, fol. 96r; ACF, vol. 4596, fols. 18r, 99r; ACF, vol. 4598, fol. 99v.
29. Winer, *Women, Wealth, and Community*, 96–99; Ifft Decker, "Public Economic Role," 58–61; Ifft Decker, "Credit and Connections," 28–30.
30. ACF, vol. 4593, fol. 16r; ACF, vol. 4599, fols. 4v–5r; ACF, vol. 4604, fol. 56v.
31. Zimmermann, "Le concept de Marca Hispanica"; Meyerson, *Jews in an Iberian Frontier Kingdom*, 2–5, 25–30; Ray, *Sephardic Frontier*, 3, 26–34; T. Barton, *Victory's Shadow*, 8–11.
32. Dillard, *Daughters of the Reconquest*, 12, 69, 73–75.
33. Freedman, *Diocese of Vic*, 20–25, 37, 147–49.
34. Assis, *Golden Age*, 168, 184; Llop i Jordana, "Les relacions entre les comunitats jueves," 211–14; Llop i Jordana, *Vides i veus*, 42–43.
35. Junyent, *La ciutat de Vic*, 111–14; Llop i Jordana and Ollich i Castanyer, "Els espais de la comunitat jueva," 67–77; Llop i Jordana, *Vides i veus*, 78–79.

36. Rich Abad, *La comunitat jueva de Barcelona*, 28–32.
37. Benedictow, *Black Death*, 80–81.
38. Ibid., 278–79; Gyug, "Effects and Extent of the Black Death"; Guilleré, "La peste noire," 106, 115–22.
39. Rodriguez, "Spain," 185–86.
40. Benedictow, *Black Death*, 281; Rodriguez, "Spain," 182; Lopez de Meneses, "Una consecuencia de la peste negra," 97–106; Rich Abad, "Able and Available," 71; Muntané i Santiveri, "Aproximació a les causes de l'avalot"; Einbinder, *After the Black Death*, 117–47.
41. Lopez de Meneses, "Una consecuencia de la peste negra," 127–29; Guilleré, "La peste noire," 140.
42. A study of the remains of mass graves, identified as the victims of the attack on the Jewish community of Tàrrega, found that young adults—perhaps recently married men and women, with no children or young children—bore the brunt of the attacks. This particular study also found a disproportionate number of women, but the authors caution that the disparity might reflect a large number of bodies of indeterminate sex: Ruiz Ventura and Subirà de Galdàcano, "Reconstrucció antropològica del pogrom," 130–32.
43. Babylonian Talmud, *Ketubot* 107a–b.
44. Widows extended 26 of 31 women's loans in Barcelona (83.9%), while an additional loan was extended by a widowed mother and her married daughter, acting jointly. Widows in Girona extended 7 of women's 9 loans (77.8%).
45. De Brocá y Montagut, *Historia del derecho de Cataluña*, 870–72; Vinyoles Vidal and Muntaner i Alsina, "Acreedoras y deudoras," 279; Mikes, "Legislació històrica de la família catalana," 183–85.
46. On April 2, 1349, Bonadona, widow of the prominent lender Samuel de Piera, collected on a debt owed to her late husband on the grounds that "in accordance with the written custom of Barcelona, I acknowledge that I possess the goods of my late husband, on account of my dowry and *sponsalicium*" (ex scripta consuetudine Barchinonense confiteor possidere bona que quondam fuerunt dicti mariti mei pro dote mea et sponsalicio meo): AHPB 18/1, fol. 8r–v.
47. In Barcelona, women's average (172 sous) and median loan (60 sous) were slightly lower than those for the community as a whole (186 sous and 80 sous, respectively), but in Girona, Jewish women extended larger average (244 sous) and median loans (150 sous) than the community at large (150 sous and 77.5 sous, respectively). On gender and loan size elsewhere: Winer, *Women, Wealth, and Community*, 88; Ifft Decker, "Jewish Women, Christian Women," 167–69.
48. Naming patterns suggest that Issach Bonjueu de Bellcaire was probably the son of Bonjueu Issach de Bellcaire. The complete lack of documentary connection between Issach and Bonjueu's widow Dura suggests that she might have been his stepmother rather than his mother.
49. Bonafilla began her career in 1347—before her husband's death—but extended 5 of her 9 new loans between 1349 and 1350: AHG Gi-5, vol. 45, fol. 72r–v; AHG Gi-6, vol. 45, fols. 21v–22r, 29r, 85r–v, 86v–87r. She also collected on 10 loans, several originally owed to her husband or father (from whom she inherited as sole heiress): AHG Gi-4, vol. 41a, fol. 20r; AHG Gi-5, vol. 45, fols. 37v, 38v, 41v, 70r, 83r, 864v, 94v–95r, 96r, 100r.
50. Rich Abad, "Able and Available," 73, 79.
51. See chapter 4.
52. Klein, "Public Activities," 61.
53. Appointed procurators acted on behalf of Jewish women in 9 of 16 women's debt collection contracts in Barcelona (56.3%) and 8 of 12 in Girona (40%).

54. Astruga, widow of Jucef de Beziers of Barcelona, returned home to Girona after her husband's death to fulfill her responsibilities as the universal heiress of her father, Bonjueu Bedoç, and one of several joint heirs to her uncle, Vidal Bedoç. She acted through an agent, Astrug Llobell Gracià, to collect on her late father's loans (for agency contract, see AHG Gi-5, vol. 45, fol. 133v–r; for quitclaims, see AHG Gi-5, vol. 45, fols. 91r–90v, 131r; AHG Gi-6, vol. 45, fols. 124v–125r). She appeared in person, but only alongside her cousins and uncles, to collect on the loans owed to her uncle (AHG Gi-5, vol. 45, fol. 69v–r, 116v, 117r, 118r–117v).
55. ACB, notaris, vol. 221, fol. 117v; AHPB 18/1, fols. 3r, 8r–9r.
56. ACB, notaris, vol. 44, fol. 81v; ACB, notaris, vol. 97, fols. 25r, 25v.
57. Bonadona does not refer to her guardianship when collecting on loans, but in late April, another Jewish woman—Astarona, wife of Issach Astrug Mercadal—collected on a loan originally owed to Issach de Piera, probably Samuel's brother and Bonadona's eventual replacement as guardian, and Bonadona, here referred to as *tutrix* of her minor son Bondia (AHPB 18/1, fol. 27r).
58. ACF, vol. 316, fol. 9r–v; ACF, vol. 378, fols. 48v–49r.
59. AHPB 18/1, fol. 66v.
60. Even Jewish widows not named as guardians probably maintained physical custody of their children as long as they did not remarry. Jewish widows who remarried lost even that right, at least in theory: Winer, *Women, Wealth, and Community*, 114–15.
61. AHPB 18/3, fols. 138r–139v; Rimentol, *El Protocol del Notari Bonanat Rimentol*, docs. 218–19.
62. Rich Abad, *La comunitat jueva de Barcelona*, 210.
63. AHPB 33/1, fol. 97v; Rich Abad, *La comunitat jueva de Barcelona*, 367.
64. Wray, *Communities and Crisis*, 102, 108.

Conclusion

1. Assis, *Golden Age*, 1.
2. Ibid., 1.
3. Assis, *Jewish Economy*, 241–42.
4. Meyerson, *Jews in an Iberian Frontier Kingdom*, 57–97; Ray *Sephardic Frontier*, 9, 71, 147–60.
5. Meyerson, *Jews in an Iberian Frontier Kingdom*, 5; Meyerson, *Jewish Renaissance*, 65–108, 157–83.
6. Siegmund, "Gendered Self-Government," 142.
7. Assis, *Golden Age*, 67.
8. Dubin, "Jewish Women, Marriage Law"; Zinger, "'She Aims to Harass Him'"; Lauer, *Colonial Justice*, 146–51, 154–58.
9. Assis, "Jewish Attitudes," 300–301; Assis, *Golden Age*, 145–60; Klein, *Jews, Christian Society, and Royal Power*, 45–50; Ray, *Sephardic Frontier*, 136; T. Barton, *Contested Treasure*, 77–78, 147–49, 167–68.
10. Baer, *History of the Jews*, 1:37, 236–42; 2:130–31.
11. An extreme and early version of this tendency can be found in Graetz, *History of the Jews*, 3:236. See critical discussions of this idealization of Iberian Jewry in Cohen, *Under Crescent and Cross*, 3–5; Ray, "Beyond Tolerance and Persecution," 2; Soifer, "Beyond *Convivencia*," 20–25; Tartakoff, "Testing Boundaries," 728–31.
12. Marcus, *Rituals of Childhood;* Nirenberg, *Communities of Violence*; Baumgarten, *Mothers and Children*; Meyerson, *Jews in an Iberian Frontier Kingdom*, 57–97; Ray, *Sephardic Frontier*, 145–72; Safran, *Defining Boundaries*; Nirenberg, *Neighboring Faiths*; Haskell, *Mystical Resistance*, 87–97.
13. Tartakoff, "Testing Boundaries," 731–33.

Bibliography

Archival Sources

Arxiu Capitular de Barcelona

Notaris, vols. 1–3, 5–9, 12–28, 32–33, 36, 39–41, 44–50, 52–53, 55, 57–58, 60–73, 75–78, 80, 88, 92–100, 113, 119, 128, 130, 134, 136–37, 220–24, 232–33

Pergamins, 1–1 series; 1–2 series; 1–6 series; 4–42 series

Arxiu Històric de Girona

Secció Girona-1, vols. 2, 7

Secció Girona-4, vols. 1–4, 6, 8, 11–12, 14, 19, 22, 38, 41a

Secció Girona-5, vols. 1, 3, 5–11, 13, 14–15, 17, 20, 22–23, 25–26, 28–29, 31–32, 34–39, 41, 43, 43bis, 45, 48, 52–55, 58

Secció Girona-6, vols. 1–2, 4–7, 9bis, 10, 12–13, 15–19, 21–26, 29–32, 34–40, 43, 45–47

Secció Girona-7, vols. 1, 3

Secció Girona-8, vols. 2, 23

Arxiu Històric de la Ciutat de Barcelona

Consell de Cent, vols. 1–7

Llibres del Consell, vols. 1–13

Arxiu Històric de Protocols de Barcelona

Manuals 1/1, 2/1, 3/1, 6/3, 10/3, 13/8, 14/2, 17/2, 18/1, 19/7–8

Arxiu i Biblioteca Episcopal de Vic, Arxiu de la Curia Fumada

Capítols Matrimonials, vols. 3301–5, 3307–8, 3311, 3314, 3317–18

Llibres Generals, vols. 5, 6, 8A, 9–11, 14–15, 17–21, 24, 27–28, 31–33, 35, 39, 41, 43, 46, 48, 51, 53, 60, 65, 70–71, 73, 75, 90, 94, 97, 105, 130, 213, 217bis, 223–24, 249, 255, 259, 263, 274, 286, 289, 292, 302, 316–17, 349, 378

Llibres Particulars, Comunitats, Judeorum, vols. 185, 4582–607

Published Primary Sources

Alighieri, Dante. *Paradiso.* Edited and translated by Robert Hollander and Jean Hollander. New York: Anchor Books, 2007.

Aquinas, Thomas. *The "Summa Theologica" of St. Thomas Aquinas.* 22 vols. London: Burns, Oates, and Washburne, 1917–25.

ben Asher, Jacob. *Arba'ah Turim*. Jerusalem: El Ha-Mekhorot, 1956–59.

Christine de Pizan. *The Book of the City of Ladies and Other Writings*. Edited by Sophie Bourgault and Rebecca Kingston. Translated by Ineke Hardy. Indianapolis: Hackett, 2018.

Eiximenis, Francesc. "Dotzè del Crestià." In *La societat catalana al segle XIV*, edited by Jill Webster, 81–82. Barcelona: Edicions 62, 1967.

Folgueroles, Pere de. *El Protocol del Notari Pere de Folgueroles*. Edited by Gener Gonzalvo, Maria Carme Coll, and Oliva Samprón. Barcelona: Fundació Noguera, 1996.

García y García, Antonio, ed. *Constituciones concilii quarti lateranensis una cum commentariis glossatorum*. Monumenta Iuris Canonici, Corpus glossatorum 2. Vatican City: Biblioteca Apostolica Vaticana, 1981.

Girondi, Nissim ben Reuben. *Derashot ha-Ran*. Edited by Leon A. Feldman. Jerusalem: Mosad Ha-Rav Kuk, 2003.

ibn Adret, Solomon. *Sefer She'elot u-Teshuvot ha-R'ashb'a*. Jerusalem: Mekhon Tiferet ha-Torah, 1988–90.

Ishbili, Rabbi Yom Tov ben Avraham. *She'elot u-Teshuvot*. Edited by Yosef Kafa. Jerusalem: Mosad Ha-Rav Kook, 1959.

Klein, Elka, ed. *Hebrew Deeds of Catalan Jews, 1117–1316*. Barcelona: Publicacions de la Societat Catalana d'Estudis Hebraics, 2004.

Maimonides, Moses. *Mishneh Torah*. Edited by Yohai Makbili, Yehiel Kara, and Hillel Gershuni. Haifa: Or Vishua Publications, 2009.

Marquès i Planagumà, Josep Maria, ed. *El "Cartoral del Rúbriques Vermelles" de Pere de Rocabertí, bisbe de Girona (1318–1324)*. Barcelona: Fundació Noguera, 2009.

Massip i Fonollosa, Jesús, ed. *Costums de Tortosa: Edició critica*. Barcelona: Fundació Noguera, 1996.

Millàs i Vallicrosa, J. M. *Documents hebraics de jueus catalans*. Barcelona, 1927.

Pons de Guri, Josep Maria, ed. *Les col·leccions de costums de Girona*. Barcelona: Fundació Noguera, 1988.

Regné, Jean. *History of the Jews in Aragon: Regesta and Documents, 1213–1327*. Jerusalem: Magnes Press, 1978.

Reyerson, Kathryn L., and Debra A. Salata, eds. *Medieval Notaries and Their Acts: The 1327–1328 Register of Jean Holanie*. Kalamazoo, MI: Medieval Institute Publications, 2004.

Rimentol, Bonanat. *El Protocol del Notari Bonanat Rimentol*. Edited by Laureà Pagarolas i Sabaté. Barcelona: Fundació Noguera, 1991.

Secondary Sources

Ackerman-Lieberman, Phillip I. *The Business of Identity: Jews, Muslims, and Economic Life in Medieval Egypt*. Stanford: Stanford University Press, 2014.

Agresta, Abigail. "The Doctor and the Notary: A Latinate Jewish Will from Fourteenth-Century Catalonia." *Viator* 46, no. 1 (2015): 229–48.

———. "'Unfortunate Jews' and Urban Ugliness: Crafting a Narrative of the 1391 Assault on the *Jueria* of Valencia." *Journal of Medieval History* 43, no. 3 (2017): 320–41.

Alfonso, Esperanza. "Medieval Portrayals of the Ideal Woman." *Journal of Medieval Iberian Studies* 3, no. 2 (2011): 131–48.

Allegra, Luciano. "A Model of Jewish Devolution: Turin in the Eighteenth Century." *Jewish History* 7, no. 2 (1993): 29–58.

Alvarez Perez, Rosa. "Next-Door Neighbors: Aspects of Judeo-Christian Cohabitation in Medieval France." In Classen, *Urban Space*, 309–29.

Angelos, Mark. "Women in Genoese Commenda Contracts, 1155–1216." *Journal of Medieval History* 20 (1994): 299–312.

Arlinghaus, Franz-Joseph. "The Myth of Urban Unity: Religion and Social Performance in Late Medieval Braunschweig." In *Cities, Texts, and*

Social Networks, 400–1500: Experiences and Perceptions of Urban Space, edited by Caroline Goodson, Anne E. Lester, and Carol Symes, 215–32. Burlington, VT: Ashgate, 2010.

Assis, Yom Tov. *The Golden Age of Aragonese Jewry: Community and Society in the Crown of Aragon, 1213–1327*. Oxford: The Littman Library of Jewish Civilization, 1997.

———. "Jewish Attitudes to Christian Power in Medieval Spain." *Sefarad* 52, no. 2 (1992): 291–304.

———. *Jewish Economy in the Medieval Crown of Aragon, 1213–1327: Money and Power*. Leiden: Brill, 1997.

———. *The Jews of Santa Coloma de Queralt: An Economic and Demographic Case Study of a Community at the End of the Thirteenth Century*. Jerusalem: Magnes Press, 1988.

———. "Els jueus de Barcelona i el comerç marítim amb la Mediterrània oriental." *Tamid: Revista Catalana Anual d'Estudis Hebraics* 2 (1998–99): 29–71.

———. "Sexual Behavior in Mediaeval Hispano-Jewish Society." In *Jewish History: Essays in Honor of Chimen Abramsky*, edited by Ada Rapoport-Albert and Steven J. Zipperstein, 25–59. London: Peter Halban, 1988.

Baer, Yitzhak. *A History of the Jews in Christian Spain*. 2 vols. Philadelphia: Jewish Publication Society of America, 1961.

Baiges i Jardí, Ignasi J. "El notariat català: Origen i evolució." In Sans i Travé, *Actes del I Congrès d'Història del Notariat Català*, 131–66.

Baiges i Jardí, Ignasi J., and Daniel Piñol Alabart. "Notariat, comerç, i cultura escrita a la Catalunya Nova (segles XIII–XV)." In *XV Congrés Internacional d'Història de la Corona d'Aragó (València, 2004)*, edited by Rafael Narbona Vizcaíno, 2:1825–38. Valencia: Universitat de València and Fundació Jaume II el Just, 2005.

Barker, Hannah. *That Most Precious Merchandise: The Mediterranean Trade in Black Sea Slaves, 1260–1500*. Philadelphia: University of Pennsylvania Press, 2019.

Bartlet, Suzanne. *Licoricia of Winchester: Marriage, Motherhood, and Murder in the Medieval Anglo-Jewish Community*. Edgware, UK: Vallentine Mitchell, 2009.

Bartoli Langeli, Attilio. "'Scripsi et publicavi': Il notaio come figura pubblica, l'instrumentum come documento pubblico." In *Notai, miracoli, e culto dei santi: Pubblicità e autenticazione del sacro tra XII e XV secolo*, edited by Raimondo Michetti, 55–71. Milan: Giuffrè, 2004.

Barton, Simon. *Conquerors, Brides, and Concubines: Interfaith Relations and Social Power in Medieval Iberia*. Philadelphia: University of Pennsylvania Press, 2015.

Barton, Thomas. *Contested Treasure: Jews and Authority in the Crown of Aragon*. University Park: Penn State University Press, 2014.

———. *Victory's Shadow: Conquest and Governance in Medieval Catalonia*. Ithaca: Cornell University Press, 2019.

Baskin, Judith R. "Dolce of Worms: The Lives and Deaths of an Exemplary Medieval Jewish Woman and Her Daughters." In *Judaism in Practice: From the Middle Ages Through the Early Modern Period*, edited by Lawrence Fine, 429–37. Princeton: Princeton University Press, 2001.

———. "Mobility and Marriage in Two Medieval Jewish Societies." *Jewish History* 22, nos. 1/2 (2008): 223–43.

Batlle i Gallart, Carme, and Maria Teresa Ferrer i Mallol. *El "Llibre del Consell" de la ciutat de Barcelona. Segle XIV: Eleccions municipals*. Barcelona: Consell Superior d'Investigacions Científiques, Institució Milà i Fontanals, Departament d'Estudis Medievals, 2007.

Baucells i Reig, Josep. *Vivir en la edad media: Barcelona y su entorno en los siglos XIII and XIV (1200–1344)*. 4 vols. Barcelona: Consejo Superior de Investigaciones Científicas, Institución Milá i Fontanals, Departmento de Estudios Medievales, 2004.

Baumgarten, Elisheva. *Mothers and Children: Jewish Family Life in Medieval Europe.* Princeton: Princeton University Press, 2004.

———. *Practicing Piety in Medieval Ashkenaz: Men, Women, and Everyday Religious Observance.* Philadelphia: University of Pennsylvania Press, 2014.

———. "'A Separate People'? Some Directions for Comparative Research on Medieval Women." *Journal of Medieval History* 34 (2008): 212–28.

Bellavitis, Anna. *Famille, genre, transmission à Venise au XVIe siècle.* Rome: École Française de Rome, 2008.

Bellomo, Manlio. *The Common Legal Past of Europe, 1000–1800.* Translated by Lydia G. Cochrane. Washington, DC: Catholic University of America Press, 1995.

Benedictow, Ole J. *The Black Death, 1346–1353: The Complete History.* Woodbridge, Suffolk: Boydell Press, 2004.

Benke, Nikolaus. "Why Should the Law Protect Roman Women? Some Remarks on the *Senatus Consultum Velleianum* (ca. 50 A.D.)." In *Gender and Religion: European Studies,* edited by K. Børresen, S. Cabibbo, and E. Specht, 41–56. Rome: Carocci, 2001.

Bennett, Judith M. *Ale, Beer, and Brewsters in England: Women's Work in a Changing World, 1300–1600.* New York: Oxford University Press, 1996.

———. *History Matters: Patriarchy and the Challenge of Feminism.* Philadelphia: University of Pennsylvania Press, 2006.

———. "The Village Ale-Wife: Women and Brewing in Fourteenth-Century England." In Hanawalt, *Women and Work,* 20–36.

———. *Women in the Medieval English Countryside: Gender and Household in Brigstock Before the Plague.* New York: Oxford University Press, 1987.

Bennett, Judith, and Amy Froide, eds. *Singlewomen in the European Past, 1250–1800.* Philadelphia: University of Pennsylvania Press, 1999.

Bensch, Stephen P. *Barcelona and Its Rulers, 1096–1291.* Cambridge: Cambridge University Press, 1995.

———. "A Baronial Aljama: The Jews of Empúries in the Thirteenth Century." *Jewish History* 22, nos. 1/2 (2008): 19–51.

———. "A Jewish Merchant in Romania: Isaac Llobell of Barcelona." In *A L'entorn de la Barcelona medieval: Estudis dedicats a la doctora Josefina Mutgé i Vives,* 137–51. Barcelona: Consejo Superior de Investigaciones Científicas, 2013.

Bermejo, Manuel Ángel. "Law, Women, and Marriage in Medieval Castile." In *Les stratégies matrimoniales (IXe–XIIIe siècle),* edited by Martin Aurell, 327–46. Turnhout, Belgium: Brepols, 2013.

Bernardi, Philippe. "En marge des contrats: Notes sur la comptabilité des notaires médiévaux et sur la rémunération des actes." In *Le notaire: Entre métier et espace public en Europe, VII–XVIII siècle,* edited by Lucien Faggion, Anne Mailloux, and Laure Verdon, 53–65. Aix-en-Provence: Presses universitaires de Provence, 2008.

Berner, Leila. "On the Western Shores: The Jews of Barcelona During the Reign of Jaume I, 'El Conqueridor,' 1213–1276." PhD diss., University of California, Los Angeles, 1986.

Blasco Martínez, Asunción. "El notariado en Aragón." In Sans i Travé, *Actes del I Congrès d'Història del Notariat Català,* 189–273.

———. "Queen for a Day: The Exclusion of Jewish Women from Public Life in the Middle Ages." In Caballero-Navas and Alfonso, *Late Medieval Jewish Identities,* 91–105.

Blumenthal, Debra. *Enemies and Familiars: Slavery and Mastery in Fifteenth-Century Valencia.* Ithaca: Cornell University Press, 2009.

———. "'With My Daughter's Milk': Wet Nurses and the Rhetoric of Lactation in Valencian Court Records." In *Medieval and Renaissance Lactations: Images, Rhetorics, Practices,* edited by Jutta

Gisela Sperling, 101–14. Burlington, VT: Ashgate, 2013.

Bonnassie, Pierre. *La Catalogne du milieu du Xe a la fin du XIe siècle: Croissance et mutations d'une société*. 2 vols. Toulouse: Association des Publications de l'Université de Toulouse-Le Mirail, 1975.

Bowman, Jeffrey. *Shifting Landmarks: Property, Proof, and Dispute in Catalonia Around the Year 1000*. Ithaca: Cornell University Press, 2004.

Bresc, Henri. "Rhétorique et culture notariale dans la Sicile des XIe–XIIIe siècles." *Provence Historique* 64, no. 256 (2014): 443–56.

Brown, Andrew. "Perceptions of Relics: Civic Religion in Late Medieval Bruges." In *Images of Medieval Sanctity: Essays in Honor of Gary Dickson*, edited by Debra Higgs Strickland, 181–205. Leiden: Brill, 2007.

Brundage, James. *The Medieval Origins of the Legal Profession: Canonists, Civilians, and Courts*. Chicago: University of Chicago Press, 2008.

Burns, Robert I. *Jews in the Notarial Culture: Latinate Wills in Mediterranean Spain, 1250–1350*. Berkeley: University of California Press, 1996.

Caballero-Navas, Carmen. "The Care of Women's Health and Beauty: An Experience Shared by Jewish and Christian Women." *Journal of Medieval History* 34 (2008): 146–63.

Caballero-Navas, Carmen, and Esperanza Alfonso, eds. *Late Medieval Jewish Identities: Iberia and Beyond*. New York: Palgrave Macmillan, 2010.

Carreras i Candi, Francesc. "Desenrotllament de la institució notarial a Catalunya en lo segle XIII." In *I Congrès d'història de la Corona d'Aragó*, 2:751–89. Barcelona: F. Altés, 1909–13.

Carvajal de la Vega, David. "La mujer castellana a fines de la Edad Media: Una firme defensore del patrimonio familiar." In *Ser mujer en la ciudad medieval europea*, edited by Jesús Á. Solórzano Telechea, Beatriz Arízaga Bolumburu, and Amélia Aguiar Andrade, 119–35. Logroño: Instituto de Estudios Riojanos, 2013.

Cases i Loscos, Lluïsa, ed. *Inventari de l'Arxiu Històric de Protocols de Barcelona*. Vol. 1, *Segles XIII–XV*. Barcelona: Fundació Noguera, 2001.

Cases i Loscos, Lluïsa, and Imma Ollich i Castanyer, eds. *Catàleg dels arxius notarials de Vic*. Barcelona: Fundació Noguera, 1986.

Castro, Américo. *España en su historia: Cristianos, moros y judíos*. Barcelona: Crítica, 2001.

Catlos, Brian A. "Contexto social y 'conveniencia' en la Corona de Aragón. Propuesta para un modelo de interacción entre grupos etno-religiosos minoritarios y mayoritarios." *Revista d'Història Medieval* 12 (2002): 220–35.

———. *Kingdoms of Faith: A New History of Islamic Spain*. New York: Basic Books, 2018.

———. *Muslims of Medieval Latin Christendom, c. 1050–1614*. Cambridge. Cambridge University Press, 2014.

Chabot, Isabelle. "Widowhood and Poverty in Late Medieval Florence." *Continuity and Change* 3, no. 2 (1988): 291–311.

Chojnacka, Monica. "Singlewomen in Early Modern Venice: Communities and Opportunities." In Bennett and Froide, *Singlewomen*, 217–35.

———. *Working Women of Early Modern Venice*. Baltimore: Johns Hopkins University Press, 2001.

Chojnacki, Stanley. *Women and Men in Renaissance Venice: Twelve Essays on Patrician Society*. Baltimore: Johns Hopkins University Press, 2000.

Classen, Albrecht, ed. *Urban Space in the Middle Ages and the Early Modern Age*. Berlin: De Gruyter, 2009.

Cohen, Mark. *Maimonides and the Merchants: Jewish Law and Society in the Medieval Islamic World*. Philadelphia: University of Pennsylvania Press, 2017.

———. *Poverty and Charity in the Jewish Community of Medieval Egypt*. Princeton: Princeton University Press, 2009.

———. *Under Crescent and Cross: The Jews in the Middle Ages*. Princeton: Princeton University Press, 1994.

Cohn, Samuel K., Jr. *Death and Property in Siena, 1205–1800: Strategies for the Afterlife*. Baltimore: Johns Hopkins University Press, 1988.

Comas, Mireia, Carme Muntaner, and Teresa Vinyoles. "Elles no només filaven: Producció i comerç en mans de dones a la Catalunya baixmedieval." *Recerques: Història, economia, cultura* 56 (2007): 19–45.

Comas i Via, Mireia. "Una adroguera barcelonina del segle XV: Isabel, vídua de Genís Solsona." *Pedralbes* 23 (2003): 337–46.

Conde y Delgado de Molina, Rafael. "Notaries i conflictes entre notaris en les ciutats i viles." In López Burniol and Sans i Travé, *Actes del II Congrès d'Història del Notariat Català*, 9–28.

Coolidge, Grace. *Guardianship, Gender, and the Nobility in Early Modern Spain*. New York: Routledge, 2011.

Corbella i Llobet, Ramon. *L'aljama de jueus de Vic*. Reprint, Vic: Publicacions del Patronat d'Estudis Ausonencs, 1984.

Cossar, Roisin. *Clerical Households in Late Medieval Italy*. Cambridge, MA: Harvard University Press, 2017.

Costa, Lluís, and Julià Maroto, ed. *Història de Girona*. Girona: Ajuntament de Girona, 2006.

Courtemanche, Andrée. "Les femmes juives et le credit a Manosque au tournant du XIVe siècle." *Provence Historique* 37 (1987): 545–58.

———. *La richesse des femmes: Patrimoines et gestion à Manosque au XIVe siècle*. Montréal: Bellarmin, 1993.

Crenshaw, Kimberlé. "Demarginalizing the Intersection of Race and Sex: A Black Feminist Critique of Antidiscrimination Doctrine, Feminist Theory and Antiracist Politics." *University of Chicago Legal Forum* 1989, no. 1, art. 8 (1989): 139–67.

Cuffel, Alexandra. *Gendering Disgust in Medieval Religious Polemic*. Notre Dame: University of Notre Dame Press, 2007.

Cutler, Allan. "Innocent III and the Distinctive Clothing of Jews and Muslims." *Studies in Medieval Culture* 3 (1970): 92–116.

Daileader, Philip. *True Citizens: Violence, Memory, and Identity in the Medieval Community of Perpignan, 1162–1397*. Leiden: Brill, 2000.

Davis, Natalie Zemon. *Fiction in the Archives: Pardon Tales and Their Tellers in Sixteenth-Century France*. Stanford: Stanford University Press, 1987.

De Brocá y Montagut, Guillermo Maria. *Historia del derecho de Cataluña: Especialmente de civil, y exposición de las instituciones del derecho civil del mismo territorio en relación con el Código civil de España y la jurisprudencia*. Barcelona: Herederos de Juan Gili, Editores, 1918.

Denjean, Claude. "Crédit et notariat en Cerdagne et Roussillon du XIIe au XVe siècle." In *Notaires et crédit dans l'occident méditerranéen medieval*, edited by François Menant and Odile Redon, 185–206. Rome: École Française de Rome, 2004.

———. *Juifs et Chrétiens: De Perpignan a Puigcerdà, XIIIe–XIVe siècles*. Canet, France: Editions Trabucaire, 2004.

———. *Le loi de lucre: L'usure en procès dans la Couronne d'Aragon à la fin du Moyen Âge*. Madrid: Casa de Velazquez, 2007.

Dillard, Heath. *Daughters of the Reconquest: Women in Castilian Town Society*. Cambridge: Cambridge University Press, 1984.

Donahue, Charles. *Law, Marriage, and Society in the Later Middle Ages: Arguments About Marriage in Five Courts*. New York: Cambridge, 2017.

Donat Pérez, Lídia, ed. *Jueus del rei i del comte: A l'entorn de les comunitats jueves de Girona i Castelló d'Empúries. Homenatge a Miquel Pujol i Canelles, Girona i Castelló d'Empúries, 19 d'octubre de 2012*. Girona Judaica 7. Girona: Patronat Call de Girona, 2014.

Dubin, Lois C. "Jewish Women, Marriage Law, and Emancipation: The Civil Divorce of Rachele Morschene in Late Eighteenth-

Century Trieste." In *Acculturation and Its Discontents: The Italian Jewish Experience Between Exclusion and Inclusion*, edited by David N. Myers, Massimo Ciavolella, Peter H. Reill, and Geoffrey Symcox, 119–47. Toronto: University of Toronto Press, 2008.

Einbinder, Susan L. *After the Black Death: Plague and Commemoration Among Iberian Jews*. Philadelphia: University of Pennsylvania Press, 2018.

———. "Pucellina of Blois: Romantic Myths and Narrative Conventions." *Jewish History* 12, no. 1 (1998): 29–46.

Emery, Richard. *The Jews of Perpignan in the Thirteenth Century: An Economic Study Based on Notarial Registers*. New York: Columbia University Press, 1959.

Engel, Diana R. "Marital Property Rights in Jewish Law: A Survey and Comparison." *National Jewish Law Review* 2 (1987): 97–122.

Epstein, Isidore. *Studies in the Communal Life of the Jews of Spain as Reflected in the Responsa of Rabbi Solomon ben Adreth and Rabbi Simon ben Zemach Duran*. New York: Hermon Press, 1968.

Epstein, Steven. "Craft Guilds, Apprenticeship, and Technological Change in Preindustrial Europe." *Journal of Economic History* 58, no. 3 (1998): 684–713.

———. *Wills and Wealth in Medieval Genoa, 1150–1250*. Cambridge, MA: Harvard University Press, 1984.

Farías Zurita, Víctor. *El mas i la vila a la Catalunya medieval: Els fonaments d'una societat senyorialitzada (segles XI–XIV)*. València: Universitat de València, 2009.

Farmer, Sharon. "Merchant Women and the Administrative Glass Ceiling in Thirteenth-Century Paris." In *Women and Wealth in Late Medieval Europe*, edited by Theresa Earenfight, 89–108. New York: Palgrave Macmillan, 2010.

———. *The Silk Industries of Medieval Paris: Artisanal Migration, Technological Innovation, and Gendered Experience*. Philadelphia: University of Pennsylvania Press, 2017.

———. *Surviving Poverty in Medieval Paris: Gender, Ideology, and the Daily Lives of the Poor*. Ithaca: Cornell University Press, 2002.

Ferrer i Juanola, Carles and Joan Villar i Torrent, "L'eclosió urbana de Girona." In Costa and Maroto, *Història de Girona*, 227–43.

Ferrer i Mallol, Maria Teresa. "L'instrument notarial (segles XI–XV)." In López Burniol and Sans i Travé, *Actes del II Congrès d'Història del Notariat Català*, 29–88.

———. "Una família de navegants: Els Marquets." In Batlle i Gallart and Ferrer i Mallol, *El "Llibre del Consell" de la ciutat de Barcelona*, 135–268.

Font y Rius, José Maria. "El desarrollo general del derecho en los territorios de la Corona de Aragón (siglos XII–XIV)." In *VII Congreso de Historia de la Corona de Aragón: Crónica, Ponencias, y Comunicaciones*, 1:289–326. Barcelona, 1962.

Freedman, Paul. *The Diocese of Vic: Tradition and Regeneration in Medieval Catalonia*. New Brunswick: Rutgers University Press, 1989.

———. "An Unsuccessful Attempt at Urban Organization in Twelfth-Century Catalonia." *Speculum* 54, no. 3 (1979): 479–91.

Fregulia, Jeanette M. "Widows, Legal Rights, and the Mercantile Economy of Early Modern Milan." *Early Modern Women* 3 (2008): 233–38.

Froide, Amy. "Marital Status as a Category of Difference: Singlewomen and Widows in Early Modern England." In Bennett and Froide, *Singlewomen*, 236–69.

Fumanal Pagès, Miquel Àngel, Joel Colomer Casamitjana, Júlia Gutiérrez Ortiz, Esther Redondo Garcia, and Francesc Florensa Puchol. "Documentant l'arqueologia: La casa de Massot Avengena a l'alfòndec del call Major de Barcelona (carrer de Sant Honorat, núm. 3)." *Tamid: Revista Catalana Anual d'Estudis Hebraics* 7 (2011): 9–71.

Furst, Rachel. "Captivity, Conversion, and Communal Identity: Sexual Angst and Religious Crisis in Frankfurt, 1241." *Jewish History* 22 (2008): 179–221.

Garcia i Sanz, Arcadi. "Precedents, origen, i evolució dels col·legis notarials." In Sans i Travé, *Actes del I Congrès d'Història del Notariat Català*, 167–87.

García Marsilla, Juan V. *Vivir a crédito en la Valencia medieval: De los orígenes del sistema censal al endeudamiento del municipio*. València: Universitat de València, 2002.

Gasperoni, Michaël. "Inheritance and Wealth Among Jewish Women in the Ghettoes of North-Central Italy (17th–18th Centuries)." *Mélanges de l'École française de Rome—Moyen Âge* 130, no. 1 (2018). https://doi.org/10.4000/mefrm.4060.

Gaulin, Jean-Louis. "Affaires privées et certification publique: La documentation notariale relative au crédit à Bologne au XIIIe siècle." In *Notaires et crédit dans l'occident méditerranéen medieval*, edited by François Menant and Odile Redon, 55–95. Rome: École Française de Rome, 2004.

Ginebra i Molins, Rafel. "Les escrivanies eclesiàstiques a Catalunya." In López Burniol and Sans i Travé, *Actes del II Congrès d'Història del Notariat Català*, 89–160.

Goitein, S. D. *A Mediterranean Society: The Jewish Communities of the World as Portrayed in the Documents of the Cairo Geniza*. 5 vols. Berkeley: University of California Press, 1978.

Goldberg, Jessica L. *Trade and Institutions in the Medieval Mediterranean: The Geniza Merchants and Their Business World*. Cambridge: Cambridge University Press, 2012.

Goldberg, P. J. P. *Women, Work, and Life Cycle in a Medieval Economy: Women in York and Yorkshire, c. 1300–1520*. Oxford: Clarendon Press, 1991.

González de Lara, Yadira. "The Secret of Venetian Success: A Public-Order, Reputation-Based Institution." *European Review of Economic History* 12, no. 3 (2008): 247–85.

Graetz, Heinrich. *A History of the Jews*. 6 vols. Philadelphia: Jewish Publication Society of America, 1956.

Green, Monica. "Conversing with the Minority: Relations Among Christian, Jewish, and Muslim Women in the High Middle Ages." *Journal of Medieval History* 34 (2008): 105–18.

Grossman, Avraham. *Pious and Rebellious: Jewish Women in Medieval Europe*. Waltham: Brandeis University Press, 2004.

———. *Ve-hu Yimshol Bakh? HaIshah beMishnatam shel Chakhmei Yisrael biYemei haBeynayim*. Jerusalem: Mercaz Zalman Shazar leToldot Yisrael, 2011.

Guerson, Alexandra, and Dana Wessell Lightfoot. "Crises and Community: Catalan Jewish Women and *Conversas* in Girona, 1391–1420." *Tamid: Revista Catalana Anual d'Estudis Hebraics* 14 (2019): 91–130.

———. "Mixed Marriages and Community Identity in Fifteenth-Century Girona." In *Women and Community in Medieval and Early Modern Iberia*, edited by Michelle Armstrong-Partida, Alexandra Guerson, and Dana Wessell Lightfoot, 132–50. Lincoln: University of Nebraska Press, 2020.

———. "A Tale of Two Tolranas: Jewish Women's Agency and Conversion in Late Medieval Girona." *Journal of Medieval Iberian Studies* 12, no. 3 (2020): 344–64.

Guilleré, Christian. *Diner, poder, i societat a la Girona del segle XIV*. Girona: Ajuntament de Girona, 1984.

———. "La peste noire a Gérone (1348)." *Annals de l'Institut d'Estudis Gironins* 27 (1984): 87–161.

Guzzetti, Linda. "Women's Inheritance and Testamentary Practices in Late Fourteenth- and Early Fifteenth-Century Venice and Ghent." In *The Texture of Society: Medieval Women in the Southern Low Countries*, edited by Ellen E. Kittel and Mary A. Suydam, 79–108. New York: Palgrave Macmillan, 2004.

Gyug, Richard. "The Effects and Extent of the Black Death of 1348: New Evidence for Clerical Mortality in Barcelona." *Medieval Studies* 45 (1983): 385–98.

Halbwachs, Verena. "Women as Legal Actors." In *The Oxford Handbook of Roman Law and Society*, edited by Paul J. du Plessis, Clifford Ando, and Kaius Tuori, 443–60. New York: Oxford University Press, 2016.

Hanawalt, Barbara. "Medieval English Women in Rural and Urban Domestic Space." *Dumbarton Oaks Papers* 52 (1998): 19–26.

———. *The Wealth of Wives: Women, Law, and Economy in Late Medieval London*. Oxford: Oxford University Press, 2007.

———, ed. *Women and Work in Preindustrial Europe*. Bloomington: Indiana University Press, 1986.

Hardwick, Julie. *The Practice of Patriarchy: Gender and the Politics of Household Authority in Early Modern France*. University Park: Penn State University Press, 1998.

Haskell, Ellen. *Mystical Resistance: Uncovering the Zohar's Conversations with Christianity*. Oxford: Oxford University Press, 2016.

Hezser, Catherine. "Roman Law and Rabbinic Legal Composition." In *The Cambridge Companion to the Talmud and Rabbinic Literature*, edited by Charlotte Elisheva Fonrobert and Martin S. Jaffee, 144–64. Cambridge: Cambridge University Press, 2007.

Hoffman, Philip T., Gilles Postel-Vinay, and Jean-Laurent Rosenthal. "Information and Economic History: How the Credit Market in Old Regime Paris Forces Us to Rethink the Transition to Capitalism." *American Historical Review* 104, no. 1 (1999): 69–94.

Howell, Martha C. *The Marriage Exchange: Property, Social Place, and Gender in the Cities of the Low Countries, 1300–1550*. Chicago: University of Chicago Press, 1998.

———. *Women, Production, and Patriarchy in Late Medieval Cities*. Chicago: University of Chicago Press, 1986.

———. "Women, the Family Economy, and the Structures of Market Production in Cities of Northern Europe During the Late Middle Ages." In Hanawalt, *Women and Work*, 198–222.

Hoyle, Victoria. "The Bonds That Bind: Money Lending Between Anglo Jewish and Christian Women in the Plea Rolls of the Exchequer of the Jews, 1218–1280." *Journal of Medieval History* 34 (2008): 119–29.

Hughes, Diane Owen. "From Brideprice to Dowry in Mediterranean Europe." *Journal of Family History* 3, no. 3 (1978): 262–95.

Hutton, Shennan. *Women and Economic Activities in Late Medieval Ghent*. New York: Palgrave Macmillan, 2011.

———. "Women, Men, and Markets: The Gendering of Market Space in Late Medieval Ghent." In Classen, *Urban Space*, 409–32.

Ifft Decker, Sarah. "Between Two Cities: Jewish Women and Exogamous Marriage in Medieval Catalonia." *Journal of Medieval History* 45, no. 4 (2019): 481–503.

———. "Credit and Connections: Jewish Women Between Communities in Vic, 1250–1350." In *Women and Community in Medieval and Early Modern Iberia*, edited by Michelle Armstrong-Partida, Alexandra Guerson, and Dana Wessell Lightfoot, 17–40. Lincoln: University of Nebraska Press, 2020.

———. "Gender, Religious Difference and the Notarial Economy in Medieval Catalonia, 1250–1350." PhD diss., Yale University, 2017.

———. "Jewish Divorce and Latin Notarial Culture in Fourteenth-Century Catalonia." In *Boundaries in the Medieval and Wider World: Festschrift in Honor of Paul Freedman*, edited by Thomas Barton, Susan McDonough, Sara McDougall, and Matthew Wranovix,

45–60. Turnhout, Belgium: Brepols, 2017.

———. "Jewish Women, Christian Women, and Credit in Thirteenth-Century Catalonia." *Haskins Society Journal* 27 (2016): 161–78.

———. "Minding Manors: Gender, Acculturation, and Jewish Women's Landholding in Medieval Catalonia." *Hispania Judaica* 14 (2019): 15–38.

———. "The Public Economic Role of Catalan Jewish Wives, 1250–1350." *Tamid: Revista Catalana Anual d'Estudis Hebraics* 11 (2015): 45–66.

Jordan, William Chester. "Jews on Top: Women and the Availability of Consumption Loans in Northern France in the Mid-Thirteenth Century." *Journal of Jewish Studies* 29, no. 1 (1978): 39–56.

———. *Women and Credit in Pre-Industrial and Developing Societies*. Philadelphia: University of Pennsylvania Press, 1993.

Junyent, Eduard. *La ciutat de Vic i la seva història*. Barcelona: Curial Edicions Catalanes, 1976.

Karras, Ruth Mazo. *From Boys to Men: Formations of Masculinity in Late Medieval Europe*. Philadelphia: University of Pennsylvania Press, 2003.

Keil, Martha. "Public Roles of Jewish Women in Fourteenth and Fifteenth-Century Ashkenaz: Business, Community, and Ritual." In *The Jews of Europe in the Middle Ages (Tenth to Fifteenth Centuries): Proceedings of the International Symposium Held at Speyer, 20–25 October, 2002*, edited by Christoph Cluse, 317–30. Turnhout, Belgium: Brepols, 2004.

Kelleher, Marie. "Later Medieval Law in Community Context." In *The Oxford Handbook of Women and Gender in Medieval Europe*, edited by Judith Bennett and Ruth Mazo Karras, 133–47. Oxford: Oxford University Press, 2013.

———. *The Measure of Woman: Law and Female Identity in the Crown of Aragon*. Philadelphia: University of Pennsylvania Press, 2010.

Kirshner, Julius. *Marriage, Dowry, and Citizenship in Late Medieval and Renaissance Italy*. Toronto: University of Toronto Press, 2015.

———. "Wives' Claims Against Insolvent Husbands in Late Medieval Italy." In *Women of the Medieval World: Essays in Honor of John H. Mundy*, edited by Julius Kirshner and Suzanne F. Wemple, 256–303. Oxford: Oxford University Press, 1985.

Klapisch-Zuber, Christiane. *Women, Family, and Ritual in Renaissance Italy*. Translated by Lydia G. Cochrane. Chicago: University of Chicago Press, 1985.

———. "Women Servants in Florence During the Fourteenth and Fifteenth Centuries." In Hanawalt, *Women and Work*, 56–80.

Klein, Elka. *Jews, Christian Society, and Royal Power in Medieval Barcelona*. Ann Arbor: University of Michigan Press, 2006.

———. "Protecting the Widow and the Orphan: A Case Study from Thirteenth-Century Barcelona." *Mosaic: A Review of Jewish Thought and Culture* 14 (1993): 65–81.

———. "Public Activities of Catalan Jewish Women." *Medieval Encounters* 12, no. 1 (2006): 48–61.

———. "Splitting Heirs: Patterns of Inheritance Among Barcelona's Jews." *Jewish History* 16, no. 1 (2002): 49–71.

———. "The Widow's Portion: Law, Custom, and Marital Property Among Medieval Catalan Jews." *Viator* 31 (2000): 147–63.

Kowaleski, Maryanne. *Local Markets and Regional Trade in Medieval Exeter*. Cambridge: Cambridge University Press, 1995.

———. "Women's Work in a Market Town: Exeter in the Late Fourteenth Century." In Hanawalt, *Women and Work*, 145–64.

Krakowski, Eve. *Coming of Age in Medieval Egypt: Female Adolescence, Jewish Law, and Ordinary Culture*. Princeton: Princeton University Press, 2018.

Kuehn, Thomas. "*Dos Non Teneat Locum Legittime*: Dowry as a Woman's Inheritance in Early Quattrocento Florence." In *Law and Marriage in Medieval and Early Modern Times:*

Proceedings of the Eighth Carlsberg Academy Conference on Medieval Legal History 2011, edited by Per Andersen, Kirsi Salonen, Helle Møller Sigh, and Helle Vogt, 231–48. Copenhagen: DJØF Publishing, 2012.

———. *Heirs, Kin, and Creditors in Renaissance Florence.* Cambridge: Cambridge University Press, 2008.

———. *Law, Family, and Women: Toward a Legal Anthropology of Renaissance Italy.* Chicago: University of Chicago Press, 1991.

Lacave, José Luis. *Medieval Ketubot from Sefarad.* Jerusalem: Magnes Press, 2002.

Lalinde Abadia, Jesús. *La Corona de Aragón en el Mediterraneo medieval (1229–1479).* Zaragoza: Talleres Editoriales Cometa, 1979.

———. "Los pactos matrimoniales catalanes." *Anuario de historia del derecho español* 33 (1963): 133–266.

Lauer, Rena. *Colonial Justice and the Jews of Venetian Crete.* Philadelphia: University of Pennsylvania Press, 2019.

Lavezzo, Kathy. "Antisemitism and Female Power in the Medieval City." *Postmedieval: A Journal of Medieval Cultural Studies* 10, no. 3 (2019): 279–92.

Lipton, Sara. *Dark Mirror: The Medieval Origins of Anti-Jewish Iconography.* New York: Metropolitan Books, 2014.

———. "Isaac and Antichrist in the Archives." *Past and Present* 232, no. 1 (2016): 3–44.

———. "Where Are the Gothic Jewish Women? On the Non-Iconography of the Jewess in the *Cantigas de Santa Maria.*" *Jewish History* 22 (2008): 139–77.

Llop i Jordana, Irene. "Les relacions entre les comunitats jueves de Vic i Girona (s. XIV)." *Annals de l'Institut d'Estudis Gironins* 42 (2001): 211–20.

———. *Vides i veus del call: Orígens i consolidació de la comunitat jueva de Vic.* Vic: Patronat d'Estudis Osonencs, 2019.

Llop i Jordana, Irene, and Imma Ollich i Castanyer. "Els espais de la comunitat jueva de Vic, entre la documentació escrita i l'arqueologia." *Tamid: Revista Catalana Anual d'Estudis Hebraics* 12 (2016–17): 65–111.

Lopez, Robert. *The Commercial Revolution of the Middle Ages, 950–1350.* Cambridge: Cambridge University Press, 1976.

López Burniol, Juan José, and Josep Maria Sans i Travé, eds. *Actes del II Congrès d'Història del Notariat Català.* Barcelona: Fundació Noguera, 2000.

Lopez de Meneses, Amada "Una consecuencia de la peste negra en Cataluña: El pogrom de 1348." *Sefarad* 19 (1959): 92–131.

Lorberbaum, Menachem. *Politics and the Limits of Law: Secularizing the Political in Medieval Jewish Thought.* Stanford: Stanford University Press, 2001.

MacEvitt, Christopher. "Processing Together, Celebrating Apart: Shared Processions in the Latin East." *Journal of Medieval History* 43, no. 4 (2017): 455–69.

Madurell Marimón, José Maria, and Arcadio García Sanz. *Comandas comerciales barcelonesas de la baja edad media.* Barcelona: Colegio Notarial de Barcelona, Departamento de Estudios Medievales, 1973.

Marcus, Ivan G. "Mothers, Martyrs, and Moneymakers: Some Jewish Women in Medieval Europe." *Conservative Judaism* 38, no. 3 (1986): 34–45.

———. *Rituals of Childhood: Jewish Acculturation in Medieval Europe.* New Haven: Yale University Press, 1996.

Marglin, Jessica. *Across Legal Lines: Jews and Muslims in Modern Morocco.* New Haven: Yale University Press, 2016.

McDonough, Susan Alice. *Witnesses, Neighbors, and Community in Late Medieval Marseille.* New York: Palgrave Macmillan, 2013.

McDougall, Sara. "Women and Gender in Canon Law." In *The Oxford Handbook of Women and Gender in Medieval Europe,* edited by Judith M. Bennett and Ruth Mazo Karras, 163–78. Oxford: Oxford University Press, 2013.

McDowell, Linda. "Place and Space." In *A Concise Companion to Feminist Theory,* edited by Mary Eagleton, 11–31. Oxford: Wiley-Blackwell, 2003.

McMillin, Linda. "The House on Sant Pere Street: Four Generations of Women's Landholding in Thirteenth-Century Barcelona." *Medieval Encounters* 12, no. 1 (2006): 62–73.

Melammed, Renée Levine. "He Said, She Said: A Woman Teacher in Twelfth-Century Cairo." *AJS Review* 22, no. 1 (1997): 19–35.

———. "The Jewish Woman in Medieval Iberia." In *The Jew in Medieval Iberia: 1100–1500*, edited by Jonathan Ray, 257–85. Brighton, MA: Academic Studies Press, 2012.

Mell, Julie. *The Myth of the Medieval Jewish Moneylender*. 2 vols. Cham, Switzerland: Palgrave Macmillan, 2017–18.

Merback, Mitchell B. "The Living Image of Pity: Mimetic Violence, Peace-Making and Salvific Spectacle in the Flagellant Processions of the Later Middle Ages." In *Images of Medieval Sanctity: Essays in Honor of Gary Dickson*, edited by Debra Higgs Strickland, 135–80. Leiden: Brill, 2007.

Meyer, Andreas. "Hereditary Laws and City Topography: On the Development of Italian Notarial Archives in the Late Middle Ages." In Classen, *Urban Space*, 225–44.

Meyerson, Mark D. *A Jewish Renaissance in Fifteenth-Century Spain*. Princeton: Princeton University Press, 2004.

———. *Jews in an Iberian Frontier Kingdom: Society, Economy, and Politics in Morvedre, 1248–1391*. Leiden: Brill, 2004.

Mikes, Tünde. "Legislació històrica de la família catalana medieval i moderna." *Bulletí de la Societat Catalana d'Estudis Històrics* 28 (2017): 163–96.

Milton, Gregory B. *Market Power: Lordship, Society, and Economy in Medieval Catalonia (1276–1313)*. New York: Palgrave Macmillan, 2012.

Mora, Victòria. "Un recorregut per la història d'antic call jueu de Barcelona." *Finestrelles* 4 (1992): 89–93.

Muir, Edward. "The Eye of the Procession: Ritual Ways of Seeing in the Renaissance." In *Ceremonial Culture in Pre-Modern Europe*, edited by Nicholas Howe, 129–53. Notre Dame: University of Notre Dame Press, 2007.

Mummey, Kevin. "Measuring the Margins: Women, Slavery, and the Notarial Process in Late Fourteenth-Century Mallorca." In *Rethinking Medieval Margins and Marginality*, edited by Ann E. Zimo, Tiffany D. Vann Sprecher, Kathryn Reyerson, and Debra Blumenthal, 111–28. London: Routledge, 2020.

Muntané i Santiveri, Josep Xavier. "Aproximació a les causes de l'avalot a Tàrrega de 1348." *Tamid: Revista Catalana Anual d'Estudis Hebraics* 8 (2012): 103–29.

Muntané Santiveri, Josep Xavier. "L'alimentació a l'aljama medieval de Tàrrega." *Urtx: Revista cultural de l'Urgell* 22 (2008): 107–27.

Nicholas, David. "Child and Adolescent Labor in the Late Medieval City: A Flemish Model in Regional Perspective." *English Historical Review* 110, no. 439 (1995): 1103–31.

Nirenberg, David. *Communities of Violence: Persecution of Minorities in the Middle Ages*. Princeton: Princeton University Press, 1996.

———. *Neighboring Faiths: Christianity, Islam, and Judaism in the Middle Ages and Today*. Chicago: University of Chicago Press, 2014.

Nussdorfer, Laurie. *Brokers of Public Trust: Notaries in Early Modern Rome*. Baltimore: Johns Hopkins University Press, 2009.

Obradors-Suazo, Carolina. "Making the Citizen, Building the Citizenry: Family and Citizenship in Fifteenth-Century Barcelona." In *Cities and Solidarities: Urban Communities in Pre-Modern Europe*, edited by Justin Colson and Arie van Steensel, 25–42. New York: Routledge, 2017.

Ogilvie, Sheilagh. *A Bitter Living: Women, Markets, and Social Capital in Early Modern Germany*. Oxford: Oxford University Press, 2003.

———. "Guilds, Efficiency, and Social Capital: Evidence from German Proto-Industry." *Economic History Review* 57, no. 2 (2004): 286–333.

Ollich i Castanyer, Immaculada. "Les taxes dels notaris de Vic al final del segle XVI." In *Homenatge a la memòria del Prof. Dr. Emilio Saez. Aplec d'estudis dels seus deixebles i col.laboradors*, 409–17. Barcelona: Institución Milà y Fontanals, Universitat de Barcelona, Centre d'Estudis Medievals de Catalunya, 1989.

Pagarolas i Sabaté, Laureà. "Gènesi i evolució dels registres notarials (segles XIII–XIX)." In López Burniol and Sans i Travé, *Actes del II Congrès d'Història del Notariat Català*, 161–84.

———. "Notariat i cultura: Els registres notarials." In Sans i Travé, *Actes del I Congrès d'Història del Notariat Català*, 333–50.

Patton, Pamela A. *Art of Estrangement: Redefining Jews in Reconquest Spain*. University Park: Penn State University Press, 2012.

Pérez Molina, Isabel. *Las mujeres ante la ley en la Cataluña moderna*. Granada: Universidad de Granada, 1997.

Perry, Micha J. "*Hatpasah*—Jewish *Translata* Documents from Medieval Catalonia: Formulae, Law, and Society." *Journal of Medieval Iberian Studies* 10, no. 2 (2018): 167–94.

Perry, Rebekah. "The Medieval Inchinata Procession at Tivoli: Ritual Construction of Civic Identity in the Age of the Commune." *Journal of the Society of Architectural Historians* 76, no. 1 (2017): 36–62.

Phillips, William D., Jr. *Slavery in Medieval and Early Modern Iberia*. Philadelphia: University of Pennsylvania Press, 2013.

Planas i Marcé, Sílvia. "Els jueus de Girona i els de Perpinyà: Relacions internes de dues comunitats bessones." In *Perpignan: L'histoire des Juifs dans la ville (XIIe–XXe siècles)*, 33–47. Perpignan: Agence Canibals, 2003.

———. "Les primeres notícies de jueus a Girona." In Costa and Maroto, *Història de Girona*, 203–24.

Planas Marcé, Sílvia. "'Only That Which I Have Lost Is Now Mine for Ever': The Memory of Names and the History of Jewish and *Converso* Women in Medieval Girona." In Caballero-Navas and Alfonso, *Late Medieval Jewish Identities*, 107–19.

———, ed. *Temps i espais de la Girona Jueva: Actes del Simposi Internacional celebrat a Girona 23, 24, i 25 de març de 2009*. Girona Judaica 5. Girona: Patronat Call de Girona, 2011.

Polonio Luque, Gloria. "Jueus i conversos en el comerç internacional barceloní de la baixa edat mitjana (1349–1450)." *Tamid: Revista Catalana Anual d'Estudis Hebraics* 9 (2013): 27–50.

Poska, Allyson. *Women and Authority in Early Modern Spain: The Peasants of Galicia*. Oxford: Oxford University Press, 2005.

Pryor, John H. "Mediterranean Commerce in the Middle Ages: A Voyage Under Contract of Commenda." *Viator* 14 (1983): 133–94.

———. "The Origins of the *Commenda* Contract." *Speculum* 52, no. 1 (1977): 5–37.

Rajabzadeh, Shokoofeh. "Alisaundre Becket: Thomas Becket's Resilient, Muslim, Arab Mother in the South English Legendary." *Postmedieval: A Journal of Medieval Cultural Studies* 10, no. 3 (2019): 293–303.

Ray, Jonathan S. *After Expulsion: 1492 and the Making of Sephardic Jewry*. New York: New York University Press, 2013.

———. "Beyond Tolerance and Persecution: Reassessing Our Approach to Medieval *Convivencia*." *Jewish Social Studies* 11, no. 2 (2005): 1–18.

———. "Images of the Jewish Community of Medieval Iberia." *Journal of Medieval Iberian Studies* 1, no. 2 (2009): 195–211.

———. *The Sephardic Frontier: The* Reconquista *and the Jewish Community in Medieval Iberia*. Ithaca: Cornell University Press, 2006.

Reyerson, Kathryn L. *The Art of the Deal: Intermediaries of Trade in Medieval Montpellier*. Leiden: Brill, 2002.

———. *Business, Banking, and Finance in Medieval Montpellier*. Toronto: Pontifical Institute of Mediaeval Studies, 1985.

———. "Land, Houses and Real Estate Investment in Montpellier: A Study of the Notarial Property Transactions, 1293–1348." *Studies in Medieval and Renaissance History* 6 (1983): 39–112. Reprinted in Kathryn Reyerson, *Society, Law, and Trade in Medieval Montpellier*. Aldershot: Ashgate, 1995.

———. *Mothers and Sons, Inc.: Martha de Cabanis in Medieval Montpellier*. Philadelphia: University of Pennsylvania Press, 2018.

———. "Women in Business in Medieval Montpellier." In Hanawalt, *Women and Work*, 117–44.

———. *Women's Networks in Medieval France: Gender and Community in Montpellier, 1300–1350*. New York: Palgrave Macmillan, 2016.

Rich Abad, Anna. "Able and Available: Jewish Women in Medieval Barcelona and Their Economic Activities." *Journal of Medieval Iberian Studies* 6, no. 1 (2014): 71–86.

———. *La comunitat jueva de Barcelona entre 1348 i 1391 a través de la documentació notarial*. Barcelona: Fundació Noguera, 1999.

Riera i Sans, Jaume. *Els jueus de Girona i la seva organització, segles XII–XV*. Girona Judaica 6. Girona: Patronat Call Girona, 2011.

———. *Els poders públics i les sinagogues, segles XIII–XV*. Girona Judaica 3. Girona: Patronat Call de Girona, 2006.

Riera Melis, Antoni. "Crisis frumentarias y políticas municipales de abastecimiento en las ciudades catalanas durante la baja edad media." In *Crisis de subsistencia y crisis agrarias en la edad media*, edited by Hipólito Rafael Oliva Herrer and Pere Benito i Monclús, 125–59. Seville: Universidad de Sevilla, 2007.

Rodriguez, Ana. "Spain." In *Agrarian Change and Crisis in Europe, 1200–1500*, edited by Harry Kitsikopoulos, 167–203. New York: Routledge, 2012.

Roth, Pinchas. "'My Precious Books and Instruments': Jewish Divorce Strategies and Self-Fashioning in Medieval Catalonia." *Journal of Medieval History* 43, no. 5 (2017): 548–61.

———. "Regional Boundaries and Medieval Halakhah: Rabbinic Responsa from Catalonia to Southern France in the Thirteenth and Fourteenth Centuries." *Jewish Quarterly Review* 105, no. 1 (2015): 72–98.

Rowe, Nina. *The Jew, the Cathedral, and the Medieval City*. Cambridge: Cambridge University Press, 2011.

Rubin, Miri. *Cities of Strangers: Making Lives in Medieval Europe*. Cambridge: Cambridge University Press, 2020.

———. *Corpus Christi: The Eucharist in Late Medieval Culture*. Cambridge: Cambridge University Press, 1991.

Rucqoi, Adeline. "Maintien et création du droit dans l'Espagne chrétienne (950–1050)." In *Guerre, pouvoirs, et idéologies dans l'Espagne chrétienne aux alentours de l'an mil: Actes du Colloque international organisé par le Centre d'Etudes Supérieures de Civilisation Médiévale, Poitiers-Angoulême (26, 27 et 28 septembre 2002)*, edited by Thomas Deswarte and Philippe Sénac, 123–40. Turnhout, Belgium: Brepols, 2005.

Ruiz Domenec, José Enrique. "The Urban Origins of Barcelona: Agricultural Revolution or Commercial Development?" *Speculum* 52, no. 2 (1977): 265–86.

Ruiz Ventura, Jordi, and M. Eulàlia Subirà de Galdàcano. "Reconstrucció antropològica del pogrom de 1348 a Tàrrega." *Urtx: Revista cultural d'Urgell* 23, no. 1 (2009): 127–37.

Safran, Janina. *Defining Boundaries in al-Andalus: Muslims, Christians, and Jews in*

Islamic Iberia. Ithaca: Cornell University Press, 2013.

Sagrera, Jordi, and Marc Sureda. "Comunitat jueva i espais urbans a Girona (1000–1500)." In Planas Marcé, *Temps i espais de la Girona Jueva*, 35–66.

Sans i Travé, Josep Maria, ed. *Actes del I Congrès d'Història del Notariat Català: Barcelona, 11, 12, i 13 de novembre de 1993*. Barcelona: Fundació Noguera, 1994.

Schraer, Michael. *A Stake in the Ground: Jews and Property Investment in the Medieval Crown of Aragon*. Leiden: Brill, 2019.

Schwartzmann, Julia. "Gender Concepts of Medieval Thinkers and The Book of Proverbs." *Jewish Studies Quarterly* 7, no. 3 (2000): 183–202.

Seal, Samantha Katz, and Nicole Nolan Sidhu. "Feminist Intersectionality: Centering the Margins in 21st-Century Medieval Studies." *Postmedieval: A Journal of Medieval Cultural Studies* 10, no. 3 (2019): 272–78.

Septimus, Bernard. *Hispano-Jewish Culture in Transition: The Career and Controversies of Ramah*. Cambridge, MA: Harvard University Press, 1982.

Shatzmiller, Joseph. *Cultural Exchange: Jews, Christians, and Art in the Medieval Marketplace*. Princeton: Princeton University Press, 2013.

———. *Shylock Reconsidered: Jews, Moneylending, and Medieval Society*. Berkeley: University of California Press, 1989.

Siegmund, Stefanie B. "Division of the Dowry on the Death of the Daughter: An Instance in the Negotiation of Laws and Jewish Customs in Early Modern Tuscany." *Jewish History* 16, no. 1 (2002): 73–106.

———. "Gendered Self-Government in Early Modern Jewish History: The Florentine Ghetto and Beyond." In *Gendering the Jewish Past*, edited by Marc Lee Raphael, 137–55. Williamsburg, VA: Department of Religion, The College of William and Mary, 2002.

Simons, Walter. *Cities of Ladies: Beguine Communities in the Medieval Low Countries, 1200–1565*. Philadelphia: University of Pennsylvania Press, 2003.

Simonsohn, Uriel. *A Common Justice: The Legal Allegiances of Christians and Jews Under Early Islam*. Philadelphia: University of Pennsylvania Press, 2011.

Skinner, Patricia. *Women in Medieval Italian Society, 500–1200*. Harlow, UK: Pearson Education, 2001.

Smail, Daniel Lord. *The Consumption of Justice: Emotions, Publicity, and Legal Culture in Marseille, 1264–1423*. Ithaca: Cornell University Press, 2003.

———. *Imaginary Cartographies: Possession and Identity in Late Medieval Marseille*. Ithaca: Cornell University Press, 1999.

———. *Legal Plunder: Households and Debt Collection in Late Medieval Europe*. Cambridge, MA: Harvard University Press, 2016.

———. "Notaries, Courts, and the Legal Culture of Late Medieval Marseille." In *Urban and Rural Communities in Medieval France: Provence and Languedoc, 1000–1500*, edited by Kathryn Reyerson and John Brendel, 23–50. Leiden: Brill, 1998.

Smail, Daniel Lord, Kathleeen Smail, and Caroline Duroselle-Melish. "Démanteler le patrimoine: Les femmes et les biens dans la Marseille medieval." *Annales. Histoire, Sciences Sociales* 52, no. 2 (1997): 343–68.

Smith, Jennifer. "Unfamiliar Territory: Women, Land, and Law in Occitania, 1130–1250." In *Medieval Women and the Law*, edited by Noel Menuge, 19–40. Woodbridge, Suffolk: Boydell Press, 2000.

Sobrequés Vidal, Santiago. "Familias Hebreas Gerundenses: Los Zabarra y Los Caravita." *Annals de l'Institut d'Estudis Gironins* 2 (1947): 68–98.

Soifer, Maya. "Beyond *Convivencia*: Critical Reflections on the Historiography of Interfaith Relations in Christian Spain." *Journal of Medieval Iberian Studies* 1, no. 1 (2009): 19–35.

Soifer Irish, Maya. *Jews and Christians in Medieval Castile: Tradition, Coexistence, and Change*. Washington, DC: Catholic University of America Press, 2016.

Soldevila i Temporal, Xavier. *Crèdit i endeutament al comtat d'Empúries (1330–1335)*. Castelló d'Empúries: Ajuntament de Castelló d'Empúries, 2008.

Stow, Kenneth R. "Ethnic Amalgamation, Like It or Not: Inheritance in Early Modern Jewish Rome." *Jewish History* 16, no. 1 (2002): 107–21.

———. "The Jewish Family in the Rhineland: Form and Function." *American Historical Review* 92 (1987): 1085–110.

———. *Theater of Acculturation: The Roman Ghetto in the Sixteenth Century*. Seattle: University of Washington Press, 2001.

Stuard, Susan Mosher. "Burdens of Matrimony: Husbanding and Gender in Late Medieval Italy." In *Medieval Masculinities: Regarding Men in the Middle Ages*, edited by Clare A. Lees, 61–71. Minneapolis: University of Minnesota Press, 1994.

———. "The Dominion of Gender, or How Women Fared in the High Middle Ages." In *Becoming Visible: Women in European History*, 3rd ed., edited by Susan Mosher Stuard, Merry E. Wiesner, and Renate Bridenthal, 129–50. Boston: Houghton Mifflin, 1998.

———. "Dowry Increase and Increment in Wealth in Medieval Ragusa (Dubrovnik)." *Journal of Economic History* 41, no. 4 (1981): 795–811.

———. "To Town to Serve: Urban Domestic Slavery in Medieval Ragusa." In Hanawalt, *Women and Work*, 39–55.

———. "Where Notaries Provided Legal Services to Medieval Townspeople." *Journal of Family History* 43, no. 3 (2018): 270–80.

Tallan, Cheryl. "Medieval Jewish Widows: Their Control of Resources." *Jewish History* 5, no. 1 (1991): 63–74.

Tartakoff, Paola. "Testing Boundaries: Jewish Conversion and Cultural Fluidity in Medieval Europe." *Speculum* 90, no. 3 (2015): 728–62.

Toaff, Ariel. *Love, Work, and Death: Jewish Life in Medieval Umbria*. Portland, OR: The Littman Library of Jewish Civilization, 1998.

To Figueras, Lluís. *Família i hereu a la Catalunya Nord-Oriental (segles X–XII)*. Barcelona: Publicacions de l'Abadia de Montserrat, 1997.

———. "Las funciones sociales del notariado en la Cataluña del siglo XIII." In *La cultura en la Europa del siglo XIII: Emisión, intermediación, audiencia (Actas de la XL Semana de Estudios Mediavales de Estella. 16 al 19 de julio de 2013)*, 169–200. Pamplona: Fondo de Publicaciones del Gobierno de Navarra, 2014.

———. "Wedding Trousseaus and Cloth Consumption in Catalonia Around 1300." *Economic History Review* 69, no. 2 (2016): 522–47.

Trivellato, Francesca. *The Familiarity of Strangers: The Sephardic Diaspora, Livorno, and Cross-Cultural Trade in the Early Modern Period*. New Haven: Yale University Press, 2009.

Vinyoles, Teresa. *Les barcelonines a les darreries de l'edat mitjana (1370–1410)*. Barcelona: Fundació Salvador Vives Casajuana, 1976.

Vinyoles Vidal, Teresa M., and Carme Muntaner i Alsina. "Acreedoras y deudoras: Mujeres y crédito en la documentación notarial catalana de inicios del siglo XV." In *Reti di credito: Circuiti informali, impropri, nascosti (secoli XIII–XIX)*, edited by Mauro Carboni and Maria Giuseppina Muzzarelli, 275–306. Bologna: Società editrice il Mulino, 2014.

Wessell Lightfoot, Dana. *Women, Dowries, and Agency: Marriage in Fifteenth-Century Valencia*. Manchester: Manchester University Press, 2013.

Wiesner, Merry E. "Having Her Own Smoke: Employment and Independence for Singlewomen in Germany." In Bennett and Froide, *Singlewomen*, 192–216.

Winer, Rebecca Lynn. "Conscripting the Breast: Lactation, Slavery, and Salvation in the Realms of Aragon and the Kingdom of Majorca, c. 1250–1300." *Journal of Medieval History* 34 (2008): 164–84.

———. "Jews in and out of Latin Notarial Culture: Analyzing Hebrew Notations on Latin Contracts in Thirteenth-Century Perpignan and Barcelona." In *Entangled Histories: Knowledge, Authority, and Jewish Culture in the Thirteenth Century*, edited by Elisheva Baumgarten, Ruth Mazo Karras, and Katelyn Mesler, 113–33. Philadelphia: University of Pennsylvania Press, 2017.

———. "Marriage, Family, and the Family Business: Links Between the Jews of Medieval Perpignan and Girona." In Planas Marcé, *Temps i espais de la Girona Jueva*, 243–56.

———. "The Mother and the *Dida* [Nanny]: Female Employers and Wet Nurses in Fourteenth-Century Barcelona." In *Medieval and Renaissance Lactations: Images, Rhetorics, Practices*, edited by Jutta Gisela Sperling, 55–78. Burlington, VT: Ashgate, 2013.

———. *Women, Wealth, and Community in Perpignan, c. 1250–1300: Christians, Jews, and Enslaved Muslims in a Medieval Mediterranean Town*. Burlington, VT: Ashgate, 2006.

Wray, Shona Kelly. *Communities and Crisis: Bologna During the Black Death*. Leiden: Brill, 2009.

Zimmermann, Michel. "Le concept de Marca Hispanica et l'importance de la frontière dans la formation de la Catalogne." In *La marche supérieure d'Al-Andalus et l'occident chrétien*, edited by Philippe Sénac, 29–48. Madrid: Casa de Velázquez, 1991.

Zinger, Oded. "'She Aims to Harass Him': Jewish Women in Muslim Legal Venues in Medieval Egypt." *AJS Review* 42, no. 1 (2018): 159–92.

Index

Printed in the USA
CPSIA information can be obtained
at www.ICGtesting.com
LVHW041205171024
793917LV00002B/29

9 780271 093307